Space, Time and Einstein

Space, Time and Einstein

An Introduction

J. B. Kennedy

McGill-Queen's University Press
Montreal & Kingston • Ithaca

ISBN   0-7735-2471-1 (bound)
ISBN   0-7735-2472-X (paper)

Published simultaneously outside North America
by Acumen Publishing Limited

McGill-Queen's University Press acknowledges the financial support of the
Government of Canada through the Book Publishing Development Program
(BPIDP) for its activities.

National Library of Canada Cataloguing in Publication

Kennedy, Jay, 1958–
    Space, time, and Einstein / Jay Kennedy

Includes bibliographical references and index.
ISBN 0-7735-2471-1 (bound).—ISBN 0-7735-2472-X (pbk.)

    1. Space and time. I. Title.

BD632.K45 2003   115   C2002-902992-9

Designed and typeset by Kate Williams, Abergavenny.
Printed and bound by Biddles Ltd., Guildford and King's Lynn.

For Carole and John Crascall

Contents

Preface and acknowledgements

The ongoing revolution in our understanding of space and time is so central to the drama of our times that no educated person can remain ignorant of it. There is no better illustration of the adventure of ideas, nor the power and practical importance of abstract thought.

Introductory texts should be brief, easy to read and seductive. This text aims to be the clearest philosophical introduction to relativity theory available. It exposes the philosophical heart of issues without jargon, mathematics or logical formulas. Our patron saint is lucidity. It is aimed at those without a background in science, mathematics or philosophy. The hope is to provide thoughtful readers with a sense of where we have come from and where we are going, and thus to offer an invitation to further studies.

This book is a threefold invitation to the philosophy of space and time. It introduces – gently and simply – the new, revolutionary ideas of Einstein. It introduces the concepts and arguments of philosophers, both ancient and modern, which have proved of lasting value. Finally, it introduces the most recent discoveries and the debates raging now, in philosophy and physics, and points out how future developments may unfold.

The text does aim to teach one skill. Careful thinking is at the core of our conception of philosophy. Now that many nations have reorganized themselves as democracies, which depend so much on reasoned debate and persuasion, careful thinking has become a foundation of our social and political lives as well. But clear thinking is an art: it requires patience, practice and cultivation. This text does not teach or use formal logic, but it pays great attention to the careful analysis and interpretation of ideas. It slows down to dissect moment-ous claims and seeks out the hidden assumptions underlying the great arguments of the past. It aims throughout to show how the analysis of arguments deepens our appreciation of philosophy, and points the way towards future progress.

This is a conservative text in the sense that it covers the standard topics, outlines mainstream debates and introduces the views of some leading contemporary philosophers. Unusually, from the outset, it emphasizes the controversy between Einstein and Lorentz over the interpretation of relativity (following essays by J. S. Bell and the more mathematical text by D. Bohm), which is now again a hot topic of debate. For accessibility, I have edited the quotations to conform to a uniform terminology, ruthlessly preferred concrete over technical terms (e.g. "rulers and clocks" rather than "reference frames") and postponed all spacetime diagrams to an appendix. In general, I have favoured bold, plausible claims and used the guide for further reading in Appendix E to point toward more advanced and nuanced litera-ture. This approach has worked well in courses I have taught at Stanford University and the University of Notre Dame in the US and the University of Manchester in the UK. There was no room for chapters on debates over space and time in the feminist philosophy of science and in art history, but some references to these are included in the guide to further reading in Appendix E.

I would like to thank the historians John Pickstone, Jon Agar and Jeff Hughes, and the philosophers Harry Lesser and Thomas Uebel for making me feel so very welcome at the University of Manchester; John Shand for his encouragement and friendship; Ian Peek, Michael Rush and Gloria Ayob for their help; reviewers for their excellent suggestions which have helped strengthen and clarify the text; E. Donegan for starting things off; Nancy Cartwright for all she has done; my teachers Peter Galison, Patrick Suppes, Tim Lenoir, Wilbur Knorr and Arthur Fine; my colleagues Ernan McMullin, Jim Cushing and Don Howard; my friends and students at Stanford, Notre Dame and Manchester; Louise for her infinite support and Lily for her smiles.

J. B. Kennedy
Manchester

PART I

Einstein's revolution

CHAPTER 1

From Aristotle to Hiroshima

Cup your hands together and peer down between your palms.

What is between them?

One answer is "air". But we think of air as composed of separate molecules, like isolated islands. What lies between the molecules?

Nothing?

The distances between the molecules differ. Could there be more "nothing" between some, and less "nothing" between others? Could nothing really exist?

The empty space does seem to be nothing. It is tasteless, colourless and weightless. It does not move, and the gentlest breeze can pass through it without resistance.

This is our first question. What is between your cupped palms? Is it space, a vacuum, a place? Is it there at all? Is it something or nothing?

Now pause silently for a moment until you can feel the blood pulsing through your hands. Time is flowing. Your brain is sensitive to the physical passage of time and as each second or so passes it rouses itself and decides to stimulate your heartbeat, sending blood coursing down through your palms.

Does time *flow* invisibly through the space between your palms, as blood flows through your fingers or as a river flows past it banks? Can you feel time flowing there? Is that the right metaphor?

Does time flow more slowly and more quickly, or at a steady rate? If steady, then steady compared to what? Does it flow at a speed of one hour per . . . hour?

If no body moves through a space does time still flow there? Can time proceed without change? This is our second question. What is the flow of time? Is it happening there in the empty space between your palms, or in the space your brain occupies? Is time the same as physical change, or is it the cause of change?

These questions about space and time seem idle at first. It is not clear even how to begin, how to get a grip on them. But we have learned otherwise.

Consider one time and place. On 6 August 1945, early on a bright sunny morning in the city of Hiroshima, tea was being made in offices, children were being bundled off to school and a lonely, propeller-driven plane buzzed unnoticed through the sky above. When the atom bomb fell, the furious, boiling ball of fire killed some one hundred thousand human beings at once. The city centre disappeared, rivers and criss-crossing canals were vaporized and buildings were blown apart for miles. Pedestrians walking across a distant bridge were suddenly sooty silhouettes on scarred concrete. Many more who at first survived the initial blast soon died horribly as their flesh peeled from their bones, and their organs were eaten away by the radiation.

The atom bombs dropped on Hiroshima and Nagasaki, like those still poised and ready in missile silos around the world today, stand as emblems of the power – of the depth and the danger – of our new ideas about space and time. The basic theory of the bombs is given by Albert Einstein's famous equation that says that ordinary matter can be converted into tremendous explosions of pure force and energy. The following chapters will trace Einstein's surprisingly simple theories, showing how new ideas about time led to new ideas about energy, and give instructions for constructing an atomic bomb. But here we should pause to contemplate the power of ideas, the possibility that seemingly idle questions may have far-reaching consequences.

Modern answers to the two questions above mix great tragedy and great beauty, and are known as the "philosophy of space and time". This subject has played a central role in European philosophy since the time of the ancient Greeks. It is sometimes traditional to divide philosophy – the "love of wisdom" – into three branches according to the three leading questions:

- *What is there?* What exists? What is reality composed of? Does it include atoms, space, ghosts, souls, Beauty, God?
- *What can we know?* Which sorts of knowledge are reliable? Can we trust our senses? Who should we believe? What is truth?

- *What should we do?* What is good or evil? Is our aim successful survival or saving our souls? Should we tell lies? Should we be guided by reason or emotion, or both?

For each question, the corresponding branch of philosophy is:

- *Metaphysics* – the study of reality
- *Epistemology* – the study of knowledge
- *Ethics* – the study of good and evil, of values

The philosophy of space and time is part of metaphysics. Some people mistakenly think that the word "metaphysics" means "after or beyond physical science", but the word is really an historical accident. Historians explain that Aristotle (384–322BCE) wrote many books, which were kept in a chest after his death in 322BCE. A later editor bound them together into volumes and gave each volume a title. One dealt with "Physics", and was so entitled. The next dealt with more basic questions but had no title. It came to be called "the book that came after the one entitled Physics", and this name, "After-the-Physics" or "Metaphysics" ("meta" being Greek for "after"), has stuck through the ages. Aristotle would have probably preferred to call it "First Philosophy", simply because it dealt with the most basic and general questions that could be asked. It was thus a deeper continuation of physics, not a separate subject.

This is important because the philosophy of space and time deals with many ideas that are part of modern physical science: it is not "after" or "beyond" physics. Here, there is no dividing line between philosophy and science.

In fact, the division between philosophy and science may have been a temporary aberration. A little history will help explain this. What we call "science" in the modern sense grew from a small movement in the 1600s led by a few philosophers, aristocrats and mechanics. At that time the new vogue in studies of nature was simply known as "philosophy". Only some two centuries later, when the trend had caught on and attracted many investigators, was a need felt for some new name for the discipline. "Science" slowly came to have the sense of a study of nature that emphasized experiment and mathematics. The word "scientist" was not coined until 1863.

These new terms signalled a novel and peculiar split between philosophy and the emergent "science"; suddenly there were two disciplines and two communities of thinkers, where before there had been one loose community of philosophers. Crudely put, the philosophers withdrew from experimenting and observing the world while scientists tried to restrict themselves to measurement, calculation and deduction. Philosophers thought in their armchairs: scientists looked through their telescopes and microscopes. The split widened so much in the twentieth century that some people complained that Europe had "two cultures": the humanities were separate and isolated from the sciences.

There are now healthy signs that this split is healing, and the philosophy of space and time is one area where philosophy and science are converging and overlapping again. After all, both are studying the same world. One reason for this convergence is an extraordinary and unexpected crisis in our understanding of space and time. Physicists had been optimistic that Einstein's theories were both correct and fundamental. Now there is a widespread sense that, although his theories make many correct predictions, they are somehow wrong and mistaken. Just as Einstein overthrew earlier physics, we may now be on the verge of a new revolution. The new problems are so surprising and so deep that ambitious philosophers have invaded physics and thoughtful physicists have begun raising broad and searching metaphysical questions again. The quantum theory of matter, the new theory of gravitation ("quantum gravity"), astronomy and attempts at unified theories of physics are all throwing up challenges to our understanding of space and time. These are deep enough to be called philosophical.

It is an exciting moment to study the philosophy of space and time. We possess deep and beautiful theories that seem right and illuminating, and make many verifiable predictions. We also know now that they are not fundamentally correct, but we do not understand why. We do not understand how to proceed.

CHAPTER 2

Einstein in a nutshell

Two theories of relativity

There are two Einsteins. For most of the world, Einstein (1879–1955) is a cult figure: the pre-eminent icon of genius. With his wispy, wild grey hair, missing socks and other-worldly idealism, he has replaced the wizards of earlier times in the popular mind. This Einstein is dangerous, a stereotype with a life of its own that distorts both the man behind it and the nature of the science that so shapes our world.

Among physicists, Einstein is at times remembered as a grumpy, cutting and arrogant fellow with little patience for family or colleagues. He so annoyed his teachers at university that he failed to secure a job in academia, and had to scramble to find low-paying work in the Swiss patent office (although some say that being Jewish hurt his chances too). During his twenties in Berne, Einstein was a fashionable man about town. His wit and violin playing brought him many dinner invitations, and he formed a reading group with friends to study the work of Kant, Schopenhauer and other philosophers. In 1905, his miracle year, he published several unrelated papers. One was good enough to win a Nobel prize, and another revolutionized our views of space and time. The 25-year-old patent clerk had remade physics in his own image.

Einstein's 1905 theory of space and time is now called the *special theory of relativity*. The word "relativity" refers to relative speeds and other relations. The theory was "special" in a negative sense: it applied only to a restricted *special case* and was not general. It has become most well known for predicting that mass can be converted directly into energy, and thus provided the theory behind atomic bombs. During the decade after 1905, Einstein struggled to broaden his theory. It was a time of frustration and false trails, of Herculean labours and wasted years. Finally, in 1916, he published his even more radical *general theory of relativity*. The special theory overthrew the classical physics of Isaac Newton (1642–1727), which had reigned for some 200 years, and the general theory overthrew Euclid's geometry, which had been considered a model of certain knowledge for more than 2000 years.

As Europe lay in ruins after the end of the First World War, an English astronomer sought observations that might confirm Einstein's radical theories. Arthur Eddington believed that a British effort to support the theories of a Swiss-German would demonstrate the internationalism of science, and promote healing among the shattered nations. He mounted an expedition to South Africa, where a total eclipse was predicted in 1919. Einstein had predicted that measurements of starlight bending around the darkened Sun would test his theory. Eddington's crude photographs made Einstein a celebrity. The results were telegraphed around the world and newspapers announced that we had entered the Age of Relativity.

Einstein became a professor of physics in Berlin, the fashionable capital of interwar Germany and a centre of modernist movements in art, literature and politics. He enjoyed his celebrity, socializing at black-tie dinners with the high and mighty, and used his fame to advance pacifism and international socialism. As the economy worsened, however, he became a lightning rod for anti-Semitic threats. A wave of frightened scientists, intellectuals and artists were then emigrating to the USA, and transforming it into a leader in scientific research. Einstein moved with his family in 1933 and took up a position at the Institute for Advanced Study at Princeton. In 1939, as the Nazis advanced across Europe, Einstein sent a now famous letter to President Roosevelt appealing for urgent research into atomic weapons. Together with pressure from their allies in Britain, this led the USA to collaborate with Britain on a huge, incredibly expensive crash programme, the Manhattan Project, which constructed the bombs dropped on Japan four years later.

In 1948 Einstein turned down an offer to become the first president of Israel, and continued his quiet life of research at Princeton. Younger physicists had moved on to more exciting developments, and at times regarded Einstein as a scientific has-been who failed to keep up with them.

Today we live in the golden age of astronomical exploration. Using the Hubble Telescope and a host of other satellites, ultra-sensitive detectors and high-speed computers, we have learned more about the universe during the past two decades than during all of history. If anything, the pace of discovery is even now accelerating. And all this is Einstein's golden age too. His ideas guide these explorations, and provide the basic framework underlying theories of the Big Bang, black holes and the birth of stars and galaxies. All the same, however, experiments now strongly suggest that Einstein's most basic views on space and time were somehow wrong: that they were fruitful half-truths. A storm of work in the foundations of physics, quantum gravity and cosmology has made this an era that once again is posing the deepest questions about space and time. Like Newton before him, Einstein now faces the prospect of being overthrown by new and deeper theories. These are exciting times.

The following chapters introduce Einstein and his special theory of relativity in a very simple way, and concentrate on two themes. First, they pinpoint the daring, conceptual leaps that lay at the heart of Einstein's theory. Einstein was not a great mathematician, and his discoveries all begin with creative insights that can be understood and appreciated without jargon. For philosophers, these flights of genius are enduring monuments to the beauty and power of thought. Secondly, the chapters return constantly to the heated controversy now surrounding the *interpretation* of Einstein's theories. Despite the myriad of successful predictions they produce, there is now real uncertainty about why his theories work, and therefore about his grand revisions in our ideas about space and time.

This approach is unusual. Most introductions to relativity hide the ongoing debates and concentrate on expounding the technical features of Einstein's theory. Here, the mathematics is set aside and we stay close to the phenomena, to the concrete predictions and observable implications of the theory. Thus we penetrate to the conceptual core of theory, and therefore to its philosophical heart.

Later in his life, Einstein distinguished between two sorts of scientific theories. *Constructive theories* begin by listing the basic things in the world, and build up or construct larger, high-level things from these. The fully developed model is then used to make predictions. Philosophers would say that such a theory begins with an ontology, and draws consequences from it.

In contrast, Einstein said, special relativity is a *principle theory*. He meant that the theory begins by listing a few high-level assumptions or isolated facts that are not supported by any model, and then uses these to make predictions. The truth of the predictions would justify the assumptions or justify relying on the facts, even if they are not clearly supported by a deeper picture of the world. A principle theory can seem very mysterious when the predictions it makes are unexpected. When a magician pulls a rabbit out of an ordinary looking hat we seek for some deeper explanation of what happened. A principle theory does not offer deeper explanations.

The special theory of relativity is a principle theory. This chapter introduces the principles and facts that Einstein used to make his startling predictions. At the end of the chapter we take a first glance at what could make all this true, and attempt to go deeper than Einstein's principles.

The general theory of relativity builds on and generalizes the special theory of relativity, but does not explain its principles.

The speed of light is constant

The central mystery is light. It is, first of all, astonishingly fast. With a flick of a switch, light floods a room. Before the rise of modern science, it was sometimes thought that light leapt magically across space without taking any time at all. This changed, however, after Galileo first turned the telescope toward the skies in 1609. Clever astronomers realized they could use the regular orbits of Jupiter's moons as giant clocks, and were able to measure the speed of light with surprising accuracy. The numbers they produced shocked people. Who could conceive of a speed of *186,000 miles per second* or *300,000 kilometres per second*?

But another, more perplexing, surprise lay in wait: the speed of light is constant. That is, all observers who measure the speed of light in empty space will find the same number no matter how fast they are moving. An observer standing still will find starlight racing by at 300,000 kilometres per second. A spaceship cruising at 200,000 kilometres per second and chasing a light beam will still find that the beam races away from the nose of the ship at 300,000 kilometres per second. This means, for example, that no one can race fast enough to catch a light beam. No matter how fast someone is moving, light will be faster by 300,000 kilometres per second.

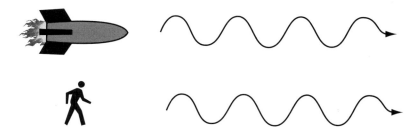

Figure 2.1 *The speed of light is constant. The speed of light is 300,000 km/s observed from the rocket, and 300,000 km/s observed by the walking figure.*

This is very peculiar. By way of contrast, consider a speeding motorist being chased along a road by the police. At the start, with the police car at a standstill at the side of the road, the speeding car zips away at 150 kilometres per hour. As the police car reaches 30 kilometres per hour, the speeding car travels only 120 kilometres per hour faster. As they accelerate, the *relative speed* of the fugitive drops down further and further, and finally dwindles to zero as the police catch up and race alongside flashing their lights. This is common sense. If the speeding car goes at 150 kilometres per hour and the police are chasing at 130 kilometres per hour, then their relative speed is 20 kilometres per hour.

But light is not commonsensical. Light races away from any standing or moving body at the same speed. The speed of light relative to *any* moving body is a constant.

This fact was discovered experimentally in the late 1800s. It was so strange there was no agreement about what it meant, or even whether the experiments could be correct. Even today we have no deep explanation of why the speed of light is constant. Many have derived the fact, but only by making other, equally mysterious assumptions. It was Einstein's great achievement to see this bizarre fact as a clue. He was able to place it at the centre of a powerful new theory, and thus opened up a new vision of our universe.

> The constancy of the relative speed of light is an experimental fact. Even today, there is no agreement about why this should be true. Einstein simply assumed it was and drew some surprising consequences.

Faster speeds, longer hours

Someone might mistakenly think that the constancy of the speed of light leads to contradictions, and therefore cannot be true. For example, suppose there are two rockets travelling through space in the same direction but at different speeds, and that there is a ray of light racing out ahead of them. Someone might think that light cannot travel 300,000 kilometres per second faster than each rocket, because the light beam would then have two speeds. But that would be a contradiction – light cannot have two different speeds. What is wrong with this reasoning?

Einstein was able to remove the appearance of contradiction by profoundly altering our view of time. To understand this, we must carefully reconsider what a contradiction would be. Plato and Aristotle were apparently the first to state what is, perhaps, the most fundamental idea in philosophy:

> *The law of non-contradiction:* Opposite properties do not belong to one and the same thing in the same respect and at the same time.

According to this law, a positive integer is never both even and odd. A newspaper can be "black and white and red all over", but not "in the same respect". It can be black here and white there and "read" throughout. It cannot be black and white at the same point since these colours are opposites. (Lukasiewicz calls this the "ontological" version of Aristotle's law: it is about properties and things. Other versions of the law concern true sentences or psychological states like belief.)

In a move of breathtaking audacity, Einstein reasoned that, since there were no real contradictions, and therefore a light beam cannot have two speeds in the same respect and at the same time, *the two rockets above must have different times*. That is, the rockets each measure the same relative speed for the light beam because *time flows differently for each rocket*.

A little story will help make this more concrete. Suppose that Jill is an astronaut flying overhead through the starry night. Jack is earthbound and working in mission control, and it is his job to monitor Jill and her spaceship carefully through a large telescope. As Jill's spaceship approaches the speed of light, Jack observes something marvellous. Jill and everything in the spaceship move in slow motion, like a film in the cinema shown at a slowed rate. The hands on Jill's wristwatch begin to crawl around the clock face. She seems to be wading through molasses. The half-hour programme she is watching on her television takes 45 minutes.

Jack is not surprised because Einstein predicted all this. As the rocket speeds up, its time flows more slowly than here on Earth. An hour on the rocket is longer than an hour on Earth. This is now called *time dilation* (to dilate is to become wider or longer), and there is a simple formula to predict how much Jill's time will slow when her rocket has a particular speed (see Appendix C).

Reasoning from the constancy of the speed of light, Einstein concluded that there was no single, universal passage of time. Rather, the flow of time depends on speeds. *Faster speeds mean longer hours.* Each body moving through space experiences the flow of time at a different rate.

This astonishing conclusion was confirmed by many experiments. One experiment by Hafele and Keating in 1971 used very accurate atomic clocks, which were carried on around-the-world flights in Boeing jets. Although the jets flew much more slowly than the speed of light, there was still a measurable time dilation. The clocks were slightly behind other clocks that remained in the laboratory, just as Einstein's theory predicted.

This can be tested at home. For example, time dilation can be used to delay getting the wrinkled hands that accompany ageing. If both hands are simply flapped up and down continuously at nearly the speed of light, they will remain young while the rest of your body ages.

Many studying relativity for the first time assume these effects are some kind of illusion that arise because of the way fast-moving objects are observed. That is, they believe that durations are *really* constant and merely *appear* to vary with speeds because they must be observed from far away. Some believe it is the lag time – the time it takes for light to travel from the object to the measurement device – that produces an illusion. This is easy to refute, and cannot be correct. For example, when the travelling atomic clocks were returned to the laboratory bench, the slight discrepancy between them and stay-at-home clocks could be read off immediately. No fancy apparatus or fast-moving objects were involved. Indeed, human observers are unnecessary. A computer could have registered and printed out the difference. Similar examples of relativistic effects are widespread in the daily work of experimental physicists. Almost everyone in the present debate agrees that the effects cannot be simple illusions.

Likewise, some beginners mistakenly believe that time dilation is just a consequence of using different units of measurement. A measurement assigns a number to a distance or duration. A tennis court is 24 metres or 78 feet long; a tennis match may last 3 hours or 180 minutes. These numbers obviously depend on conventional units of measurement: on, say, whether metres or feet are used. When international organizations change the definitions of the units, the numbers assigned to bodies change too. But time dilation occurs even when everyone agrees on and uses the same units of measurement. Jack and Jill compare their rulers and synchronize their watches before the spaceship leaves Earth. Even so, Jill's watch will run more slowly relative to Jack's when she increases her speed. In short, time dilation is a real effect, and is neither an illusion nor a difference in the choice of measurement units. The flow of time depends on speeds.

If two rockets flying at different speeds are chasing the same light beam, the light will indeed travel 300,000 kilometres per second faster than each of the ships. But there is no contradiction. The light beam has opposite properties but not "at the same time"; each ship has its own time.

> Time dilation was inferred from the constancy of the speed of light and other assumptions in order to avoid contradictions, and was later confirmed by many experiments.

The lazy ship

When Einstein published his ideas about time dilation in 1905, he limited his predictions to a special case: to special sorts of measurements. As mentioned above, special relativity is special because it is limited to special cases. To understand these important limitations, we must consider some simple facts about motion.

Suppose a ship is sailing very smoothly down a wide river at a constant speed and in a fixed direction. Suppose some budget travellers have cabins below deck without windows, and so cannot see the river banks sliding slowly by the ship. When they wake up in the morning such passengers will not be able to tell whether the ship is moving or standing still. In fact, no observation or experiment performed within the cabin can measure the ship's motion: without looking outside steady speeds are undetectable and unmeasurable.

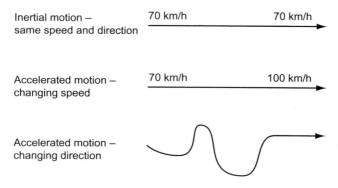

Figure 2.2 *Inertial and accelerated motion.*

This is very peculiar. If the passengers are really moving, they should be able to discover it without looking elsewhere. Philosophers and scientists discussed this riddle so often that they gave steady motion a special name:

Inertial motion: Motion at a constant speed along a straight line.

"Inertial" comes from the Latin word for inactive, sluggish or lazy. Thus, during inertial motion the ship is lazy in the sense that it just keeps doing what it was doing: it does not change speed or direction.

The opposite of inertial motion is *accelerated motion*, and that is easy to detect. For example, when a car accelerates, the passengers are pushed back against their seats. If the ship were to slow down or speed up, the passengers below deck might spill their coffee and would immediately conclude that the ship's speed was changing. The word "acceleration" is used to mean a *change in speed or in direction* (or both). Thus, steering a car to the left without touching the accelerator pedal is also an acceleration in this sense.

Distances and durations are measured with rulers and clocks. Einstein limited his special theory to the case where the rulers and clocks used in measurements were at rest or moving inertially. In short, *the special theory applies only to "inertial measurements"*. The object that is measured may be accelerating – it may be turning loops or flapping up and down – but the measuring devices must be resting or moving steadily.

We can now state Einstein's claims about time dilation more precisely:

Time dilation: Take as a standard a clock that is at rest or moving inertially. Other clocks moving relative to the standard will have longer hours (i.e. "dilated hours"). Furthermore, all physical processes moving relative to the standard clock will take longer than if they were at rest relative to the standard.

That is, it will take more than an hour on the inertial, standard clock for an hour to pass on a clock moving relative to it or, for example, for a moving video player on the spaceship to show an hour-long programme. (The special theory can be applied to accelerating measuring devices by using approximations. If the period of acceleration is divided into short intervals, the device can be treated as moving inertially during each interval. By adding the changes during each of these intervals together, the change during the entire acceleration can be approximated. But, strictly speaking, the special theory applies only to measurements made by devices moving at constant speeds in a straight line.)

The principle of relativity

Einstein's central idea is that there is *democracy among all inertial measurements.* Any measurement made by a set of rulers and clocks moving at a steady speed in a fixed direction is equally as good as a measurement made by any other set.

Suppose that there are two sets of rulers and clocks moving relatively to each other, and each is measuring the speed of a passing spaceship. The results of the measurements will differ, but Einstein insists each result may equally claim to be "the" speed of the ship. There is no physical way to show that one speed is more correct than the other.

Suppose that the budget travellers below deck on the ship work hard to discover their speed by doing all sorts of experiments in their cabin. For example, they drop objects and discover that they fall faster and faster the longer they fall. In fact, every second of fall increases their speed by 32 feet per second. This law is the same in the cabin as it would be on shore. That is, *even laws of physics are unaffected by the ship's speed through the river.* Thus Einstein's democracy extends even to laws; they are the same for all observers moving at steady speeds in a fixed direction.

Einstein called this sort of democracy his special principle of relativity: the laws of physics are the same for all observers moving at a steady speed along a straight line. That is, regardless of your relative speed, the laws of physics are the same. As Einstein said:

> This postulate we call the "special principle of relativity." The word "special" is meant to intimate that the principle is restricted to the case when the [measuring devices] have a motion of uniform translation . . . and does not extend to the case of non-uniform motion.

What is a law of physics? When we plan a journey by car, we all use the simple law that "distance *equals* speed *multiplied* by time": an average of 90 kilometres an hour for five hours will cover 450 kilometres. Here we have a law that connects three things: distance, speed and time. Each of these can easily be measured with, say, the speedometer of the car, a wristwatch and a good map. This suggests that a law is a relation between measurements. The relation in this law is represented by the italicized words above. In every motion, the relation between distance traversed, speed and time taken will be the same.

Some laws contain constants. For example, when we drop something to the floor, its speed increases by 9.8 metres per second during every second it falls. Thus, in general, a *physical law is a relation, involving constants, between measurement results*.

Measurements made at different speeds lead to different results. Birds flying alongside a car sometimes seem to stand still: their measured relative speed is zero. But a pedestrian watching the birds swoop by would disagree, and insist that their relative speed was, say, 40 kilometres per hour. The difference between a speed of zero and 40 kilometres per hour reflects the speed of the measurer. Both the driver and the pedestrian, however, will agree that the distance covered by the birds is given by their speed multiplied by the time taken.

Einstein's principle of relativity can now be stated more clearly. He says that, while the *measurements* made by different sets of rulers and clocks will differ and depend on speed, *relations* between the measurements will be the same for all sets moving inertially. Likewise, any physical constants in laws will be the same. Measurement results are relative; laws are not.

Physics is about relations.

Special relativity is derived from two principles. Both are experimental facts boldly assumed to hold universally. The first says that physical laws are the same for all observers. The second says it is a law that light travels at 300,000 kilometres per second.

Faster speeds, shorter lengths

Using his two principles, the constancy of the speed of light and relativity, Einstein made a second, astonishing, prediction. As Jill's spaceship speeds up, earth-bound Jack will find that its length *shrinks*. If the spaceship had the shape of a long sausage with fins when it blasted off, at high speeds it will contract lengthwise into the shape of a disc or pancake. As Jill faces forwards out of the window on the ship's nose, her shoulders will remain the normal distance apart but her belly button will be very close to the skin on her back. This is called *length contraction*.

For another example, suppose that someone with more money than sense buys a Jaguar on impulse, but returns home to find that the six-metre car will not fit into the three-metre garage. By driving the car at nearly the speed of light towards the open door of the garage, it is actually possible to fit it snugly inside. Of course, the brakes should be applied before hitting the rear wall.

Actually, physicists have found it difficult to confirm length contraction directly. Time aboard a speeding spaceship can be measured by exchanging light or radio signals, but it is harder to measure lengths by pulling alongside the spaceship with a yardstick. However, length contraction is considered a confirmed effect.

The famous experiments by the Americans Michelson and Morley in 1887 are taken as strong evidence for length contraction. Simply put, they used a long rod moving in the direction of one of its ends. When they shone a ray of light along the rod and reflected it back to its source, they discovered that the ray took slightly less time for the

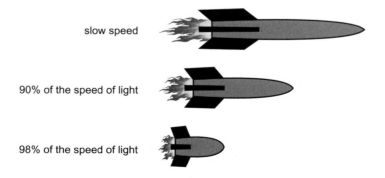

Figure 2.3   *Contraction in the direction of travel.*

18

return trip than expected. Einstein and other physicists concluded that the rod must have shrunk.

Just as with time dilation, these contractions seem strange to us only because we are such slow-moving creatures. The fastest human beings run 100 metres at the Olympics in about ten seconds. If we were many millions of time faster than that, and could flit around the world in a flash, shrinking lengths and slowing times would be an ordinary part of our lives. On Saturday nights, we could become thinner (and dizzy) just by constantly rushing back and forth past our dates. But a professor who paced back and forth in front of the blackboard at near light speed might take hours and hours to finish a lecture.

To summarize, with faster speeds, lengths become shorter in the direction of travel. This can be put more precisely:

Length contraction
Take as a standard a yardstick at rest or moving in a straight line at a constant speed. Other yardsticks moving relatively to this inertial standard will contract in the direction of their travel. That is, the contracted yardsticks will measure only a fraction of the standard yardstick. In fact, the length of all moving objects will contract relative to the standard.

Thus, faster speeds imply shorter lengths.

Length contracts only in the direction of travel: a sausage becomes a pancake, but its diameter remains the same.

The relativity of simultaneity

Before Einstein, physicists thought that time flows at the same rate everywhere. There was supposed to be, we might say, a "universal Tuesday": if it were Tuesday here on Earth, it was Tuesday throughout the entire universe. That is, it was believed that one and the same instant of time occurred simultaneously throughout the universe, and was then followed by the next instant everywhere at once.

Einstein quickly realized that his theories ruled out such a universal simultaneity. This is easy to see. Suppose Jack and Jill synchronize their watches at noon and plan to speak again an hour after Jill has blasted off in her spaceship. At 1 pm on Earth, Jack waits by his radio but Jill fails to make contact. Jack checks his watch against those of his colleagues in mission control, and finds that they all show the same time. Jill is, however, blissfully unaware of her rudeness: her hour has dilated and only a part of her stretched out hour has passed. Jill's 1 pm is not simultaneous with Jack's 1 pm; instead, say, Jill's 12.45 pm is simultaneous with Jack's 1 pm Since time flows differently for bodies moving relatively to each other, they disagree about which events are simultaneous. Thus, according to Einstein, *simultaneity is relative.*

Interpreting relativity

Everyone now agrees that special relativity is well confirmed by experiment. But there remains stark disagreement about why length contraction and time dilation occur – about what is going on behind the scenes to produce such startling effects. This may come as a surprise. Einstein's theory is 100 years old. Surely scientists and philosophers would have clearly understood it by now?

But the popular image of science is often different from the way it really works. Consciously or unconsciously, scientists are propagandists. To the outside world, they present science as a series of great discoveries, as smooth upwards progress towards truth. But inside science, fierce debates and controversies rage constantly. The public is shielded from these in several ways. First, scientific language is often technical and difficult for non-scientists to penetrate. Secondly, science textbooks used everywhere from elementary school to university tend to conceal disagreement. This helps students by simplifying the material, but it also serves to reinforce the image of science as "objective truth" above all questioning, and thereby reinforces the enormous social and political authority of science.

Disagreement about the interpretation of scientific theories is normal. No major theory of science is free of debate about its truth, meaning and implications.

One task that philosophers perform is the conceptual interpretation of theories in physics. That is, they exploit their talents for clear reasoning and careful definitions to explore what the formulas in physics mean, to unveil what the symbols say about our world. Physicists today are trained to calculate numbers rather than analyse conceptual arguments, and their verbal interpretations of their own theories are often unreliable. Despite their technical skills, as soon as physicists stop calculating they are sadly quite mortal.

The purpose of interpreting scientific theories is twofold. Science is partly an intellectual quest to understand the world around us, but as science became more successful at making predictions it also became more obscure, technical and mathematical. Thus progress in understanding the world now often depends on first interpreting and thereby understanding the scientific theories we already possess. The second purpose of interpretation is more practical. Advances in science come in many ways. Some are the result of blind trial and error, and some arise when patterns in data are first discerned. Historically, interpretation and conceptual analysis have been one important route forwards towards new theories and better science. Many of the important concepts that lie at the foundations of contemporary science were first created by philosophers. Thus today's philosophers can hope to contribute to our intellectual understanding of the world, as well as to the advance towards better and deeper theories.

Relativity theory so shocked everyone that many different interpretations of the above effects have been advanced and defended. During the 1920s and 1930s, most physicists accepted relativity theory and it became a routine part of their work. Controversy, however, raged loudly and ceaselessly. A number of physicists flatly rejected the theory and concocted paradoxes to show that it could not be true and must be self-contradictory and incoherent. Outside science, quacks and disgruntled cranks barraged scientists with "proofs" of Einstein's errors. In Nazi Germany, the Nobel-prize winner Johannes Stark bizarrely condemned Einstein's theories as "Jewish physics", and used his political power to push research in other directions. In retrospect, those turbulent times were a learning period. Mainstream physicists rebutted the paradoxes, and deepened our understanding of relativity.

During the Cold War, from the 1950s through the 1980s, special relativity was gospel. It was considered the best confirmed of theories, and provided foundations for all advanced work in theoretical physics. Controversies over the interpretation of the theory subsided, and textbook presentations of the theory were standardized. Then came the surprise. Beginning in the 1980s, philosophers and some physicists began to realize that certain experiments (discussed below) were a new and unexpected challenge to our *understanding* of relativity. That is, while still accepting that the theory worked at a practical level, increasing numbers began to doubt that the standard interpretation was correct.

Similar sorts of interpretational problems arise with ordinary maps. A map of the world may be useful for navigation even though it grossly distorts the shape of the continents and portrays the spherical Earth as if it were a two-dimensional plane. Special relativity makes predictions that turn out to be true, but we can still ask how well it pictures reality.

There are many examples in history of theories that made good predictions but fundamentally misdescribed reality. A simple one is the theory that the Sun will rise every morning. This theory leads to the prediction of a general brightening in the sky at about 6 am, which will be well confirmed. But the theory is false because the Sun does not rise: Earth rotates.

Two key distinctions, or pairs of words, are at the centre of debates over special relativity: "relative" versus "invariant" and "appearance" versus "reality".

"Relative" means related to or dependent on something else. When used as a noun, "relative" means something involved in a relation, which is why we call our cousins relatives. The word "invariant" is used very often in debates over relativity. In this context, a property is invariant when it is *independent of the set of rulers and clocks that is used for measuring it*. Suppose that different sets of rulers and clocks are all moving relatively to each other, and are used to measure some one property. If all the sets give the same answer, then the property they are measuring is invariant and independent of how it is measured. Physicists sometimes use the word "absolute" as a synonym for "invariant", but history has encrusted "absolute" with so many different meanings that we will avoid it in these introductory chapters.

The philosophy called "Relativism" holds that *truth and values depend on personal beliefs or cultural conditions*. Relativism is not the same as Einstein's theory of relativity. As will be discussed below, Einstein's relativity theory does not reject objective truth altogether. It argues that some properties we thought were invariant are not, and introduces new sorts of invariants. In fact, the name "theory of relativity" was not Einstein's first choice; it was coined by another physicist (Poincaré).

The second distinction between appearance and reality is familiar. Hallucinations and mirages are cases where appearances diverge from reality. A straight stick appears bent when half submerged in water, even though it is really straight. This distinction is also central to modern science. Earth appears to be flat and motionless, but science tells us this is not really so. For another example, colours are mere appearance. The atoms that make up the objects around us are colourless, and appear coloured only because they reflect light of different wavelengths into our eyes.

Note that, as defined above, the question of whether a property is invariant or not is a question about appearances. A physicist can test whether lengths are invariant merely by making observations, and need not speculate about whether those measurements faithfully report what is real. *Appearances may have the property of invariance.* In debates over special relativity, most people accept that the theory correctly describes appearances. That is, the predictions it makes have so far, without exception, been confirmed. The question that remains is over the reality behind the appearances. What is happening behind the scenes? Can we describe or build models of a world that would explain our observations of length contraction and time dilation?

A theory may make good predictions even though it wrongly describes reality.

The mainstream interpretation

A tennis court appears to have a length (24 metres) and a tennis match appears to have a duration (say three hours). Likewise, a shoe appears to have a definite size, and the wink of an eye seems to take less than a second. The key question is about these distances and durations. Bodies appear to have lengths; events appear to have durations. Are these real properties of bodies and events, or are they mere appearances, like the flatness of the earth? Or are they something else altogether?

Of course, science has no pope. No one imposes uniform views on physicists, and every shade and variation of opinion on this issue has been asserted at one time or another. Nonetheless, there are two chief answers to these questions. The first is accepted – implicitly or explicitly – by most mainstream physicists. Therefore, for our purposes, call it the "mainstream interpretation". This view denies the existence of real distances and durations. More precisely, a body does not have a real length and an event does not have a real duration that is independent of other things. Since, as experiment and observation confirm, there appear to be no invariant distances and durations, these are not real properties of physical things. This is a radical claim but it is orthodox within the mainstream.

For comparison, consider the case of a controversial portrait hanging on the wall of an art museum that is variously thought to be beautiful, ugly or indifferent. Suppose that, over the centuries, judgements have always been mixed but tended to shift with the prevailing fashions. Some would conclude that beauty or ugliness is therefore not a property of the painting. Since the painting is the same but judgements of it vary, the judgements seem not to reflect any inner quality of the painting at all.

The mainstream interpretation relies on a similar argument. When astronauts watch a video, it takes 90 minutes according to their watches, but earth-bound observers say it lasted two hours. Since one drama cannot last both 90 minutes and two hours, these durations are not properties of the video. Physicists use a very short argument to buttress this conclusion. Recall that a property is invariant when all sets of rulers and clocks report the same measurement results:

Argument against distances and durations

A. If a property is not invariant, then it is not real. (P)
B. Distances and durations are not invariant. (P)
C. Therefore, distances and durations are not real
   properties. (from A,B)

That is, if measurements of distances and durations produce different results depending on which set of rulers and clocks is used, then distances and durations are not real properties of individual things (like beauty in the painting).

The first premise in the argument, A, is key. It moves from a claim about what we observe and measure to a claim about nature itself: from appearances to realities. This is a very big assumption and is, strictly speaking, not a part of Einstein's theory of relativity. It is a part of the *interpretation* of that theory: the attempt to clarify what the theory says about our world. But the first premise seems reasonable. If a property really belongs to an object, then different measurements should all faithfully report the same result.

The second premise, B, is just the assumption that observations confirm the occurrence of length contraction and time dilation. That is, it assumes that Einstein's predictions turn out to be true, which is widely accepted.

Together, the two premises produce a startling conclusion. According to the argument, relativity theory implies that shoes do not have sizes! A tennis court does not have a definite length; a tennis match in itself never lasts three hours.

Of course, the claim that distances and durations are not real properties is merely negative: it makes an assertion about what does not exist. But the mainstream interpretation also makes positive claims about what does exist instead of distances and durations. A comparison will help make this clear.

Suppose that, at a large family reunion, someone is variously introduced as a brother, son and cousin. Should we conclude, as in the case of the painting, that these various attributions are not all correct? Since being a brother, being a son and being a cousin are not the same, should we conclude that the introductions were mistaken? Clearly not. The reason is that being a brother, and so on, depends on the kind of *relation* to other people. One person can be at once a brother to a sister, son to a father and cousin to a cousin because he enters into various relations with different people.

According to the mainstream interpretation, the relativity of distances and durations seems revolutionary only because of an error. We thought that they were real properties of individual things, but actually they are each a kind of relation (technically, a "projection onto a coordinate system"). Lengths vary because they are like family relations to the surrounding bodies and measuring instruments. We mistakenly assumed that lengths are properties of individual things only because our ordinary experience involves objects moving far more slowly than the speed of light. Since we are also moving slowly, we all have the same low speeds relative to such objects. Since our relations are thus all the same, we overlooked their key role. A later chapter explains this strange world of relativity further, and explores this positive side of the mainstream interpretation.

In sum, the mainstream interpretation denies that real distances and durations are properties of individual bodies or events. It asserts, instead, that distances and durations are kinds of relations. A shoe has one length relative to one set of rulers and another length relative to a different set of rulers (like the brother who is a cousin), but no particular length of its own.

Properties belong to one thing, relations to two or more. Although distances and durations are not real properties, they are also not mere appearances: they are real relations.

The minority interpretation

The young Einstein was a rebel, moving from job to job and scrambling to find a secure job. The great father figure in physics at that time was the famous Dutchman Hendrik Lorentz. A generation older than Einstein, and a picture of prosperous, upper-middle-class respectability, Lorentz had played a major role in the discovery of the electron, for which he received one of the first Nobel prizes in 1902. He had come within a hair's breadth of discovering special relativity, and yet always praised and encouraged the young upstart who scooped him. Some measure Lorentz's greatness by his ability to recognize in Einstein an unusual and unconventional genius so very different from his own. In fact, Lorentz became one of Einstein's earliest promoters, and generously helped him find positions that enabled him to continue his research. For his part, Einstein seems to have idolized Lorentz. He once wrote to a friend, "I admire this man as no other. I would say I love him". Decades later, shortly before his own death, Einstein voiced an extraordinary sentiment about his older colleague: "He meant more to me personally, than anyone else I have met in my lifetime."

Later in his career, Lorentz loomed over the world of physics as a wise and benevolent grand old man, perhaps the leading physicist of his generation. But historians have been less kind. In the aftermath of the relativity revolution, Lorentz has often been portrayed as a sad figure, with a mind mired in the comfortable past and simply unable to comprehend the dazzling world unveiled by Einstein's theories. The historian Thomas Kuhn wrote chillingly about older scientists who were left behind by scientific revolutions, and quoted the physicist Max Planck: "A new scientific truth does not triumph by convincing its opponents and making them see the light, but rather because its opponents eventually die, and a new generation grows up that is familiar with it."

For many people, Lorentz is perhaps the most prominent example of a great scientist who died clinging to his outmoded theories. His case provides extra evidence of the depth of Einstein's reworking of our concepts of space and time: even a Lorentz, they say, could not make the revolutionary leap into the strange new world of relativity theory. Today, however, as doubts about the foundations of Einstein's theories multiply, Lorentz appears very differently. We now have more sympathy for his position, and even honour him for clinging to insights that time has rehabilitated. With Einstein, he is a hero in our story.

In particular, Lorentz helped begin a tradition of seeking deeper explanations of relativistic effects such as length contraction and time dilation. While Einstein simply derived these from the principles he assumed, Lorentz insisted that we press more deeply and uncover their causes. He was thus the founding father of what, for our purposes, we will call the minority interpretation.

The momentous debate between Einstein and Lorentz pitted two of the greatest physicists against each other. Their respect and affection for one another should not disguise how cutting their disagreement was. Both men had dedicated their lives to physics. If Lorentz proved correct, Einstein's historic first discovery would be denied him. If Einstein triumphed, Lorentz's whole approach to physics, his life-work, would be dismissed as old-fashioned, mechanical and metaphysical.

Einstein's mainstream interpretation is dramatic. With a single sweep, it eliminates features of our world that seemed obvious and indispensable, and tumbles us headlong into a new world where distances and durations are not real properties. This has been the dominant view since the triumph of Einstein's 1905 paper on special relativity. According to the minority interpretation first developed by Lorentz, however, each object does have a definite length of its own, but it varies with speed. That is *lengths are real but variable properties of individual bodies*. Similarly, an event such as the wink of an eye or a tennis match does have a definite duration, but the duration will dilate or shrink with speed. A tennis match on a large ship will really take longer than the same match would in a court at rest; a moving clock will really run more slowly. Thus the minority interpretation breaks the democracy among inertial measurements. It says that some measurements reveal the *real distances and durations*, while some instruments are distorted by the effects of their own high speeds and report merely apparent distances and durations.

Historically, Lorentz and other advocates of the minority interpretation were motivated by the following sorts of ideas. Just as water waves are disturbances travelling through water, they reasoned, light waves must be disturbances travelling through some very thin fluid filling all of space. They called this fluid the "ether", which is Greek for flame or fire. Although there was no direct evidence for the existence of such an ether, it conveniently explained length contraction. Just as a ship ploughing through water will feel a resistance that rises with speed, all objects that move in space are resisted by the ether. Since it is so thin, we are normally unaware of this, but at high speeds it would pile up against bodies and cause them to contract in the direction they are travelling in. A similar but more complicated argument explained time dilation as another effect of this resisting ether wind.

Thus the ether is important because it gave a physical explanation of length contraction and time dilation. Einstein and the mainstream interpretation simply deduce these effects from the mysterious constancy of the speed of light and the relativity principle, but do not explain them.

In fact, the minority interpretation has a very different view of the speed of light. It is well known that ordinary waves travel at the same speed in the same medium. Thus waves in water always travel at a characteristic speed. The reason is that each medium has a certain "bounciness" or elasticity that determines how quickly it pushes back when disturbed. Such a wave is, for one example, a push alternating downwards and upwards, so the degree of "bounciness" sets the speed of waves as they progress through the medium. In water, therefore, waves from a high-power racing boat and from a small pebble dropped in a pond both travel at the same speed. The minority interpretation argues that light is just an ordinary wave that travels in the ether, and thus *really* always has, regardless of its source, the same speed relative to the ether.

But the peculiar thing about light is that measurements of its relative speed always give the same result. According to the minority interpretation this is mere appearance and not really true. Actually, the speed of light relative to a spaceship *does* depend on how fast the spaceship is moving. If the spaceship is moving at half the speed of light, then a light beam racing ahead is gaining ground at only half the speed of light. The relative speed of light merely *appears* to be constant because of distortions due to length contraction and time dilation. Thus the minority interpretation removes the central mystery of Einstein's theory by explaining the constancy of light's relative speed, but it replaces it with the mystery of the ether.

Mainstream physicists have always been sceptical of the minority interpretation. They have great difficulty with these "real but variable" distances and durations. Since inertial movement is undetectable, passengers in a cabin below deck cannot tell how fast they are really moving, and likewise we cannot measure our real speed through the ether. Thus we cannot say how strong the ether wind is, and how much contraction it causes.

Physicists dislike properties that they cannot measure. The minority interpretation offers neat physical explanations but introduces unmeasurable and undetectable properties into physics.

There is a second, related reason why the mainstream never embraced the minority interpretation: it leads to no new predictions. Although it is quite radical, Einstein's theory is conceptually clean and very clear, whereas the minority interpretation is messy. It asserts the existence of real but unmeasurable lengths. It asserts the existence of the ether or some other cause of contraction and dilation, but provides no new or independent evidence for it. It asserts that these effects will coincidentally just match those predicted by Einstein, but seems to construct its theories just to produce this match. Physicists might accept this mess if the minority interpretation led to new ideas and made new predictions that would distinguish it from Einstein's theory. But so far it has not.

Before we needed to explain length contraction and time dilation we believed that distances and durations were *real* and *constant* properties. Now we must choose between two interpretations of these observations:

- *Majority interpretation:* distances and durations do not exist as real properties of individual things (a shoe has no size)
- *Minority interpretation:* distances and durations do exist and vary with speed through the ether; they are real but variable properties of individual things (a shoe has a variable size)

As we shall see, many other important consequences flow from this fundamental difference between the two interpretations.

The mainstream and minority interpretations lead to the same predictions. The mainstream interpretation is far more economical and cleaves closely to the results of measurement. The minority interpretation offers physical explanations and realistic pictures of the cause of length contraction and time dilation, but at the cost of introducing into physics unmeasurable properties and a ghostly, undetectable ether.

However, the debate between these two interpretations has heated up again in the past decade. In the following chapters we will explore the various advantages and disadvantages of these two interpretations. Chapter 17 will outline new experiments that seem to favour the minority interpretation, and that have triggered a renewed assessment of it merits.

The minority interpretation is committed to real, physical lengths and therefore to real, physical length contraction, but not to any particular cause of that contraction. The ether is only one possible explanation of contraction.

CHAPTER 3

The twin paradox

Symmetry

Among physicists, the word "symmetry" means "sameness across difference". The prefixes "sym" and "syn" mean "same", so "symphony" means "many musicians making the same sound" and "synchrony" means "same time". "Metry" comes from the Greek word for "measure" (as in "metric") and here means "size" or "shape". Thus a face has a symmetry when it has the same shape on different sides, but the charm of a human face often lies in its slight asymmetries.

One of the most outrageous aspects of Einstein's theories is their unexpected symmetries. Suppose that two identical spaceships, A and B, are approaching each other and will pass each other in empty space, and each is moving inertially at a steady speed along a straight line. Spaceship A will find that that spaceship B's lengths are contracted and hours are dilated. Everything in stubby spaceship B happens in slow motion. *But*, Einstein said, spaceship B is also moving inertially and it can also make measurements. According to *its* rulers and clocks, spaceship A is contracted and slowed. There is a perfect democracy among sets of rulers and clocks. That is, according to Einstein, spaceship A is shorter than spaceship B *and* spaceship B is shorter than spaceship A. Hours on spaceship A are longer than those on spaceship B *and* hours on spaceship B are longer than those on spaceship A. Time dilation and length contraction are symmetric. The different measurements show the same effects.

This prediction seemed to be complete nonsense to many physicists when they first learned of Einstein's theories: it seemed to be a blatant contradiction. But Einstein was able to explain that it did make sense, and was not at all contradictory. Understanding this will help us learn to envisage the new nature of space and time discovered by Einstein.

Measuring spaces in time

How can one spaceship be shorter and longer than the other? Is there a contradiction? The short answer is no. For a contradiction, opposite properties must belong to one thing at the *same* time, but this is not the case. The different spaceships have *different* times.

Consider how the lengths of moving bodies are measured. For concreteness, imagine that a Jaguar is on a road that is covered by alternating black and white squares like a chess-board. If the Jaguar is standing still, its length is easy to measure: just count the number of squares between the front and the back wheels. If the Jaguar is moving, however, the wheels are at different places at different times. For a meaningful measurement, we must count the squares between the locations of the front and the back wheels *at the same time*.

The general point is, therefore, that length measurements depend on a definition of simultaneity. Suppose that there are two observers. If they disagree about which events are simultaneous, they will disagree about where the wheels are "at the same time". Thus they will disagree about the length of the car.

Einstein suggested a practical method for measuring the speed of moving objects: a clock must be set up in each square of the chess-board, and all the clocks must be synchronized to show the same time simultaneously. To measure the length of a speeding Jaguar, we simply agree to mark the location of its wheels at the same time, say, precisely at noon, and count the intervening squares.

But how should the clocks be synchronized? If we collect them all together, synchronize them, and then move them back to their squares, the movement will cause time dilation and destroy their synchronization. Just as Jack in Houston and Jill in her spaceship experienced different flows of time, the moving clocks will show divergent times.

Einstein suggested that each clock be left sitting in its own square, and that a light beam be used to synchronize them. Suppose a flash of light travels across the chess-board, and that light takes a billionth of a second to cross one square. Then, if the flash of light strikes one clock at noon, it should strike the next at noon plus a billionth of a second, the next at noon plus two billionths of a second, and so on. The clocks can be adjusted to show these times, and thus will be synchronized. Since light always travels at the same speed, there are no distorting effects to disturb the clocks. The same sort of procedure can be used for making length measurements with a moving yardstick. Tiny clocks can be set up at regular intervals along the stick, and a ray of light travelling along the beam will synchronize them.

Einstein stressed that our intuition about measuring lengths cannot be trusted. Great care must be taken to measure the front and back locations of moving objects at the same time, and to use clocks synchronized with light beams.

Measurements of space depend on time.

The garage

An illustration will help bring these points home. According to Einstein, length contraction will permit us to house the six-metre Jaguar in a three-metre garage, as mentioned above. By driving at 85 per cent of the speed of light, the car will contract by some 50 per cent. We can drive the car into the garage and quickly slam the door. Does this show that the contracted car is really shorter than the garage? How could there be symmetry here? Could the car also be longer than the garage? (The discussion below is repeated in Appendix A.)

Since we do not have everyday experience of cars moving so fast, we have to be very careful when thinking about lengths. If measurements are made using rulers at rest inside the garage, they will indeed find the car shorter than the garage. That is, the front of the car and the rear of the car will both be within the garage *at the same time*. Since the car is moving so quickly, however, it will almost instantly thereafter smash into the back wall of the garage and explode. The explosion will first consume the nose of the car, and then a shock wave will travel along the body of the fast-moving car as its rear end continues to slide towards the flames. Finally, the car, rulers and garage will all be vaporized.

In sum, five events have the following order, according to clocks and rulers at rest in the garage:

1. The front of the car enters the garage.
2. The rear of the car enters the garage.
3. The door is slammed shut.
4. The front of the car is consumed by the explosion.
5. The rear of the car is consumed by the explosion.

The car is entirely inside the garage (or what is left of the garage) from the second event onwards.

The driver of the car, however, uses rulers and other equipment within the car and reports a very different sequence of events. According to the driver, the *garage* is approaching at 85 per cent of the speed of light, and therefore the garage is contracted to 50 per cent of its ordinary length. Thus the three-metre garage is only 1½ metres deep. Unable to stop the oncoming garage, the driver sees the nose of the six-metre Jaguar hit by the approaching back wall. At this same time, the rear of the car is still sticking 4½ metres out of the garage door. The resulting explosion at the nose creates a shock wave that travels down through the car as it crumples against the moving back wall. However, the garage is moving so quickly that it continues to slide past the car during the explosion. Just as the garage door passes the rear of the car, the garage door is slammed shut, and then the whole is consumed by the explosion. The door was indeed slammed

Moving car, stationary garage

Stationary car, moving garage

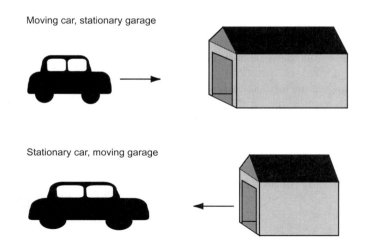

Figure 3.1 *Length contraction. From the perspective of a stationary garage and from the perspective of a stationary car.*

after the rear of the car was in the garage but, according to the driver, the explosion had already started and destroyed the front of the six-metre car.

In sum, there are again five events, but the driver records them in a different order:

1. The front of the car enters the garage.
2. The front of the car is consumed by the explosion.
3. The rear of the car enters the garage.
4. The door is slammed shut.
5. The rear of the car is consumed by the explosion.

The car is longer than the garage but fits inside because the explosion consumes the front of the car before the rear enters.

According to Einstein, it is generally true that events in different places may have no definite order in time. For example, suppose there are two distant places and that three events happen in each place. Say events X, Y and Z happen on the left and events A, B and C happen on the right. According to one set of clocks, the events may happen in the order ABCXYZ, while another set of clocks may record the order AXBYCZ. Thus *events separated in space may have different orders in time*, depending on which set of rulers and clocks is used to measure them. This is just a consequence of time dilation: the relative stretching out of time intervals at high speeds.

Two events have a fixed and definite order only when one is the *cause* of the other. For Einstein, causes always precede their effects. But when neither light nor any other causal process can travel fast enough to pass from one event to another, there is nothing to determine their order. Thus if, on the right, A causes B, which causes C, then no clock could record their order as BAC.

To summarize, time passes in different ways. When events are separated in space, different sets of clocks will find they occur in different orders. The order of events differs. The car is shorter than and longer than the garage, but not "at the same time". There is symmetry of effects but no contradiction.

Interpreting symmetry

Both the majority and minority interpretations agree that measurements show that one ship is longer *and* shorter than the other, or that the car is longer *and* shorter than the garage, depending on which set of rulers and clocks is used. That is, they agree that appearances are symmetric. They also agree that there is no contradiction because different times are involved.

Symmetry is, however, a key test case for the two interpretations. When we push beneath observations and measurements and ask what is really happening behind the appearances the two interpretations dramatically diverge. For many physicists, symmetry shows just how unappealing and unwieldy the minority interpretation can be.

The majority interpretation can explain symmetry quite briefly. Recall that there is a democracy among sets of rulers and clocks that are moving inertially (principle of relativity). Therefore, when one set finds that objects moving past are shorter than when at rest, then other sets will also find that objects moving past are shorter. Different sets of rulers and clocks are governed by the same laws and should see the same effects – even when two spaceships are measuring each other. This is a beautifully simple and clear account of a very perplexing phenomenon. At once, the outrageous surprise of Einstein's symmetry seems to dissipate. Symmetry seems natural: it is just a consequence of the principle of relativity. Moreover, the majority interpretation adds, there could be no contradiction in saying that one ship is shorter and longer than the other. Since lengths are not real properties, the ship does not have two opposite properties at once. Lengths are relations, and a ship can have two lengths in the same way a person can be a brother and cousin.

For advocates of the minority interpretation, this is all deeply unsatisfying. They assert that lengths are properties, and that there is a fact of the matter about which of two objects is shorter and which is longer. Explaining the symmetry is a serious challenge for the minority interpretation. According to this interpretation, the ether is at rest and other objects have definite speeds relative to it. Thus, for example, someone might say that the garage is really at rest and the Jaguar is moving towards it. This means that their real speeds relative to the ether are different or "asymmetric" (there is no sameness across difference). Usually, an asymmetry cannot explain a symmetry; usually, different causes have different effects. Thus explaining Einstein's symmetries is difficult for the minority interpretation.

It succeeds because there is a second asymmetry. According to the minority interpretation, the lengths are really different. The moving Jaguar is really contracted. Thus both the lengths and the speeds are asymmetric. Roughly put, these two asymmetries cancel each other out: the effects of two compensating asymmetries can be symmetric.

To see this, consider the moving Jaguar. According to the minority interpretation the Jaguar is really contracted, but measurements made by the driver perversely indicate instead that the garage is shorter. How can this be? Suppose the driver uses the car itself as a ruler. To measure the length of moving objects, the driver must determine when it is *the same time at opposite ends of the car*. For that purpose, the driver briefly turns on a dashboard light at the mid-point of the car; the moments when the flash reaches the front and rear end of the car are "simultaneous". Unbeknown to the driver, however, the minority interpretation insists that the car is really moving as the light is travelling. This shortens the time required for the light to reach the oncoming rear. But the front of the car is racing away from the flash. If the car is travelling at nearly light speed, it will take a very long time for the flash to catch up with the car's front. Crucially, the fact that the car is moving means that the two events in which the light reaches its end-points are actually very far apart in space: much farther than the real length of the car.

But the driver thinks the length of the car is unchanged. The driver thinks that the very large distance between the two events is just the ordinary length of the car. By comparison, stationary objects seem shorter than the Jaguar because the method of measurement makes the distance between the moving ends of the car seem much larger. Thus, *the driver grossly under-reports the lengths of bodies* passed by the Jaguar. Measurements made from the car will show that the garage is contracted.

According to the minority interpretation, the symmetry of length contraction is partly an illusion. The moving car is really contracted, as measurements made by stationary rulers and clocks in the garage correctly show. But measurements made by rulers and clocks moving with the contracted car are fooled by the motion, and underestimate the lengths of passing bodies.

Miraculously, this mixture of real contraction and illusory measurements produces exactly the symmetry predicted by Einstein (details in Appendix B). In the end, the two interpretations are exactly equivalent.

Although both the mainstream and minority interpretations predict the symmetry of relativistic effects, the issue has been a tremendous psychological boost for the mainstream view. Where the minority interpretation seems a mad conspiracy of inelegant complications, the mainstream interpretation is sweet and clear.

Both interpretations agree that appearances are symmetric. The majority interpretation says lengths are real relations, and these relations are really symmetric. The minority interpretation denies there is any real symmetry: the moving spaceship is really shorter than a resting spaceship. In one case appearances reflect reality; in the other, there are compensating real asymmetries that deceptively produce symmetric appearances.

A fountain of youth?

The most famous of the problems prominent in the early controversies over relativity was the twin paradox. It is easy to state but exposes some very deep issues, and so hundreds of papers have been written about it over the decades. Now that the dust has settled, it is clear that the paradox does contain a profound lesson. It does not show that relativity is nonsense, but helps us sharpen our intuitions about life at the speed of light.

Suppose that Jack and Jill are twins. Jack still works in Houston for NASA, and Jill is an astronaut embarking on a long journey to some distant star. If her spaceship travels at nearly the speed of light, the clocks and other processes on board will slow because of time dilation. For Jill, the astronaut twin, the journeys out and back again will both be fairly brief. But on Jill's return, stay-at-home Jack in Houston will be a grey grandparent, and many years "older" than his twin.

As the experiment with the atomic clocks showed, this is not a fairy tale. If long space journeys occur in the future with very fast spaceships, such discrepancies in age will become common. Many generations of workers may retire from mission control before a crew of youthful astronauts return from a single journey.

Why did early critics believe this was a paradox that disproved relativity? Because, they argued, the theory is symmetric. According to Einstein, the spaceship's clocks are slower than those on Earth *and* the earth-bound clocks are slower than those on the spaceship. If both these are true, then why should only the twin in Houston be so old? Whatever happens, shouldn't the twins' experiences be symmetric, that is, the same despite their different journeys?

These critics have made a mistake. There is a big difference between the twins: the astronaut twin *accelerates*. Remember that

Einstein's special theory of relativity is special because it applies only to rulers and clocks moving steadily in the same direction, that is, moving inertially. Jill climbs into a rocket that accelerates to leave Earth and our solar system. In the middle and again at the end of her trip, further accelerations are needed to land at home again. Since these accelerations are asymmetric and experienced only by one twin, there is no reason to expect that their ages will remain the same. Asymmetric causes imply asymmetric effects.

Steady motion is not detectable by experiment. Thus when two bodies approach each other inertially, no experimental evidence will show whether one or the other or both are moving. Acceleration, however, is not inertial movement, and is easy to detect. Those who drink hot coffee in a suddenly braking car will soon have the experimental evidence in their laps. As a car moves inertially, the surface of the liquid remains flat; but with any acceleration – speeding up, slowing down or turning – the liquid will slurp over to one side of the cup. Acceleration has dramatic effects, and the difference in the twins' ages is one of them.

Of course, the acceleration does not *directly* cause the asymmetry. The acceleration determines the path of the astronaut twin, and it is this path that determines the age difference. The asymmetry of the acceleration causes an asymmetry in the motions of the twins, and this causes the asymmetry between their ages.

In retrospect, the twin paradox is so prominent in the literature on relativity because many believe that Einstein showed that "everything is relative". But this is not true even for motions. Inertial motions are relative, but *accelerations are physical*. Regardless of which set of inertial rulers and clocks is used, if the distance between two bodies changes with accelerating speeds, then experiments will quickly decide which body is moving. The lesson of the twin paradox is that, even in relativity theory, not everything is relative.

Speed reflects the distance covered during a duration of time; acceleration is a change in speed. It is surprising that accelerations have physical effects even though distances and durations are not physical properties.

CHAPTER 4

How to build an atomic bomb

A few months after Einstein published his first paper on relativity in 1905, he sent in a sort of extended footnote to the same journal. His theory had an odd little consequence. It seemed so strange that he phrased the note's title as a question: "Does Mass Depend on Energy?" To leaf through the next four flimsy pieces of paper and contemplate all that followed is to feel the power of ideas. For better or worse, Einstein had unlocked the secret of the atom. Here was the destruction of Hiroshima and Nagasaki. Here were 40 years of fear and tension as Cold War superpowers pursued their policy of mutual assured destruction, insisting on arsenals so large that even after a first strike they could reduce their adversary to bouncing rubble. Here was the promise of infinitely renewable energy, and the curse of Chernobyl. Here was the first explanation of the Sun's ceaseless light and the starry heavens. Although it is true that chemists had stumbled upon radioactivity before Einstein, and might have developed atomic power without him, Einstein's theory was the torch that led the way. His ideas shaped a century we were lucky to survive.

Einstein concluded his short note by deriving the most famous physics equation of them all,

$$E = mc^2$$

(pronounced "ee equals em sea squared"): the only equation we will meet in the main text of this book. Here, E stands for energy, m for mass and c for the speed of light. In short, it means that energy can be converted into mass, and mass into energy. In some sense, they are just different forms of the same thing.

Just after deriving this formula, in the last lines of his note, Einstein raised the question of whether his far-fetched idea might have experimental consequences: "It is not impossible that with bodies whose energy-content is variable to a high degree (e.g. with radium salts) the theory may be successfully put to the test." That is, Einstein already glimpsed in 1905 the possibility that radioactive elements like radium or uranium might easily exhibit conversions of mass into energy. This was 40 years before Hiroshima and Nagasaki were bombed. Even now, thousands of nuclear missiles sit steaming in their silos poised for launch. A dozen countries are pressing ahead with their weapons programmes. Einstein's ideas haunt us still.

Faster speeds, greater masses

Energy is the "amount of motion". Suppose that two identical cars are racing down a road; the faster car has more energy. Suppose that a truck and a small car are travelling side by side along the road and at the same speed; the truck is heavier and therefore has more energy. It is harder to stop. Thus, in moving objects, more speed or more mass means more energy. As a car accelerates or as we push a body along, it gains more energy.

Einstein discovered that a moving object weighs more than the same object at rest; that is, an object with more energy also has more mass. As the speed of an object increases, its mass increases. As objects move faster and faster and approach the speed of light, their mass becomes nearly *infinite*. This effect is called "relativistic mass increase". There are various ways of describing this but the one adopted here is the simplest and most common.

Energy can also be stored inside objects. Suppose we hold the ends of an elastic band in our hands. As we move our hands apart, they have motion and thus energy. As the band stretches to its limit, our hands slow down and the band absorbs their energy. The energy or motion is clearly in the band. If we relax and let the band pull on our hands, they will move together again. This inward motion has the energy that was stored in the band. Thus the band is a device for absorbing, storing and releasing energy.

Stored energy also has mass. When the elastic band is stretched or a spring is compressed it weighs more. Likewise, a new battery weighs slightly more than a used battery. Like time dilation and length contraction, this mass increase is not noticeable in everyday life. The extra mass is only significant when bodies move at enormously high speeds. The motion of our hands stored in the elastic band is so slow that no device yet invented is capable of measuring the mass increase.

To summarize, with faster speeds bodies weigh more, that is, they have more mass. More precisely:

> *Relativistic mass increase:* Assume an apparatus at rest or moving at a steady speed in the same direction is used to measure the mass of passing bodies. A given body that is measured at several speeds will have higher masses at faster speeds.

The celestial speed limit

Imagine trying to run if every faster stride made your legs heavier and even sprinting speeds turned them into lead weights. Increasing a body's speed requires some kind of push or force. Increasing the speed of heavier bodies requires stronger and harder pushes. If a body's mass approaches infinity, then further increases in speed would require forces that approach infinity. But no rocket engine and no explosion can produce *infinite* forces: nothing finite and limited can produce something infinite. Thus no force existing in the universe can push a body all the way up to the speed of light. In short:

Argument that the speed of light is a maximum

A. If a mass reaches the speed of light, then an infinite force exists.	(P)
B. No infinite force exists.	(P)
C. Therefore, no mass reaches the speed of light.	(from A,B)

The first premise, A, is part of relativity theory. The second, B, seems secure because an infinite force would require infinite energy, which is not available in any finite portion of our universe.

Thus Einstein discovered that physical laws impose a speed limit on all movements: no body can attain or reach the speed of light. This is the famous "celestial speed limit". There is some talk of spaceships with "warp drive" engines, or of imaginary particles called "tachyons" that travel faster than light, but, if Einstein is right, these will remain the stuff of science fiction.

Why is light capable of travelling at the maximum speed? Einstein's recipe for finding the mass of a moving object says first weigh the object on a bathroom scale when it is at rest, and then multiply by a number like 2 or 15 or 20,000 (higher numbers for faster bodies) to find its mass when moving. That is, the mass at high speeds depends on the mass found when the body is measured at rest, that is, on its *rest mass*. More precisely, the mass at high speeds is a *multiple* of the rest mass.

Interestingly, a ray of light is pure energy and has no rest mass at all. Thus if the rest mass is zero, then multiplying by 2 or 20,000 or infinity will still leave zero. A multiple of zero is still zero. Unlike ordinary bodies, light can travel at the maximum speed without becoming infinitely heavy.

This celestial speed limit for ordinary bodies is more than disappointing. Although almost every physicist believes that faster-than-light travel is impossible, perhaps someone someday will discover a way to circumvent Einstein's prohibition. Recent experiments (see below) hint that there is a loophole.

Mass is energy: energy is mass

Einstein had a mind that leapt nimbly from one new idea to the next. His powerful sense of intuition steered him to a safe landing and a new discovery. These leaps make his scientific essays miniature works of art. They are simple and graceful, but reveal a mind dancing among the deepest ideas. One example of such a leap is his claim that energy and mass are the same thing. Strictly speaking, relativistic mass increase says only that a given hunk of mass will gain or lose weight as its speed changes: more or less speed is more or less mass. Strictly speaking, this does not imply that *all* mass is made up of energy. For example, just because blowing air into a balloon or releasing it from the balloon changes the size of the balloon, we do not say that the balloon is entirely made up of air. The red plastic must be there first.

But Einstein leapt. If *some* mass is produced by increased energy then, he claimed, *all* mass is just energy. Thus his famous formula does not say that adding energy produces a change in mass – as adding air swells a balloon. It just says that energy is mass, and mass is energy. It took some time before other physicists were convinced that Einstein was right. Now they routinely transform mass into energy and vice versa in their experiments. It is even common to transform solid matter into nothing but pure energy.

43

Thus the first important idea contained in Einstein's short formula is that energy can be converted into mass and vice versa: the *interconvertibility* of mass and energy. This interconversion has an important consequence; it shows that the law of conservation of energy and the law of conservation of mass are false. In classical physics before Einstein, these were regarded as fundamental. But when mass is converted into energy, the total amount of mass in the universe decreases just as the total amount of energy increases. Thus neither total is conserved. To save the general idea of conservation, physicists combined the two laws. After Einstein, they said that the total amount of mass and energy together is conserved when all measurements are made by the same set of rulers and clocks. This new idea is called the *law of conservation of mass–energy*. (Physicists discovered later that this law holds only *on average*: for short times the total amount of mass–energy can fluctuate up or down.)

Einstein's formula also contains a second idea lodged in the little letter *c*. It is this which makes the formula so dangerous, and so profoundly shaped the twentieth century. How much energy comes from a given hunk of matter? Suppose we have one ounce or one gram of matter and convert it into energy. How much oomph do we get?

The formula makes the calculation easy. For the letter *m* substitute the amount of mass to be converted. Then multiply by *c* squared to get the energy. This looks very innocent, but in fact *c* squared is a very big number: 9,000,000,000,000. In words, this is nine trillion (using units of metres per second squared). Thus one gram of matter, about the weight of a feather, will produce an explosion about the same size as *20,000 tons* of exploding dynamite! This was the size of the atomic bomb dropped on Hiroshima. If the energy trapped in your body were suddenly all released, Earth would be shattered.

Chain reactions

Atomic bombs are dangerous because they are so simple. As far as we know, every nation that has attempted to build and explode them has succeeded. Relatively crude technology will do. The first bombs were built in the early 1940s before transistors and computers were invented. Think of an old radio or automobile from that time: the same technology was used to build the first bombs.

The central idea is this. Suppose that we have small but strong steel springs that can be compressed and latched. Since they store energy when latched, they are slightly heavier. Suppose, however, that the latches are fragile and barely manage to keep the spring from extending out again. With the slightest jar or bang, the latches may break and release the spring. Thus the compressed and latched spring is *unstable*.

Suppose that we collect hundreds of such latched springs, pack them tightly in a barrel and screw the lid down. They may sit there peacefully for a while. But suppose that someone bumps the barrel, or suppose that a latch somewhere spontaneously breaks apart. If just one spring is released the commotion may give its neighbours a knock. They too will burst their latches, and knock their neighbours in turn. Soon the barrel will be rocking and bouncing with uncoiling springs. Perhaps all of them will expand and explode the barrel.

This is an atomic bomb: unstable units packed together tightly and then disturbed. Each unit releases energy as it breaks apart, and this energy disturbs its neighbours, releasing even more energy. If each exploding unit causes more than one of it neighbours to burst apart, then the numbers of bursting units will rise rapidly. This is the famous *chain reaction*. Atoms are used instead of steel springs because they are very small. Enormous numbers of them can therefore be packed into a bomb small enough to be carried by an aeroplane or truck.

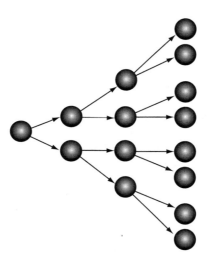

Figure 4.1 A chain reaction. An example where each atom releases energy and causes two more atoms to break apart, releasing even more energy.

Not all kinds of atoms are appropriate "fuel" for an atom bomb. The core or nucleus of each atom contains particles called protons. These particles all powerfully repel each other and are always struggling to escape and run off in all directions, but they are held in place and bound together by strong forces, which usually keep the atom quite stable. However, in very large atoms, there are so many protons that their repulsion from each other is almost as powerful as the attractive forces that knit them together. These large atoms are unstable. A nudge or shock may break them apart and liberate the protons.

If many large unstable atoms make up a hunk of matter and a single one disintegrates, the liberated particles may knock a neighbouring atom and cause its disintegration. If each atom destabilizes and destroys more than one of its neighbours, the chain reaction would soon "avalanche" and cause much of the hunk of matter to explode.

Unluckily for us, atoms just right for making atomic bombs are lying around in nature, and can be mined in the deserts of South Africa or the western United States. The most well-known is uranium, a yellowy heavy metal. Its nucleus can contain 238 large particles, which makes it very large and very fragile. Even sitting in the desert, some of its atoms decay spontaneously and send particles shooting outwards. But they usually escape without hitting and destroying a neighbouring atom (the ordinary matter around us and in our bodies is 99.99 per cent empty space). In a bomb, largish hunks of uranium are put together so that escaping particles have a high probability of hitting a neighbouring uranium atom and starting a chain reaction.

There is one important trick needed to make an atomic bomb. Suppose a chain reaction starts. One atom breaks apart and particles shoot outwards and break two neighbouring atoms apart. The particles expelled from these two atoms break four more apart, and the chain reaction proceeds, affecting 1, 2, 4, 8, 16, 32, 64 atoms, and so on. This series of mini-explosions will release heat and energy, and this will cause the metal to melt and ooze down into a puddle. As it does so, the atoms will separate from each other: heat causes expansion. In turn, this will make it less likely that the escaping particles will bump into a neighbouring atom. Thus the chain reaction will fizzle, affecting, say, 64, 32, 27, 16, 5, and eventually 0 atoms. The uranium will melt and become white hot but nothing more.

This is where the physicists call in the engineers. To sustain the chain reaction, the uranium atoms must be held together tightly for just long enough for the chain reaction to proceed. This is a delicate feat of engineering. In one design, unstable atoms are formed into a ball and surrounded by dynamite. Just as the chain reaction is sparked off, the surrounding dynamite is exploded. The inward compressing force of the ordinary explosion holds the uranium together for just long enough (only a small fraction of a second) for the chain reaction to race through the entire core. Even though the metal becomes incredibly hot, the atoms remain close enough to sustain the chain reaction. Suddenly, so much energy is released that the compressing force is brushed aside and a huge explosion is unleashed.

The recipe for an atom bomb is thus simple physics and delicate engineering. First, obtain and purify a few pounds of uranium or plutonium. Keep the material in small samples so that no chain reaction begins spontaneously. Place them gently together in a bomb. At the desired instant, compress the samples together and trigger a chain reaction, say by sharply striking the metal. Hold the compressed sample together for long enough for the chain reaction to consume large numbers of unstable atoms.

In a way, we cannot comprehend the horror of these bombs. The city of Hiroshima has erected a museum and left a few shattered buildings untouched since 1945. This is a moving reminder that science threatens us, and continues to threaten us with annihilation. It is not clear how we will cope in the long run. Our hopes depend in part on the same intelligence that has endangered us, and on a vigilant understanding of these weapons and the physics behind them. Against the horrors of the Second World War, we can now weigh one shining, collective achievement. For more than half a century, no one has dropped an atomic bomb on another human being. Every year that ticks by adds to this fragile miracle.

Interpreting mass–energy

The interconvertibility of mass and energy is a shock. We are accustomed to thinking that the world consists of some sort of stable stuff. It can move back and forth in space, or clump together and fall apart, but somehow survives all such rearrangements. What does it mean to say that this stuff is composed of motion? More poetically, are our bodies just forms of trapped motion? Are our movements just streaks of evaporating matter? Einstein's equation does not answer these questions. It simply reports the fact that matter and energy can be converted into each other.

Lorentz's minority interpretation offers an interesting explanation of why mass increases with speed. The idea that someone jumping from a skyscraper reaches a maximum velocity may be familiar. As the body rushes earthwards more and more quickly, it tries to push the air out of its way. But the faster the push, the more the air resists it. Eventually there is a balance. Gravity tries to pull the body down even faster, but the air pushes back and prevents any more acceleration. The body plummets downwards at a constant velocity, which physicists call (no pun) its "terminal velocity".

There is an alternative interpretation of this. Instead of saying that the resistance of the air increases with the body's speed we could insist that the mass of the body increases with the body's speed. Both of these would imply that gravity would find it more difficult to further accelerate the falling body. Both of these are in accordance with the observed facts.

In more detail, near the top of the skyscraper gravity initially succeeds in accelerating the body. But as the body falls more rapidly we could say it responds less and less to the force of gravity and continues moving downwards only because of inertia. Since it is more difficult to make heavy bodies speed up, we could say *that the body effectively gets heavier and heavier as it speeds up*. That is why its acceleration dwindles to zero even though the downward force on it stays the same. In fact, at the maximum, terminal velocity, we could say that the body is infinitely heavy, since it no longer responds to the force of gravity at all.

If we did not know about the resistance of the air, and had no other way of sensing air, we might have found it natural to say that mass rises with velocity. This second interpretation is well known to physicists who study the way ships and submarines move through water. They say that such bodies have an *effective mass* that rises with velocity through a fluid. Interestingly, the same is true of electrons and other charged particles travelling through electromagnetic fields. The faster the electron moves, the heavier it seems. It becomes more and more difficult to accelerate through the field. Physicists sometimes say that its effective or *electromagnetic mass* rises with velocity.

Lorentz suggested that the relativistic increase of mass was just such an effect. Since he believed in the existence of the ether, he concluded that rising effective masses were caused by its resistance. That is, the ether behaves like other fluids and resists being shoved aside as bodies pass through it. Since there is so little ether in any volume of space, we do not ordinarily observe this resistance; only as bodies move extremely fast, say at nearly the speed of light, would its effects become significant.

As before, the minority interpretation is appealing because it offers a neat and persuasive explanation, but it depends on an undetectable ether.

CHAPTER 5

The four-dimensional universe

The views of space and time which I wish to lay before you have sprung from the soil of experimental physics, and therein lies their strength. They are radical. Henceforth space by itself, and time by itself, are doomed to fade away into mere shadows, and only a kind of union of the two will preserve an independent reality. (Minkovski, 1908)

Three years after Einstein published his paper on special relativity, his former teacher Hermann Minkovski forever transformed our view of the universe. Einstein had predicted length contraction and time dilation, but Minkovski drew out their radical implications. As the famous quotation above suggests, Minkovski (pronounced Min-koff-ski) showed that space and time were mixed together in a sort of "union". We do not live in a three-dimensional universe with time flowing through. Instead, we live in a *four-dimensional spacetime*. Time is the fourth dimension.

These are strange claims. To assess them, the next two sections lay out some important philosophical issues in general terms. The following sections return to Minkovski and relativity theory.

Is the world made of events?

A tennis ball is real. A tennis court and tennis players are real. But is a tennis match real? Common sense and philosophers like Aristotle assert that the basic things in the universe are ordinary objects like human beings, tennis balls and trees. Modern science disagrees, and says instead that atoms or quarks are basic; human beings and tennis balls are built up from these smaller particles. Both of these views, however, are examples of ontologies in which *the basic objects persist through time*. That is, a tennis ball or an atom exists at one moment, and the next, and the next. Loosely put, one and the same object moves through time.

Some physicists and philosophers think that relativity has definitively shown that our world does not consist of persistent objects: there are no such things. Tennis balls and tennis courts are not real. Instead, the basic objects are events like tennis matches, elections or weddings. These are fixed at a particular time and place and never occur at another time and place. These are the basic objects of an *event ontology*. According to this view, the ordinary objects that appear to persist through time are really just collections of events. We see a tennis racquet striking a ball, a ball in flight, a ball nipping a net, a ball skidding on a court and a ball hitting the opponent's racquet. This sequence of events is usually believed to involve one and the same ball. But in an event ontology, these events are each real and distinct. Events are not made up of persisting objects. There is no single ball moving through the events. Rather, there is a similar-looking, yellow fuzzy patch in each of a series of events.

Philosophers usefully distinguish between *persistence* and *endurance*. An object that moves through time from one moment to the next persists. A sequence of similar but distinct events that creates the illusion of persistence is called an "enduring object". Events are sometimes thought of as *parts of the enduring object*, which is itself just a long-lasting event. In debates over relativity, an enduring object is sometimes called a *spacetime worm* because it is a consecutive series of events snaking through space and time. Thus, in an event ontology, both people and quarks are reinterpreted as spacetime worms.

Compare this to a reel of film shown in the cinema. Each still photograph on the reel is the picture of an event at a particular time and place. The photographs do not change, but the sequence creates the illusion of motion. An event ontology is similar: in reality there are only unchanging events in fixed sequences and, therefore, the illusion of motion, change and persistence through time.

But surely we experience motion and change? We see it all around us! Defenders of event ontologies agree that we have an *illusion* of movement and change, but deny their actual existence. The sensation of movement that we might experience in a moving car is just that – a sensation. It occurs at an instant in our minds, and is not itself direct evidence for motion outside our minds. Even common sense agrees that there can be sensations of motion without real motion, as when someone is sick with vertigo.

Likewise, defenders of event ontologies argue that, strictly speaking, we do not in fact see motion. We see an object at one place and have a memory of a similar object in another place; the visual image and the memory together, they argue, produce an impression of motion. The existence of the memory is a fact about the present, and not itself direct evidence for true motion. Moreover, since motion occurs across time, we could not experience it directly. That would imply experiencing a past moment in the present. In short, defenders of an event ontology say that all experience occurs at a moment in time, and such experience cannot be direct evidence for motions and changes that stretch out through many moments. *Thus an event ontology is compatible with all our direct experience, and therefore strictly in accordance with all observation and experiment.*

Some philosophers criticize event ontologies, saying that they make the similarity of events in a sequence an incredible accident. Why should the event of the racquet striking the ball be followed by another event that includes the ball? This makes sense if the ball moves through time to the next event. But if there is no true movement and change, why should consecutive events be similar at all? Could a ball at one moment be followed in the next by a swallow in mid-flight? Why do we not see series of events that look like "cuts" in a film, in which the scene changes instantly and there is no relation between consecutive stills?

The answer to this objection is interesting. Defenders of event ontologies admit that the similarity of events that follow one another has no physical explanation: it is just a "brute fact" about which nothing more can be said. Perhaps God just decreed that events have a pleasing order. But, the defenders continue, in the common-sense universe, where objects are supposed to be real and persist through time, there is a corresponding mystery. Physical laws account for movement through time, and these are also just brute facts. Thus both views have to accept unexplainable brute facts.

In an event ontology, there is no explanation for similarities among sequences of events; in a common-sense universe, the movements of persistent objects are explained by laws, but these laws themselves – at some level – have no explanation. Thus in both there remains a mystery about the nature of movement and change. (Moreover, some philosophers say that such laws are just regular patterns of events, which would make the mystery of laws identical to the brute mystery of ordered events.)

In short, event ontologies seem peculiar but are surprisingly coherent and compatible with all our experience. Does relativity theory decide the question of whether persistent objects or events are real?

Do the future and past exist now?

Most of us believe that only the present exists. Events in the future will exist, and events in the past did exist, but neither future nor past events exist now. This view is called *presentism* and treats time and space in very different ways. The different parts of space all coexist in a present moment, but only one part of time exists; namely, the present.

Presentism is compatible with either the existence of persistent objects moving through time or with an event ontology. A presentist merely insists that "only the present exists now" and is indifferent to what the present consists of, that is, whether it is persistent objects or events.

Many interpreters of relativity have asserted that the theory proves that presentism is false. Instead, the past and future coexist with the present, and are just as real as the present. This is strange and perhaps even frightening. It means that past wars are still being fought, and that every step of our future lives is already happening in some sense. In debates over relativity theory, such a world is called the block universe, because the entire four-dimensional universe, including the past and the future, seems to be like a giant block of ice: all events in the past, present and future coexist and are frozen in their locations in space and time.

For our purposes, we will assume that either presentism or the block universe view must be true. That is, other combinations (like an existent present and past, but nonexistent future) will be ignored.

Metaphors are often used to help us mentally picture a block universe. It has been compared to a loaf of bread or bologna. The present moment is a slice across the middle of the loaf; the future and the past lie on either side. Of course, the loaf is only a three-dimensional object, and the block universe is four-dimensional. Thus slices of the block universe would each be a three-dimensional world at an instant: just like the world we see around us now. The series of such three-dimensional "slices" – past, present and future – together make up the whole four-dimensional block.

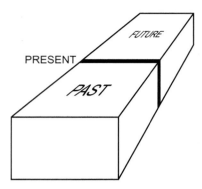

Figure 5.1   *The block universe. A frozen four-dimensional world of events.*

Since each slice of the block universe is a complete world-at-an-instant, it contains all objects that exist at the time. This is, again, like cinema film: each still photograph in the film is a picture of a scene at an instant, and the sequence of all the stills makes up the entire film. If the still photographs were cut apart and bundled together in a pile, we would have yet another image of the block universe.

If it is true that we live in a block universe, then there are no objects persisting through time. That is, *a block universe implies an event ontology*. This is because there is no real motion or change in a block universe. True motion occurs when a body now in one place occupies another place in the future: that is, when one and the same body moves from one location to another as, for example, when someone walks across a room. This could not happen in a block universe, where future events already exist. In a block universe, future events have an existence that is just as real and full-blooded as present events.

Advocates of the block universe also claim that the movements and changes we see around us are all a kind of illusion. The star of a film may occur in every still on the reel, and may appear to be moving when the film is shown, but actually does not move at all: each still is fixed. Similarly, the slices in a block universe are each slightly different. If we believe that someone is walking across the room, there is actually a series of slices each with a walker in slightly different positions. In each slice, the walker is standing stock still like a sentry. Thus both the event ontology view and the block universe view assert that motion is just a series of fixed events, like a sequence of still photographs. In the block universe all the events in the series exist at once: from the past, to the present and into the future.

When discussing the block universe or event ontologies, philosophers sometime find it awkward to use expressions like "the past exists now" or "the future has already happened". The reason is that verbs like "to exist" include a reference to the passage of time, that is, they are past, present or future tense. Thus, to say "the past exists" seems like a contradiction because the verb is in the present tense. To avoid this, philosophers tend to talk about *tenseless existence*, that is, a way of existing that does not imply a flow from the past into the future but is instead eternally static. Thus they say that, in a block universe, the past and the future "exist tenselessly", and mean that "exist" here is not to be understood as a verb in the ordinary present tense.

A final distinction that is important for understanding the block universe view is that between Laplacian determinism and fatalism:

- *Laplacian determinism*: the view that conditions at the present moment together with physical laws determine all future events. That is, laws ensure that the future can happen in only one way.
- *Fatalism:* the view that all future events are fixed, but not necessarily by physical laws. That is, the future can happen in only one way, but there may be no regular or law-like patterns in future events. Perhaps God or fortune has decreed that a series of miracles or physically uncaused events come about.

The block universe view is fatalistic. In a block universe, there can be only one future because it is already there, and in some sense has already happened. But the block universe view does not depend on the existence of laws, or any regularities between slices. Laplacian determinism may be true in a block universe, or may not be.

It was believed that classical physics before Einstein provided evidence for the truth of Laplacian determinism, but many now believe that twentieth-century physics disproved this view and showed that there is true randomness in microscopic events. The defeat of Laplacian determinism, however, would not count against the block universe view. (Thus the block universe view is compatible with probabilistic interpretations of quantum theory.)

Spacetime

Upon giving up the hypothesis of the invariant and absolute character of time, particularly that of simultaneity, the four-dimensionality of the time–space concept was immediately recognised. It is neither the point in space, nor the instant in time, at which something happens that has physical reality, but only the event itself. There is no absolute relation in space, and no absolute relation in time between two events, but there is an absolute relation in space and time . . . Upon this depends the great advance in method which the theory of relativity owes to Minkovski. (Albert Einstein, *Meaning of Relativity*)

Before relativity, it was thought that the world and objects in it were all three-dimensional. This meant everything had a length, breadth and height. It is hard to say what a dimension is. We picture a dimension as a long, straight line. If three straight lines can be drawn at right angles to each other, the space they are drawn in is three-dimensional. On a piece of paper, only two straight lines can be drawn at right angles, so the paper is two-dimensional.

Lines through space can be used to name the locations of objects. On the two-dimensional surface of the earth, places can be located by their latitude and longitude. In three-dimensional space, we can name places using the three coordinates (x, y, z). What would it mean to say that the world is really four-dimensional? It is easy to locate all events in space and time because each has a place and a date. Each event could therefore be given four coordinates (x, y, z, t). In effect, we routinely recognize that events have four dimensions when we agree to meet someone for coffee at a certain place and time. Thus it is true but trivial to say that events have four coordinates. When some physicists say the world is four-dimensional they are making a different and much stronger statement. To understand their claim, we begin with a fact, and then consider its interpretation.

Suppose there are two events, A and B, each at a different place and time. Using rulers and clocks we could measure the distance between the two places and the duration between the two times. These two numbers indicate how separated the events are in space and time. But, as we have seen, these distances and durations are not invariant and therefore are not real properties of anything. Now something magical happens. Although neither the distance nor the duration is invariant, together they do form an invariant number. They are combined using a peculiar recipe. The distance and duration are treated as if they were two sides of a right-angled triangle. Using a formula very similar to Pythagoras' theorem, we calculate the length of the "third" side of the triangle. This new

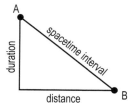

Figure 5.2 *The spacetime interval. A number calculated from the distance and time elapsed between events A and B that expresses how far apart they are in spacetime.*

number is *invariant*. Since it is some kind of combination of space and time, it is called the *spacetime interval*.

Measurements of distances and durations depend on speeds, since they will contract or dilate, but the spacetime interval between two particular events is always the same: everyone who measures and calculates will find the same number. This is surprising. How do two variable numbers combine into a constant? One way of thinking of it is that, at higher speeds, the lengths shrink and the times elongate, and these variations compensate for each other. All physicists agree that the invariance of spacetime intervals is a fact. That is just a statement about numbers that we calculate from measurements. But what does this imply about reality? How should we interpret that invariance?

As we have seen, the mainstream interpretation of relativity denies the existence of real distances and durations. They are not real properties of individuals. This is, however, a purely negative doctrine. But clearly things are separated from each other in space as well as in time. What are they separated by? The mainstream physicist answers that, while neither space nor time exists in its own right, the combination of them does. Things are separated from each other by stretches of spacetime.

The central argument for the reality of the spacetime interval was made by Hermann Minkovski. In essence, he argued that if all measurements give the same value for a property, then the property must be real. If there were a painting so beautiful that everyone fell down instantly babbling about its beauty, then we would conclude that beauty really was a property of the painting. Likewise, Minkovski argues that if the spacetime interval appears the same in all measurements, then it must be real.

The positive doctrine of the mainstream interpretation is thus found in the following argument:

Reality of the spacetime interval

A. The apparent (measured) spacetime interval is
   invariant.   (P)
B. If an apparent property is invariant, then it corresponds
   to a real property.   (P)
C. Therefore, the spacetime interval is a real
   property.   (from A,B)

It is now clear that the mainstream interpretation denies three-dimensional distances and durations, which are not real properties of individual things, but affirms the existence of four-dimensional spacetime intervals, which are real properties of events.

Minkovski helped clarify the meaning of the spacetime interval with his well-known *rotation analogy*. Consider some three-dimensional object such as a sculpture of Venus. As we view it from different angles, its width may change. It may seem wide when viewed from the front, but seem narrow when viewed from the side. Minkovski said that spacetime is real, but that different sets of rulers and clocks are all "viewing it from different perspectives". According to one set, a spacetime interval may appear short in space and long in time, but another set may find it long in space and short in time. More crudely, it might be said that when we treat distances and durations independently, we are arbitrarily chopping up a spacetime interval into so much space and so much time. Another observer may choose to chop it up differently, into less space and more time.

This rotation analogy also explains what it means to say that *distances and durations are relations*. Suppose that the sculpture of Venus sits in a space, and that we choose three lines in the space to be the mutually perpendicular x-axis, y-axis and z-axis. Given these lines, we can say the sculpture has, say, a length of two metres along the x-axis and three metres along the y-axis. But these lengths are *relations* between the three-dimensional shape of the statue and certain lines. If we chose different lines to be our axes, then the "length along the x-axis" would change. In short, "length along the x-axis" is not a property that depends only on the individual statue; it is a relation between the statue and a direction.

Likewise, the mainstream interpretation asserts that *four-dimensional* "shapes" and intervals are real. Choosing an x-axis in space and a time axis defines the distance and duration of a four-dimensional shape (an event). But if the directions of these axes change, then the distance and duration change. They are relations between the four-dimensional shape and certain directions.

Spacetime intervals may also be helpfully interpreted as "sizes" of events. In three-dimensional space, volume is length multiplied by breadth multiplied by height. Likewise, in four-dimensional space, the four-dimensional volume is duration multiplied by length multiplied by breadth multiplied by height. Thus a tennis match may take three hours and fill a tennis court, and we can calculate the four-dimensional volume of this event. This region of spacetime has an invariant volume, even though the length of the court and the duration of the match are relative to the clocks and rulers used to measure them.

To summarize, the mainstream interpretation makes several claims:

- distances and durations are not real properties of individuals
- nor are they mere appearances
- spacetime intervals are invariant and therefore real
- distances and durations are relations between spacetime intervals and directions in spacetime.

Einstein always insisted on the first two ideas, and later accepted Minkovski's interpretations of the spacetime interval.

The minority interpretation accepts, of course, the fact that the spacetime interval is invariant, but it interprets it as a mathematical accident. Movement through the ether causes lengths to contract and clocks to slow. Since these two processes have "opposite" effects, we should not be surprised that, if we combine both in a calculation, they cancel and leave a constant. Lorentz never thought that the invariance of the spacetime interval was important.

The block universe argument

Some physicists believe that relativity theory has proved that the past and future exist in a giant four-dimensional block universe. Although his views changed during his career, Einstein, for example, made the following statement in 1952, a few years before he died. He argued that the relativity of simultaneity implies a block universe:

> The four-dimensional continuum is now no longer resolvable objectively into slices, all of which contain simultaneous events; "now" loses for the spatially extended world its objective meaning . . .

Since there exist in this four-dimensional structure no longer any slices which represent "now" objectively, the concepts of happening and becoming are indeed not completely suspended, but yet complicated. It appears therefore more natural to think of physical reality as a four-dimensional existence, instead of, as hitherto, the evolution of a three-dimensional existence.

(Einstein, 1952)

Although his language is cautious here, Einstein's meaning is clear. There is no physical "evolution" through time, that is, no change or persistence; instead, a static four-dimensional block exists. He says that becoming is not "completely suspended" because there is a residue of change in a block universe; namely, the adjacent, static slices differ slightly, and this creates an illusion of becoming and change.

It should be emphasized first that most physicists regard the entire issue of the block universe as speculative, and simply have no opinion about the matter. For them, it is simply not a scientific question since we cannot experiment directly on the past and future. However, many physicists, such as Einstein, Hermann Weyl and others, thought that relativity theory did prove that our world was a block universe. A number of philosophers have also thought so, although there is naturally disagreement in the details of their views. For example, Bertrand Russell and Hilary Putnam have argued that relativity theory implies some kind of block universe.

Arguments about the block universe all arise from attempts to *interpret* the special theory of relativity, and all go beyond Einstein's 1905 theory by adding new premises. In particular, all attempt to say what reality is like if simultaneity is relative. Einstein's *theory*, on the other hand, does not mention reality; it merely describes relations between measurements, that is, between appearances. Thus different interpretations of relativity theory will imply different views about the block universe. As pointed out below, the minority interpretation escapes this strange consequence.

The quotation from Einstein above contains a short but very powerful argument for the block universe. According to his theory, simultaneity is relative. That means that different sets of rulers and clocks, moving relatively to each other, will find that different sets or different "slices" of events are simultaneous. In this sense, to say that two distant events are simultaneous is merely a convention or arbitrary agreement, and has no physical or "objective" meaning. If different clocks were chosen, different events would be simultaneous. As Einstein interprets it above, this fact already implies that we live in a block universe.

Einstein's friend and colleague at Princeton, the logician Kurt Gödel, filled in more detail in a 1949 essay. According to him, the relativity of simultaneity seems to lead to:

> an unequivocal proof for the view of those philosophers who, like Parmenides, Kant and modern idealists (such as McTaggart), deny the objectivity of change and consider change as an illusion or appearance. The argument runs as follows: Change becomes possible only through a lapse of time. The existence of an objective lapse of time, however, means that reality consists of an infinity of layers of "now" which come into existence successively. But, if simultaneity is relative, reality cannot be split up into such layers in an objectively determined way. Each observer has his own set of "nows" and none can claim the prerogative of representing the objective lapse of time.
>
> (Gödel, 1949)

The similarity of this passage to some of Einstein's writings suggests that he and Gödel had been discussing this issue.

This short argument turns upon the idea that true physical change implies profound differences between the past, present and future. During change, one and the same object loses some properties and gains others. It also persists through time, moving from one moment, which ceases to exist, into the next moment. But if simultaneity is human choice – mere agreement about which rulers and clocks to use – then there is no real difference between the present and the past or future. These labels, "past", "present" and "future", are merely human names that reflect no physical difference in the events they describe. Thus we have:

Short argument for block universe

A. If simultaneity is relative, then there is no physical difference between the past, present and future. (P)

B. Simultaneity is relative. (P)

C. Therefore, there is no physical difference between the past, present and future. (from A,B)

D. But, if there is no physical difference between the past, present and future, then there is no true change. (P)

E. Therefore, there is no true change. (C, D)

The last line means that we live in a block universe. If there is no true change, then any event that ever existed always exists: it cannot change from existent to nonexistent.

By way of analogy, consider a map of Earth showing the equator. We could travel there and find many physical differences between the northern hemisphere and southern hemisphere on either side of the equator (trade winds in different directions, etc.). Likewise, some claim that relativity theory provides a realistic map of our four-dimensional universe. They insist, however, that unlike the equator, its lines of simultaneity correspond to no physical difference in the universe. We find on the four-dimensional map no objective dividing line between the past and the future, and are supposed to believe that no such line exists in nature.

In other words, a realistic interpretation of the relativity of simultaneity is incompatible with presentism. This doctrine implies that the present "slice" of simultaneous events is the only existent slice. The past slices have ceased to exist, and future slices do not yet exist. According to presentism, change is the passing away of one slice and the emergence of the next. But if Einstein's theory is a good map of reality, then there is no physical difference between the present slice of events and past or future slices. In particular, the conventional labels "past" and "future" do not imply the physical label "non-existent".

Much of the literature on the block universe concerns another, related argument that involves three events, and therefore can be called the *triangle argument* . This argument begins with the premise that, since *some* distant events coexist with me, *at least* events simultaneous with me at the present moment exist.

Solipsism is the belief that only I exist. That is, the universe consists of me and nothing else; all other things and space itself are an illusion of some sort in my mind. Surely, however, we deny solipsism. But then *some* other bodies or events must coexist with me. The only question is which events are the coexistent ones.

The triangle argument is aimed at those who accept coexistence but will not at first agree that past and future events exist now, and resist attempts to drive them to this conclusion. Suppose, the argument begins, that past and future events do not coexist with me at the present moment. Then, since some events do coexist, it must be simultaneous events that coexist. The argument shows, however, that even this modest beginning leads back to the coexistence of the past and the future, and thus to the block universe.

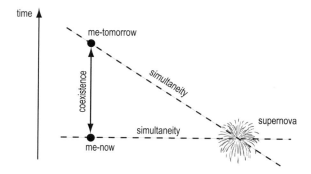

Figure 5.3 *The triangle argument. The dotted lines indicated simultaneity (which implies coexistence), and the two-headed arrow indicates the derived coexistence relation.*

Suppose that there are three events: me-now, me-tomorrow and a distant supernova. Suppose that, according to one set of rulers and clocks, me-now is simultaneous with the distant supernova, but that, according to a different set of rulers and clocks, me-tomorrow is simultaneous with the supernova. Then we have the argument:

Triangle argument for block universe

A. If an event exists and it is simultaneous with another
   event, then the other event also exists.   (P)
B. Me-now exists; me-now and the supernova are
   simultaneous.   (P)
C. Therefore, the supernova exists.   (from A,B)
D. But, the supernova and me-tomorrow are
   simultaneous.   (P: according to other clocks)
E. Therefore, me-tomorrow exists.   (A,C,D)
F. If one event exists and another event exists, then
   they co-exist.   (P)
G. Therefore me-now and me-tomorrow co-exist.   (B,E,F)

This means that the self I am now and feel to be real (me-now), coexists with myself tomorrow (me-tomorrow), which is just as real. Of course, since we could have chosen *any* pair of events far away enough from the supernova, the conclusion means that the present and the future coexist, and thus that the entire future and its past coexist. Thus we live in a block universe.

Clearly the first premise, A, is very suspicious. It moves from a conventional label, "simultaneous", to an assertion about physical existence. This is precisely the inference that Einstein's theory is supposed to deny. But the only alternative (short of solipsism) is to concede that some events in the past and future do coexist, and the argument is aimed at those who wish to deny this.

The fourth line of the argument, premise D, has troubled some critics. It implies that two sets of clocks and rulers, and therefore two definitions of simultaneity, are used. In the context of this argument, however, this is legitimate. Briefly put, premise A says that simultaneity is good evidence for objective existence. Once we know something exists, we are free to use other definitions of simultaneity, and that subjective choice will not affect what objectively exists.

Note that the coexistence does not imply simultaneity. Me-now and me-tomorrow are not simultaneous.

The importance of the triangle argument is that it creates an embarrassing dilemma for interpreters of relativity theory. If they deny solipsism, they must agree that some events coexist. But if they deny that the past and future coexist with the present, then all the coexistent events must be in the present. But this minimalist idea together with the relativity of simultaneity drives them back to the idea that the past and future coexist. *For those who interpret relativity, it seems that there is no middle ground between solipsism and the block universe.* Any attempt to restrict robust existence to some single slice of the four-dimensional world is the assertion of some privileged or absolute simultaneity, and is profoundly at odds with the mainstream interpretation of relativity theory.

Indeed, one philosopher has argued that relativity theory does imply something very close to solipsism. Howard Stein severely criticized arguments for a block universe, and spelled out in detail which events he believes coexist with me-now. According to his view, only me-now and certain past events coexist. An event in the past coexists with me-now if light from the event *could* reach me, that is, past events that could have causally influenced me still exist. This appears to be a very strange view. Other people do not exist now, but their past selves may exist and therefore coexist with me. Stein's view shows that although relativity theory makes good predictions, it appears to be very difficult to spell out what it implies about the nature of reality.

In the end, it is very difficult to interpret the relativity of simultaneity without embracing some form of block universe. If this seems implausible, then there is extra reason to consider the merits of the minority interpretation. According to this, the relativity of simultaneity is mere appearance; in reality, only clocks at rest in the ether show true time and can be used to judge which events are really simultaneous. Thus Lorentz and other defenders of the minority interpretation can naturally say that only the present is real. *The minority interpretation is compatible with presentism.*

CHAPTER 6

Time travel is possible

Causal order

The iron chains of causality link events together into a definite order: a cause always precedes its effect. If, however, there are distant events that do not influence each other, what decides their order?

As noted above, time dilation implies that different sets of rulers and clocks moving relative to each other will assign different orders to distant events. Consider, for example, three events: event A, which causes event B, and a distant event, X. Since A and B are connected by some causal process, their order is fixed. But if event X is distant enough from both, then different clocks may register any of the three orders

A, B, X   or   A, X, B   or   X, A, B

That is, the distant event may follow both A and B, happen between them or precede both.

According to the mainstream interpretation of special relativity, durations and other temporal intervals are not invariant, and are therefore not real. According to this view, there is no fact of the matter about which of the three orders above is real and physical. The events all occur and are all real, but there is no physical fact that makes X later or earlier than the others. Just as there are no unicorns or pink elephants, there is no order between distant events that do not influence each other.

Consider another illustration. Suppose that there are two long queues leading into two doors at a club or music concert. Within each queue the order is clear. The people closer to the door will enter first. But as the two queues shuffle past each other, sometimes one is faster and sometimes the other. Thus there is no clear order between people in different queues. In the future, when they meet inside the club, they will influence each other, and they may have influenced each other in the past. But while they are separated from each other in different queues there are no influences, and therefore no meaningful order between them. According to the mainstream interpretation, events in our world are like this. Some are linked in chains of causes, but between the parts of chains that do not influence each other there is no definite order.

Which events are chained together into an order by causes, and which are not? Since causes are carried by things with energy or mass, and these cannot travel faster than the speed of light, no cause can propagate faster than light. Thus if light cannot pass from one event to another, then no causal influence can and the pair of events is not causally ordered. There is no fact of the matter about which is earlier and which is later. Thus, according to the mainstream interpretation, if light emerges from a distant star and travels this way but cannot reach Earth before the next election, then the emission of the light was neither earlier nor later than the next election. Similarly, it would take light about a billionth of a second to cross an object the size of a human brain. If two synapses fire in such a way that light could not travel from one firing to the other, then there is no physical order between these events.

Killing grandmothers

> Using faster-than-light velocities we could telegraph into the past.
> (Einstein, quoted by Sommerfeld, 1908)

If you could travel faster than light, you could kill your grandmother before she gave birth to your mother. Since this is impossible, we have a second argument for the celestial speed limit. The strategy of the argument is a *reductio ad absurdum*. That is, the assumption that faster-than-light travel is possible is shown to lead to nonsense, and thus must be discarded.

Take as the three events above your grandmother's adolescence (A), the present moment (B) and a distant exploding star, that is, a supernova (X). Suppose that the explosion is so far away that its light does not reach Earth for many centuries from now. Thus the explosion is earlier or later than your grandmother's adolescence, *or* the explosion is earlier or later than the present moment, depending on which set of rulers and clocks is used. Now assume, *contrary to the theory of relativity*, that a magical rocket is somehow capable of travelling faster than light. This means that it can, for example, travel from Earth out to the exploding star and return again before light from the explosion manages to reach Earth for the first time. In fact, it would enable you to board the rocket and travel for a sightseeing tour of the explosion. Since the explosion is "later" than the present, your trip would seem like an ordinary trip: the arrival at the star would be after the departure from Earth. Since the explosion is also "before" your grandmother's adolescence, however, you could instruct the pilot to return to visit your 13-year-old grandmother and kill her. Such a return trip would also seem like an ordinary trip: from one event to another in *its* future.

In effect, the magical rocket is a time machine. Since relativity theory says that distant events are not ordered in time, the rocket can travel backwards in time by hopscotching across to a distant event and then returning to the past. Faster-than-light speeds would not enable a trip directly into your past; it would be necessary to visit distant places that are outside your time order, and then re-enter your time order.

In the example of the queues above, this would be like jumping between the two queues. By shifting back and forth, you could enter

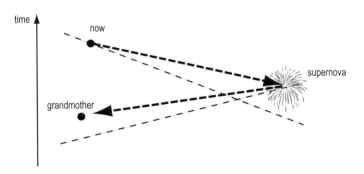

Figure 6.1 *Killing your grandmother. Each dotted line connects events that are simultaneous. Each dotted arrow is a faster-than-light rocket trip into the future (the arrows can be above the lines of simultaneity and yet slope downwards on the graph because of the high speed).*

the club earlier than someone directly in front of you, and thus jump ahead in time (or later, if you were unlucky and jumped to a slower queue).

But, as the example shows, time travel leads to contradictions. If you are reading this, your grandmother did give birth to your mother. But if the magical rocket makes time travel possible, you could kill your adolescent grandmother before your mother's birth. Thus your mother would be born and not born. There's clearly something wrong about all this, and it leads to the following argument:

Time travel is contradictory

A. There is faster-than-light travel. (P: leads to absurdity)
B. Some distant events have no definite order in time. (P)
C. If there is faster-than-light travel and distant events have no definite order, then there is time travel. (P)
D. So, there is time travel. (from A,B,C)
E. If there is time travel, then there are contradictions. (P)
F. So, there are contradictions. (D,E)
G. But there are no contradictions. (P)
H. So, there is no faster-than-light travel.

The last line does not follow rigorously. When an argument crashes into contradiction, one or more of the preceding premises must be thrown out. But it is sometimes not immediately clear which premise is the culprit responsible for the contradiction. Additional arguments may be needed to justify pointing the finger of blame at a particular premise.

In this case the second and third premises, B and C, are consequences of relativity theory, and the last, G, is our bedrock assumption. If we stand by these, then we must reject either faster-than-light travel (premise A), or the idea that travel back in time would produce contradictions (premise E).

Most philosophers do reject time travel because it would lead to contradictions. In a surprising essay, however, the metaphysician David Lewis argued that time travel would not lead to contradictions. In brief, he says that any visit to the past has already happened, and thus could not change the way the past happened. If it is a fact that your grandmother gave birth to your mother, then it is a fact that any time traveller who happened to be there did not kill her first. A murderous time traveller would find that quite ordinary circumstances contrived to forestall her death: the gun misfired, and so on. If

Lewis is correct, then there is no logical argument – like the above – against time travel. We can throw out premise E instead of the first premise, and still avoid the contradiction. Philosophers often describe something as "possible" if it is not contradictory. Something may be logically possible in this sense, even though physical laws forbid it. Lewis can therefore conclude that "time travel is possible".

Physicists are more interested in the question of whether time travel is *physically possible*. Most would quickly say "no", but an intriguing line of research was opened up by Kip Thorne and others in the early 1990s. He asked whether, if space can really bend and curve as Einstein says (see Chapter 13), it is so flexible that "tubes" or "tunnels" could connect the present to the past. If so, then anything travelling down through the tube would emerge at an earlier time, and time travel would in fact be physically possible. Although surprising progress was made on the theory of such *wormholes* through spacetime, most physicists remain sceptical. But the final word is not yet in.

CHAPTER 7

Can the mind understand the world?

We have studied the elements of Einstein's special theory of relativity, and can now put them together into a more panoramic view. He began by assuming the truth of two principles, both drawn from experience and experiments: the principle of relativity; and the constant speed of light. From these two central principles, Einstein and his followers *deduced* a series of stunning consequences, of which we have met several in turn during the previous chapters:

- time dilation
- relativity of simultaneity
- length contraction
- symmetry of effects
- relativistic mass increase
- energy–mass conversion
- celestial speed limit
- invariance of the spacetime interval.

These are predictions about what observation and measurement will discover, that is, about phenomena and appearances. We have not explored the details of the arguments Einstein gave for deducing these effects from his principles. It is enough here to state that they are consequences of the principles and have been confirmed by experiments.

These two principles and their predicted consequences together form the *theory*: Einstein's special theory of relativity. Note that this deals only with measurements made by equipment moving inertially (say, carried by a coasting spaceship). Einstein removed this restriction in his general theory, which we will examine in Chapter 13. Clearly, there is much that is puzzling and mysterious about the special theory of relativity. Why is the speed of light, unlike all other moving things, constant? Why are steady speeds undetectable? Why are physical laws the same regardless of speed? Why do distances and durations and masses depend on speed? Einstein's theory does not answer these questions. At best it explains one mystery only by postulating another. It is content to assume its principles, make predictions and subject those to experimental test. This has frustrated many physicists and philosophers, who have therefore gone beyond the bare bones of the theory by *interpreting* it, and saying what it implies about the reality beneath appearances. We can now compare the two interpretations we have studied.

The mainstream interpretation:
- was originated by Einstein in 1905 and Minkovski in 1908
- asserts that distances and durations are not real properties – they are relations
- and therefore asserts that there is no objective present
- and therefore asserts that we live in a four-dimensional universe
- and therefore favours the block universe view – the past and future exist
- and therefore favours an event ontology without real change or movement.

As emphasized earlier, not all of those who defend the mainstream view accept all these points. Most physicists probably accept that distances and durations are not real properties, that there is no objective present and that we live in a four-dimensional universe. However, most do not speculate about the existence of the past or the future. As the arguments above showed, though, if simultaneity is really relative, the block universe view may be unavoidable – as several prominent physicists have thought.

The mainstream interpretation seems to adhere cautiously to Einstein's theory. For example, since the theory predicts that times depend on who measures them, it concedes that these are not real and objective. But any attempt to spell out what this implies about change and the reality of a four-dimensional spacetime soon encounters unpleasant implications. What begins as a minimalist interpretation seems, by the end, implausible.

It should be noted that Einstein's own views were always complicated and shifted considerably during his long career. It is best to be careful and not assume that he finally favoured any single interpretation of relativity.

The minority interpretation:
- was developed by Lorentz and defended with variations by others
- asserts that distances and durations are real properties, but vary with speed (relative to the ether, etc.)
- asserts that we live in a three-dimensional space with time flowing
- asserts that there is an objective present
- and therefore is compatible with presentism – only the present exists
- and therefore is compatible with an ontology of persistent, changing objects.

The minority interpretation proposes an elaborate ontology that leads to many satisfying explanations, but also creates new puzzles without leading to any new predictions and experimental support.

In 1913, after years of struggle with special relativity, Lorentz rather wistfully summarized the debate between the two interpretations – a debate he was losing:

According to Einstein, it has no meaning to speak of [the true] motion relative to the ether. He likewise denies the existence of [invariant and] absolute simultaneity. It is certainly remarkable that these relativity concepts, also those concerning time, have found such a rapid acceptance.

The acceptance of these concepts belongs mainly to epistemology [i.e. to philosophy, since no experiment yet compels us to adopt one view or the other]. It is certain, however, that it depends to a large extent on the way one is accustomed to think whether one is most attracted to one or another interpretation. As far as this lecturer is concerned, he finds a certain satisfaction in the older interpretations, according to which the ether possesses at least some substantiality, space and time can be sharply separated, and simultaneity is not relative.

Finally, it should be noted that the daring assertion that one can never observe velocities larger than the velocity of light contains a hypothetical restriction on what is accessible to us, a restriction which cannot be accepted without some reservation.

(Lorentz, 1913)

This last point shows extraordinary foresight. Lorentz did not know that, some 80 years later, new experiments would hint at the existence of faster-than-light effects and revive his interpretation of relativity in some quarters. These historic experiments have weakened the dominance of the mainstream interpretation and have renewed hopes for the minority interpretation, as we investigate below. The debate over relativity theory is very much alive, and perhaps will only be settled by readers of this book and the coming generation. This is a time of great progress, and of deepening mysteries.

PART II

Philosophical progress

The relativity revolution has left in its wake a topsy-turvy world of immense power and immense insecurity, and a sense of both progress and perplexity. We have learned the most profound secrets about space and time, only to be confronted by renewed mystery. Is matter a form of motion? Do the past and future exist now? Is there change? Why is the speed of light constant? Does the very length of a body depend on how it is measured? Do the past and future exist now? Is time travel possible?

From the eclipse expedition in 1919 through to today, this revolution has sent philosophers scurrying backwards to deepen our understanding of the nature of space and time. They have returned to the earliest debates of about 500BCE in ancient Greece and the great feuds over the new discoveries made during the scientific revolution in the 1600s. This research has substantially advanced our understanding of the origins of key concepts, and of the interpretation of Einstein's theories.

The following chapters pursue three key themes:

- *Paradox as a source of innovation*
  Long before experiments were conducted, key concepts emerged as solutions to philosophical problems.
- *The metaphysics of space*
  Do space or spacetime exist in their own right, as a kind of container, over and above bodies?
- *The rise of the relational worldview*
  Natural science has shifted the way philosophers think about relations, the glue that holds the cosmos together.

Throughout, the aim will be to show that insights accumulate. The lessons learned from studying the ancient paradoxes will provide fresh perspectives on the interpretation of general relativity and contemporary debates.

CHAPTER 8

Who invented space?

Some 5,000 or 6,000 years ago, early societies living in Turkey and Armenia spoke Indo-European: the language from which modern European languages have descended. Their vocabulary for concrete objects and simple actions paints a vivid picture of prehistoric life: "bear", "wolf", "monkey", "wheat", "apple", "wheel", "axle", "tree", "father", "carry", "see", "know", and so on. Words for less concrete aspects of the world were a long time coming. The adjective for "big" in Indo-European, for example, was "mega": the root of our "megabyte". This is an abstract word because it can apply to many different kinds of concrete objects; both bears and wheels can be big. Many centuries passed before humans were able to extend this to the very abstract concept of "bigness" or "size": a general noun for an abstract quality. In Homer, who composed his poems about 3,000 years ago, the noun "bigness" (*megathos*) refers only to the height of human bodies; the word is still tethered to specific and concrete objects.

Several centuries later, there was a breakthrough when the philosopher Zeno of Elea (*c*.490–*c*.430BCE) used "bigness" to mean something like the expanse or dimensionality of all existence: that is, he began to liberate extension from concrete things. Each time the word was stretched, and each advance toward greater abstraction was a tiny victory for poetic genius, and contributed to the richness and power of our language today. Every time we buy a shoe or a dress by asking for a certain "size" we draw on the slowly accumulating creations of these ancient word-artists.

But the concept of "space" was very different. It did not grow gradually by stretching earlier meanings over many centuries. It appeared as an act of deliberate creation in ancient Greece during the greatest philosophical controversy of the sixth century BCE. In fact, some historians assert that European philosophy itself was born in the heat of this debate, as it slowly emerged out of religion, mythology and folk history. The controversy centred on what is perhaps the oldest and most venerated problem in European philosophy: the famous *problem of change*. In this chapter, we study the problem not only because it is beautiful and deep, but because it puts the invention of "space" into a new perspective. By studying the way earlier cultures came to their concepts of space, we begin to see how fragile and strange our own concept is.

Ambitious students are sometimes advised to avoid the "hard old problems" that have been lying around for a long time. They may be advised that new advances and discoveries come not from beating dead horses but by entering quickly into the fray of contemporary controversy. But in philosophy there is a catch. The newest problems, if they are really deep and interesting, are often found to have the oldest problems lurking underneath. Progress in philosophy sometimes comes from piercing through a new puzzle and discovering its tangled relations to well-explored regions like the problem of change or the problem of universals. Thus the "hard old problems" are philosophy's hidden shoals; success depends on a talent for navigating through and around them. Records of past struggles with these problems are precious charts – treasure maps of diagnoses and solutions that every ambitious philosopher will master.

Certain sects of philosophers once dismissed these old debates in philosophy as mere "pseudo-problems". They believed that any problems that so stubbornly resisted solution must be mere confusions or artefacts of our inadequate language. But these views have now been discredited. Battles with the problem of change led to concepts that form the foundations of our modern physics. Today the ongoing research on these problems continues to generate new insights and deepen our appreciation of these precious resources.

The problem of change

It is something of a mystery why wealthy young Greeks, clad in their toga-like robes and sitting around on stone benches in the town square, began to argue over subtle philosophical questions. There was a general quickening in the pace of life. Growing cities were sending out small fleets across the Mediterranean to start new daughter cities. A new alphabetic writing had been learned a century or so earlier from Phoenician traders sailing from ancient Lebanon and Israel. The arts of sculpture, architecture, painting and poetry all began to flourish. The upper classes still owned slaves and women led severely restricted lives. Perhaps this is because these elites lacked the concepts of universal justice and human rights; it was they who began to invent these concepts some centuries later. In the midst of this general revival from about 600BCE onwards, some enquiring minds began debates that were to lay the foundations of European philosophy, science, law, politics, art and literature. We are all in their debt.

One of the reasons the problem of change is so beautiful is that change is all around us. It takes a very subtle mind to notice that something so ordinary and common conceals, just beneath the surface, a fundamental mystery. What is change? It is as everyday as a leaf turning from green to yellow, and as intimate as your eyes shifting along this line of text. Change involves *difference*: the leaf is first green and then not green. It involves *newness*: the yellow that comes to be did not exist beforehand. It thus involves succession in time: green is followed by yellow. But change is not mere replacement. If one green leaf is simply removed and another yellow leaf is substituted, the first green leaf has not changed. It has merely been replaced. Thus change involves *persistence or sameness across time*. And finally change itself is some *process* or *transition*: the green leaf changes when it *becomes* yellow.

The Greeks used the same word to describe both motion from one place to another and change in the properties or nature of a thing. Movements and changing colour – kissing and blushing – were both examples of change for the Greeks. The word they used, *kinesis*, is the root of our "cinema", where we watch moving pictures.

What could the problem with change be? The ancient Greeks saw that the process of change, the way something came to be something else, was puzzling. They were first struck by the newness that change produced. Where was the yellow before the leaf changed its colour? In general, *where did the new quality or state come from?* We may think this question has an easy answer, but let's pause to ponder the question for a moment. It has surprising depths.

Some philosophers have interpreted this first version of the problem of change as groping towards our laws of conservation, so let us label it the "problem of change from conservation". In philosophy, discussions can often be kept simple by creatively using labels for ideas, and we will cultivate the habit here. This problem about the newness that change involves is really just the idea that "no one can pull a rabbit out of a hat". But it is important enough to give it a fancy name and carefully examine the ideas involved:

The problem of change from conservation

A.	If there is change, then something new comes to exist that did not exist before.	(P)
B.	If something did not exist before, then it was nothing.	(P)
C.	So, if there is change, then something new comes to exist from nothing.	(A,B)
D.	But it is not the case that something new comes to exist from nothing.	(P)
E.	So, there is no change.	(C,D)

This is a startling and daring conclusion. How could anyone doubt the change that occurs all around us? If you are certain that there is change, and wish to rescue it from this attack, you must find some error in the above argument.

This little argument is valuable because it points at two profound issues. First, it led the Greeks to express the idea that "nothing comes from nothing" (as the slogan goes). Thus the fourth sentence, D, is a deep and far-reaching idea. Our experience tells us that objects just do not simply appear or disappear: rabbits do not emerge from empty hats; pink elephants do not materialize in my bedroom at night. It is the same reassuring habit of things that modern scientists rely on when they formulate their conservation principles. Here, however, accepting this idea leads to trouble. If we accept this, are we forced to agree that there is no change?

Secondly, this argument is valuable because it makes us question the first sentence, A. It exposes a *tension* in our concept of change. Does change really produce something new? In a sense it obviously does. But we do not believe that the new aspects emerge "out of nothing". So the results of change are new, but they were also there before in some way or some form. They are somehow new, but also somehow old. We must explain this to avoid the preposterous conclusion that there is no change.

The idea that "nothing comes from nothing" became important again about 1,000 years later. Philosophers were debating with members of the new Christian religion in the early centuries after the birth of Christ. The Christian doctrines proudly asserted that God created the world "from nothing" (in Latin, *creatio ex nihilo*). At times, the theologians used this as a dig against the pagans. Without revelation, it was said, the pagans could not imagine creation from nothing, and ignorantly supposed even a god could not perform such a miracle.

> The problem of change from conservation is important because it articulates early notions of conservation and because it exposes a strange tension, a new-oldness buried deep in the nature of change.

Another problem of change

As the ancient Greeks struggled to detail a theory of change they stumbled on a more subtle issue that might be called the problem of change from contradiction (Sorabji calls it "the problem of stopping and starting"). There are some curious illustrations of the problem.

Did you know it is impossible to jump off a bridge? If you are on the bridge, you have not yet jumped. If you are off the bridge, you have already jumped. But there is nothing "between" being on or being off the bridge. You cannot be both on and off the bridge, and you cannot be neither on nor off the bridge. So there is no such thing as jumping off bridges.

Likewise, it is impossible for trains to start. Before they start, they are at rest. After they start, they are in motion. But the train cannot be at rest and in motion, and it cannot be neither at rest nor in motion. So trains do not start – ever.

These may seem to be merely silly or irritating riddles, but their ancestors opened up a deep chasm that many philosophers, mathematicians and scientists have struggled to cross. They point to difficulties in giving a "micro-theory" of the process of becoming, or of the transition from one state to another. It is worth dissecting this problem more clearly to get at the underlying issues.

The problem turns on the idea of opposites like "being on" and "being off" or "being at rest" and "being in motion". The Greeks distinguished between different kinds of opposites. Some pairs of opposites are *mutually exhaustive*. That is, every relevant thing must be one or the other: there is no alternative or intermediary. An integer greater than zero is either odd or even; there are no other options. A

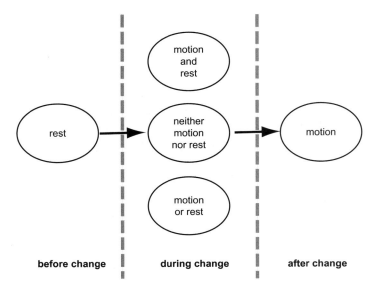

Figure 8.1 *The problem of change from contradiction. What is the transition between rest and motion? None of the intermediate states are satisfactory. The top two are ruled out by logic and the lowest is the same as either the initial or final state, and therefore is not change.*

train must be either at rest or in motion (i.e. not at rest). This kind of opposite is called a *contradictory*. Even and odd are contradictory properties among positive integers. The idea that something must have one or the other of two contradictory properties is called the *law of excluded middle*: there can be no third thing "between" two contradictories.

Not all pairs of opposites are mutually exhaustive. Black and white are opposites but they are not mutually exhaustive because something may have a colour "between" black and white; namely, grey. Such an opposite is merely a *contrary* and not a contradictory.

The second version of the problem of change is strongest when phrased in terms of contradictory properties:

The problem of change from contradiction

A. If a thing is changing from one property to its
   contradictory property, then the thing has exactly one,
   or both, or neither of the properties.   (P)

B. Such a changing thing does not have exactly one of the properties, because it is then either before or after the change. (P)

C. Such a changing thing does not have both of the properties, because they are opposites. (P)

D. Such a changing thing does not have neither of the properties, because they are contradictories and therefore mutually exhaustive. (P)

E. Therefore, it is not the case that a thing is changing from one property to its contradictory property. (from A–D)

Thus the would-be jumper cannot get from being on the bridge to being not on the bridge, and the train cannot start.

> When philosophers attempted to give a micro-theory of the process of change or becoming, they encountered "gaps" when neither property applied or "overlaps" when both did. But these are impossible.

Parmenides

The first and most famous solution to these problems of change was advanced by Parmenides of Elea, who lived in a Greek colony in southern Italy about 650BCE. Although his surviving writings are all fragments of poetry, he is now revered as the first philosopher in the European tradition. At the time, however, the word "philosopher" had probably not yet been invented, and there was no European culture.

Parmenides' solution was dramatic. The fury it triggered propelled many developments in philosophy, and it will not be reassuring to those frustrated with the problems above. In short, Parmenides caved in, accepted the arguments and declared that there was no change! He asserted that the everyday appearance of change around us is some sort of illusion. If we could penetrate through these appearances we would see that the world is really static and frozen without movement of any kind. Thus, according to Parmenides, there is no error in the above arguments. The only "problem" is our mistaken idea that change and movement are real.

More extremely, Parmenides not only rejected change through time, but also seemed to assert that there is no "change through space". That is, there are no differences between things. Everything is the same, completely homogeneous, and in fact *just one thing*. The world is like a geometric point, and has no parts or other distinguishable features. We are all one and the same person, and identical with the material world. This philosophy is known as *monism*, since it insists that everything is one.

For most people, Parmenides' solution is extreme and even insane, but he nonetheless remains enormously important. His solution grew out of his heroic commitment to clear thinking. After much study, when he could discover no error in the arguments against change, he instead rejected the plain evidence of his five senses. He championed clear, abstract thinking long before its value had been proved in science or mathematics. More deeply, his solution grew out of belief that the world must be intelligible, that it must be understandable. When the arguments above convinced him that change was contradictory, he threw out change. If change could not be understood, it could not be part of the world. Parmenides is a hero to philosophers for these commitments and for proclaiming them so vividly. In an odd way, he did much to inspire subsequent philosophy and science because he challenged everyone else to say clearly why his solution was wrong. We hope, however, to honour his principles and yet find some way to understand change.

> Parmenides' story has a very surprising ending – he may have been right. His conception of a changeless world was different from the block universe debated above, but both reject motion and change. Did Einstein vindicate Parmenides?

The invention of space

The first recognizable concept of space was created as part of a solution to the problem of change. The solution is ingenuous and was indeed the product of great genius, and its distant cousins are taught in every secondary school today.

Several philosophers, now called the *atomists*, developed a comprehensive theory of reality to eliminate the problem of change. At the time it was remarkable for its clarity and depth, and served as a model for later scientific theories. The following contains the central doctrines of the three thinkers: Leucippus, Democritus and Epicurus.

Democritus is honoured as the main founder of atomism; his portrait appeared on modern Greek coins before the Euro was adopted. The atomists' theory had three principles:

The metaphysics of atomism
I. *Atoms and the void*: changeless atoms and a changeless void exist. Both are eternal; only they exist.
II. *Motion*: change is the motion of atoms through the void, that is, their rearrangement.
III. *Bonds*: the atoms have "hooks and barbs" and can clump together into stable, large bodies.

These ideas were so novel in 600BCE that the atomists needed to coin new words to express them. Their atoms were supposed to be very tiny, and impossible to break or cut. The first syllable of "atom" means "not", just as in the English word "amoral" and the second syllable "tom" is from the Greek verb "to cut". So "atom" literally meant the "uncut" or "uncuttable".

In this system, the change of a leaf from green to yellow was easily explained as the rearrangement of the atoms or chemicals within the leaf. This is, in essence, similar to the view of modern chemistry and biology. Thus, the atomists could brag, there was no mysterious emergence from nothing.

Their second new idea led to a furious controversy in which many of the themes of this book were voiced for the first time. What does it mean to say that the void exists? If a void is just emptiness, can emptiness exist? In struggling to answer these questions, atomists finally developed a concept of the void that was an important forerunner of our modern "space". The word the atomists used for void, *kenon*, was quite ordinary. It named the inside of an empty cup or container, which might later be filled. That is, it chiefly meant the "vacant inside of a container". But the atomists were stretching the meaning of the word in a very creative way. Their void was the whole universe. It was pure emptiness. It was not inside a container: it was the inside without the container. The atomists knew this was strange, but went out of their way to emphasize the new meaning they were giving to the word "void". Their language became quite vehement when they asserted that the void was "nothing" and that "nothingness exists".

Although radical, the atomists' metaphysics was a brilliant proposal for solving the problem of change. They argued that larger bodies were built up from atoms. The changes we see around us are mere appearance: a kind of optical illusion. In reality, there was no change at all. The atoms never change and the void, as a mere nothing, certainly cannot change. Moreover, since there was no real change, there was no problem of change. This solution also nicely captures our sense that change involves both something new and something old. The arrangements of the atoms are new, but the atoms are eternal and never come into existence. Thus the atomists can claim to have saved the principle that "nothing comes from nothing".

In a way, however, the atomists resembled Parmenides. Like him, they had so much regard for the problem of change that they saw no recourse but to deny the existence of change. Despite its attractions, atomist metaphysics struck many as an entirely absurd proposal. Who could believe that the void, a mere nothing, *exists*? Why were the atoms uncuttable and unchangeable? What prevented them from breaking down further or simply eroding away?

> The atomists may be interpreted as substituting one paradox for another: instead of the problem of change, we have a nothing that is a something.

Aristotle's common sense

Plato (*c*.428–*c*.348 BCE) is held to be the greatest philosopher of ancient times. His devotees say he combined a mind as deep as Einstein's with the literary powers of a Shakespeare. But Plato's student Aristotle has been by far the most influential European philosopher. For many centuries, Plato's writings were almost entirely lost, and Aristotle came to dominate European thought. He was known simply and affectionately as "the Philosopher". His works were considered almost as true as the Bible, and anyone who claimed to find obscurities or mistakes in Aristotle was considered a poor interpreter. In a way, this was very fortunate. Aristotle is the great champion of common sense. He fought off the paradoxes and contradictions that seduced his predecessors, and grounded his philosophy firmly on everyday experience.

Aristotle was the last of the three great philosophers of ancient Greece: Socrates, Plato and Aristotle. Socrates (*c*.469–399 BCE) was a poor stone-cutter who wandered barefoot through Athens posing uncomfortable ethical questions to his social betters. Traditionally compared to Jesus Christ, he was a charismatic and inspiring figure who transformed the history of philosophy, even though he left no writings. The Athenians finally voted to put him to death in 399BCE for "corrupting the youth". Plato, a wealthy aristocrat devoted to Socrates in his youth, went on to found the school known in Greek as the Academy, where philosophy, mathematics, language and astronomy were studied. This was perhaps Europe's first university and managed to survive in some form for a thousand years. Aristotle was Plato's most famous student, and studied in the Academy for about 20 years. When he left, he founded his own school, called the Lyceum. Aristotle's father had been court physician to the Emperor Phillip II, and Aristotle became tutor to Phillip's son, who is known to history as Alexander the Great: he conquered the known world, at least from Italy to India, before dying at the age of 33. Aristotle is regarded as the first scientific biologist because of his careful studies of animals and their development, but he is important here because of his emphatic rejection of the atomists' concept of space. Aristotle's arguments and his enormous authority meant that "space" was frequently considered to be an entirely incoherent notion during much of the next 2,000 years.

In response to the atomists and other early philosophers, Aristotle also advanced a comprehensive theory of the world. His metaphysics, only part of which we study here, was founded on the notion of substance:

Aristotle's metaphysics

I. *Substances and properties*: the basic things are the concrete bodies and objects we encounter in our ordinary experience: humans, horses, trees, rocks and so on. They have properties like "being rational", "being two-legged", "being an animal" and so on.

II. *Actuals versus potentials*: in addition to their actual properties, substances have potential properties "inside" them. Change occurs when a potential property becomes actual: a green leaf has potential yellowness, and changes colour when that potential becomes actual yellowness.

III. *Plenum*: all substances touch and are surrounded by other substances. There is no empty space. Like a fish moving through water, motion occurs when the substances ahead are shoved aside and other substances fill in behind.

SPACE, TIME AND EINSTEIN

Later, Latin translations of Aristotle's new terms became some of the most important in European philosophy. The word "substance" literally means whatever "stands under" a thing's properties. For example, an egg has the properties of whiteness, hardness and so on; these properties belong to its underlying substance, which holds them together. "Potential" means "could be or might be". It comes from the Latin translation for the Greek word for capability or power (as does the English "potent"). Potential properties have the power to become actual, but are not yet so. "Plenum" describes that which is full and has no gaps (like the English "plenty" or "plentiful").

It is important to see here how Aristotle thought he had solved the problem of change without invoking the idea of space. His strategy became a model for later philosophers who denied the existence of space. Aristotle argued for substances by appealing to common sense. We should base our philosophy on what seems most secure and irrefutable, namely the existence of the objects around us. We should not speculate about mysterious and invisible atoms, nor make them the foundation of our metaphysics.

Likewise, his common sense led him to agree that "nothing comes from nothing". The new end products of change had to exist in some form before change. They were new but also old. Thus he posited his potential properties. Aristotle does not say exactly what these are, but simply insists that they must be there to avoid the paradoxes. They are ghostly, shadowy properties that are there but that do not show or exemplify themselves. Potential yellowness is not coloured; it does not appear in any way until it becomes actual. Thus, Aristotle claims, the problem of change is solved. The new results of change do not come from nothing; they come from potential properties.

At times Aristotle thought of potentials not as ghostly properties but as the powers or capacities or "dispositions" to do or become something. The green leaf must *be* capable of turning yellow; otherwise it could not. Thus this capability exists in its substance. The results of change emerge, not from nothingness, but from capacities.

Although there is something correct in Aristotle's solution to the problem of change, he has in fact shifted the question. The earlier philosophers were led to doubt and deny the very existence of change, and challenged Aristotle to defend it. Aristotle just sets this aside. He argues that not everything can be proved. Instead, he assumes it is obvious that change occurs and asks what follows from this. Thus, he argues, *since* change occurs, *then* potential properties or capacities must exist to avoid the paradoxes. As a cautious and conservative philosopher, Aristotle constructed theories to redeem common sense and simply found the paradox-mongers distasteful.

> Aristotle says that substances are the common-sense things we see around us; but his concept of a substance, which seamlessly unifies its actual and potential properties, is not commonsensical.

Criticism

The problem of change spawned a great rivalry at the heart of the metaphysical tradition in Europe. It led to the invention of the first concepts of space, to the assertions that "nothing exists" and to the forceful reaction embodied in Aristotle's common-sense substances. *Both space and substance were thus born as solutions to the problem of change.* The following chapters will trace the fortunes of these two antagonistic worldviews. Both solutions failed to resolve the problem of change. It is important to see why.

By making the atoms and the void eternal and unchanging, the atomists attempted to solve the problem of change by eliminating change altogether. Instead, however, they simply concealed change. The atomists gave no name to the relation between the atom and the bit of the void it sits in, but it later become known as the *occupancy relation*. They might have imagined that this relation was nothing at all. It appears, for example, that no concrete tie of any sort relates an ordinary stone to the ground it sits on. But this relation is real; it is where change in the atomists' system lies concealed.

One argument for the reality of the occupancy relation relies on the *Truthmaker Principle*, which simply asserts that if some sentence is true, then something makes it so. This is a useful way to express the transition from truths we know to assertions about reality, that is, from epistemology to metaphysics. Thus:

Argument for the reality of the occupancy relation

A. If some sentence is true, then something makes it so. (P)
B. It is true that "an atom is related to the bit of space it occupies: it is *in* a place". (P)
C. Thus something relates an atom to space. (from A,B)

The argument does not tell us much about the structure of this occupancy relation, but simply that it exists. The atomists simply overlooked it, and trusted to their intuition that things simply sit in places without any real tie between them. The argument here is an antidote to such naivety. Once we recognize the reality of the relations between atoms and the void, whatever these relations may be, it becomes obvious that this is the place or *locus* of change in the atomists' system. When atoms move through the void and are rearranged, what changes are the occupancy relations. That is, the relational tie between an atom and its place is broken, and new ties in new places are formed.

If it is true that occupancy relations change, then the problem of change is resurrected within the atomists' system. The new occupancy relations are new, and therefore they emerge from "nothing", or did not emerge at all and so on. As Barnes says, atomism is "fundamentally a flop, it does not answer Parmenides".

Thus the initial persuasiveness of atomism depends on a confusion about relations. Our ordinary experience with moving objects suggests that no palpable thing relates a body to its place. The relation is invisible and seems almost nothing at all. The atomists hid real change in this relation; they swept the problem under the rug, and thus did not solve but only suppressed the problem of change.

The fatal flaw in Aristotle's solution to the problem of change is remarkably similar. In his plenum of substances jostling against each other, Aristotle takes it for granted that substances will touch. But he does not stop to analyse this relation, called the *contiguity relation* ("contiguity" is "the quality of touching"). It has obvious problems.

Intuitively, when two things touch, no third thing is brought into existence; there seems to be no "touching" relation over and above the things that touch. This intuition is again based on our ordinary experience; we never see some new entity created by touching. The truthmaker principle, however, again tells us that something must make it true that things are touching. What could this be?

The atomists might answer that touching occurs when two atoms occupy adjacent places, and these places are held together in a unified space. Thus the touching relation is really two occupancy relations plus whatever holds space together. But touching is very difficult to explain within Aristotle's system. If only substances exist, is the touching relation another substance? If not, and touching is not a new entity, what "holds" substances next to each other? What does it mean for them to be "next to each other"? Aristotle cannot say that they sit in adjacent bits of space, because he denies the existence of space. This difficulty came to the fore in the philosophy of Leibniz, a later Aristotelian, discussed below.

Just as the atomists hid real change in occupancy relations, Aristotle hides change or motion in these contiguity relations between substances. He does not spell out what touching is, nor how touching relations change during movement within the plenum. He relies instead on ordinary intuitions about touching. Thus Aristotle too merely conceals and suppresses the problem of change.

There is a similar difficulty with Aristotle's notion of potential properties, which are meant to explain change within a substance. Aristotle does not and cannot account for the *inherency relation* between a substance and its properties, and understandably resists calling this a relation at all. But change in properties involves a change in inherency relations, and thus triggers another, new version of the problem of change. In sum, Aristotle hides the problem of change in two new sorts or relations, contiguity and inherency, but never explains how these are immune to the problem of change.

The problem of change survived these first onslaughts. The dragon waits to be slain.

CHAPTER 9

Zeno's paradoxes: is motion impossible?

Counting things was the beginning of mathematics. The integers came first: 1, 2, 3, ... Later the need to measure straight lines and flat areas led to the study of geometry in ancient Egypt and India. But mathematics stumbled when it came to curves, spheres, continuous quantities and smooth changes. Early mathematics could not grasp our more fluid world, could not bring its changes and subtleties to life. Mathematics had to learn about change and infinity. It had to enter the labyrinth of the continuum.

Zeno's famous paradoxes may seem to be merely teasing riddles or bewildering games, but they are much, much more than that. They provoked the first great debates over infinity in the European tradition. Two thousand years later, students were still immersed in study of the paradoxes, and one of them, the Englishman Isaac Newton, grew up to create a new kind of mathematics of change: the infinitesimal calculus. Today, the jets we fly in, the bridges we cross and the devices that play our music were all designed using Newton's calculus.

Since space, motion and time are often thought of as continuous and infinite, Zeno's paradoxes were also the first deep enquiry into their structures. Philosophers, however, have tended to study Zeno's paradoxes of motion as if they were primarily about space, motion and time. Plato portrayed Zeno as Parmenides' younger lover, and historians have tended to agree that Zeno's paradoxes were an indirect defence of his friend's strange philosophy. Analysis of the paradoxes confirms this, and opens up broader ways of thinking about Zeno's work.

The arrow and the dichotomy

Zeno argued that an arrow shot from a bow never moves during its entire flight. This has become known as the *paradox of the arrow*. His idea is deceptively simple:

The paradox of the arrow

A. At each instant of its flight, the arrow is in a place exactly its size. (P)

B. If a thing is in a place exactly its size, it is motionless. (P)

C. So, at each instant, the arrow is motionless. (from A,B)

D. If something is true for each instant during a period, then it is true for the entire period. (P)

E. So, for the entire period of its flight, the arrow is motionless. (C,D)

(Zeno's paradox did not mention instants of time, and the above is only one interpretation of his words.)

Although almost everyone agrees Zeno's conclusion is daft, there is no agreement about why. Each of the premises has been attacked.

Some philosophers have thought that the problem occurs at the outset with the idea of "instants". They have denied that time is composed of separate instants. Instead, they supposed that time had to be composed of small stretches of time. But there are difficulties here. If an arrow moves during the smallest stretch of time, then the stretch has parts, and is not the smallest.

Others rejected that idea that "to be in a place exactly its size" implies that a thing is motionless (B). But during motion a thing passes through different places; if it is in motion, it cannot be in just one place.

The shift from each instant to the entire period (E) is also suspicious. There are many cases when something that is true of the parts is not true of the whole, and vice versa. Each individual in a human population is a person, but the population is not a person. Objects composed of atoms are coloured, but no atom is coloured. With the arrow, though, Zeno seems safe. If the arrow is motionless in each instant, when could any motion occur?

These considerations immediately show the value of Zeno's paradoxes. They forced philosophers to develop ideas about the nature of time and its continuous structure. Before giving a deeper diagnosis of the paradox, let's examine another famous paradox about infinity. According to Zeno's paradox of the dichotomy, you cannot walk to the nearby wall you are facing. Here "dichotomy" means "cutting in two" ("dicho" means "in two" and "tom" means "cut" – as in "atom"). The argument runs as follows:

The paradox of the dichotomy

A. If a runner reaches the end-point of a distance, the
runner also visits its mid-point. (P)
B. If the runner visits the mid-point, then the runner
visits a point half way to the mid-point. (P)
C. Thus, if a runner reaches the end-point, the runner
visits an infinity of points. (from A,B, induction)
D. But it is impossible to visit an infinity of points. (P)
E. Therefore, the runner does not reach the end-point
of the distance. (C,D)

This is obviously a general argument and, if it holds at all, implies that you cannot walk to a nearby wall. In fact, you cannot even move an inch in that direction.

The last premise, D, seems very suspicious, but the idea behind it is simple. "Infinite" literally means "without end" (Latin "in" means "not" and "finis" means "end"). So to finish visiting an infinity of points would mean coming to the end of what does not have an end.

Deeper questions lurk in the transition to the third sentence. How do we get from the idea that "each interval has a mid-point" to an infinity of points? This is a leap. Today logicians and mathematicians usually consider this leap acceptable and call it "mathematical induction" (but there is still a leap of some sort).

> The problem is not that Zeno's conclusions are true, but that there is no agreement about why they are false.

Aristotle banishes infinity

Before getting further tangled in Zeno's paradoxes, we should pause at the brink to consider what infinity might be. For many classical thinkers, at least from the time of Aristotle, there was no such thing. Infinities were pathologies: signs that a theory or line of reasoning had gone wrong somewhere.

Aristotle defined orthodox thought about infinity for some 2,000 years. He first admitted that there were powerful reasons for supposing that infinities existed. The integers seem to be infinite, and the universe may be infinite in extent. Time seems to go on and on, and thus would also be infinite. But infinity was notoriously paradoxical. Even in classical times there were a number of well-known puzzles. As above, to say that an infinity existed, and was wholly present, seemed to assert that something without end had come to an end. But the incomplete could not be complete, and thus there could be no infinity. There were also problems with parts and wholes. Consider the integers, 1, 2, 3, . . . The even integers, 2, 4, 6, . . ., are only a part of all the integers, yet for every integer there is one corresponding even integer: its double. Thus there is a one-to-one correspondence between integers and even integers, and there is the same number of each. But then the part is equal to the whole! Since this cannot be, there cannot be such a thing as an infinity.

Aristotle laid down the orthodox doctrine. He had used the distinction between potential and actual to solve the problems of change. It explained how the results of change could be both new and old. Now he proposed to use the same distinction again to resolve tensions surrounding infinity: we had some reasons to suppose it existed, but other reasons to deny its existence altogether.

According to Aristotle, *there is no actual infinity*: no existing thing is infinite. Thus the paradoxes are avoided. However, there may be *potential infinities*. If we can always add 1 to an integer to produce the next integer, then the integers can potentially go on and on. If one day can always be followed by the next, then days are potentially infinite. No integer and no day, no existing thing, is ever infinite.

This famous doctrine had wide ramifications for Aristotle's metaphysics. He denied, for example, that the universe was infinite. It also explains in part his hostility to Zeno's paradoxes. His distinction did not, however, lead him to a satisfactory resolution. He appears to have changed his mind and gave incompatible solutions to the paradoxes in different places.

Aristotle's insistence that there are no actual infinities makes us even more suspicious of Zeno's reasoning in the paradox of the dichotomy, but leaves the enigma intact.

Paradoxes of plurality

Bertrand Russell, the most prominent Anglo-American philosopher of the twentieth century, said that every generation solves Zeno's paradoxes, and every following generation feels the need to solve them again. Rather than advancing one more supposed solution, perhaps we can develop a deeper perspective on why they are so difficult to disentangle. What issues lie beneath Zeno's paradoxes?

Plato portrays Zeno as indirectly defending Parmenides. Instead of arguing positively that all reality is one and unchanging, Zeno argues negatively that reality could not be many things. Most historians agree that this interpretation of Zeno is correct, but philosophers still tend to treat the above paradoxes as if they were merely puzzles about motion through space and time. According to this view in Plato, Zeno's deeper concern was more general, and focused on aspects of the so-called *problem of the one and the many*. Aristotle mentions that this was already an "ancient" problem in his time, and the problem of unity in diversity continued to dominate Greek metaphysics for the next thousand years after Plato and Aristotle. Can we interpret Zeno's paradoxes as manifestations of this more fundamental tension between unity and plurality?

To be one thing and to be many things are contradictories: something cannot be both one and many in the same respect and at the same time. But as we look around us, almost everything we see is both one and many. An egg is one and yet is many properties, such as hardness and whiteness. Space is one and yet is made up of many places. An army is one and yet is many soldiers. How do all these manage to be both one and many?

The first, obvious answer is that they are one and many *in different respects*. An egg is one as substance, but has many properties. A space is one as a whole but has places as parts. An army is one as an army, but as soldiers many. This simple response, however, merely pushes the problem down one level, for how can one thing comprise many "respects" and yet remain one? This is a tough question. The quick answers fail to dissolve the tension between the contradictories, and simply push the problem around.

This central tension between one-ness and many-ness is the core of the problem, but like other deep problems it can be manifested in a bewildering variety of ways. The phrase "problem of the one and the many" has come to stand for this hornets' nest of related problems. Some philosophers use it to refer to the conflict between two basic sorts of ontologies: pluralism says that there are many things or many kinds of elements, while monism says that there is only one thing or one kind of thing. But the one–many conflict is more general than this, and infects all metaphysical questions.

Plato's dialogues return to these problems of unity and diversity again and again, and at times they portray it as the central problem of metaphysics. Although only fragments of Zeno's writings have survived as quotations in other books, several of these fragments are *paradoxes of plurality*, and make it clear that the many-ness of things was one of Zeno's main targets. Indeed, Plato says in the *Phaedrus* that Zeno made "the same things seem like and unlike, and one and many, and at rest and in motion". As one example, we find Zeno advancing the following paradox. This passage, from a book by Simplicius, is thought to be a genuine quotation, and may be the earliest, recorded "argument" in European philosophy:

> In proving once again that if there are many things, the same things are limited and unlimited, Zeno's very own words are as follows.
>
> "If there are many things, it is necessary that they are just as many as they are, and neither more nor less than that. But if they are as many as they are, they will be limited.
>
> If there are many things, the things that are are unlimited; for there are always others between the things that are, and again others between those. And thus the things that are are unlimited."

Zeno's point is that if many things are both unlimited and limited, they are contradictory. But, since there are no contradictions, there are not many things and reality must be just one thing. The thinking behind the second half of this argument probably goes as follows. If things are many, they cannot seamlessly touch or overlap. Thus they must be somehow separated from each other, say by boundaries or by intervening things. And these separators too must be distinct from the things they separate (if not, there is no separation), and are therefore just more things among the many. But then they in turn must be separated from the others, and an infinite regress follows: they are unlimited in number. (This puzzling argument has some strength. Note that we cannot answer it by assuming that things or their separators are wholes made of parts or that space is continuous, because these presume some sort of many-ness.)

Without examining the depths of this argument, it is clear evidence that Zeno was attacking plurality. Is it possible to show that the above paradoxes of motion are also rooted in similar puzzles about unity and diversity? Zeno's paradoxes are very controversial and have been interpreted in many ways. Here we can only suggest that this is a fruitful way of thinking about the underlying issues.

The nub of the paradox of the dichotomy is the infinity of points that must be traversed. What is the source of this infinity? Why do we agree there is an infinity of points before the end-point? Why is there a mid-point between any two points? One answer is that there could not be *nothing* between the two points, because then they would not be separated, and would not be *two* points. This sort of answer shows an immediate link to the paradox of plurality above, and suggests that the paradoxes of motion are related to the deeper problem of the one and the many. Indeed, Simplicius quoted the passage above to make that point.

Today, we might say there is an infinity of points because the intervening space is smooth and *continuous*. However, any attempt to spell out what we mean by this would again encounter the one–many conflict. Even in modern mathematics, theories of the continuum have been beset by difficulties, and some suggest these are technical analogues of the problem of the one and the many.

The paradox of the arrow can be understood in the following way. A motion seems to involve both diversity and unity. It is easy to see how diversity is involved because the motion traverses many places or takes many moments. It is less easy to see the role of unity. A motion can be a smooth and unbroken whole, as Aristotle thought, and it traverses its whole route during a whole period of time. But it is hard to see how the unity combines with the diversity of places and times to constitute a motion.

Since the role of unity is hard to express or even articulate, it is easy for Zeno's argument (a body does not move in a place its size, etc.) to conclude that there is no unity at all. But stripped of unity, we have no motion at all. When a motion is broken down into many instants without connection, into a "pure diversity", then motion itself disappears. The strength of the paradox does not lie, therefore, in the rather dodgy argument for breaking down motion into static instants, but in the difficulty we have in articulating how motion can be both a one and a many. Unless we have a clear idea of how motion unites its diverse instants, we will fall back into a picture of motion as pure diversity and thus into Zeno's lair.

The German philosopher Hegel made a bizarre suggestion in the early 1800s, which may help to illustrate the kind of solution which would fend off Zeno's attack on motion. Hegel said that a moving body is actually in two places at once. Perhaps he meant the two places were almost entirely overlapping, and that motion just was a strange ability to unite the diverse. If so, Hegel can answer Zeno by saying that a body in a place exactly its size can be moving; namely, when it is also in another place at the same instant! Whether or not this makes sense, Hegel at least aims at a concept of motion that explicitly fuses the many into one, and this is the sort of picture that is needed to rebut the paradox of the arrow.

Russell gave a solution to the paradox of the arrow that was influenced by mathematics and relativity theory. In essence, he gave in to Zeno, and agreed that motion just was many motionless instants. If time really flows, then his solution is very much like the films, mentioned earlier, where a sequence of still photographs constitutes motion (sometimes called "cinematic motion" or "the staccato universe").

> Zeno's paradoxes can be interpreted as manifestations of the problem of the one and the many. If many things are somehow unified, a relation does the work.

What are relations?

Space and time are composed of relations, and so they are in a way the subject of this book. The thrust of this chapter and Chapter 8 is that the struggle to conceptualize change, motion, space and time stumbled upon deeper issues with the ontology of relations. The atomists and Aristotle suppressed the problem of change only by sweeping the real change in their systems into occupancy and inherency relations. Zeno exploded notions of space and time by teasing out the implications of the one–many-ness residing within all real relations. Before our investigation of space and time continues, we should consider some general issues and views about the nature of relations.

The primitive tendency to think that everything that exists is an individual object obstructed enquiry into relations. Many philosophers have even denied that relations have any existence of their own, over and above the things they relate. Crudely put, those who think of relations as real tend to think of them as something like a great stone bridge stretching between two cliffs, and somehow connecting or uniting them. In this picture, a relation connects two particular things, the cliffs, but has some extra being of its own, the mortar and stones in the arch. Russell called these "real relations", and meant thereby that relations had some reality distinct from what they related. Thus this view can be called *realism* about relations.

Other philosophers have maintained that only particular things exist and would favour pictures like the following. One tree is taller than another tree because the first has a height of 10 metres and the second has a height of 15 metres. That is, the relation "is taller than" is just an awkward way of talking about the properties belonging to individual trees. The only things that exist are the individual trees and the properties in them; nothing stretches between the trees when one is taller than the other. This is sometimes described as *reductionism* since the relations are "reduced to" particular things and their individual properties.

Despite prominent exceptions, it is fair to say that for some 2,000 years, from Aristotle to Russell, reductionist views dominated among philosophers. Aristotle rejected realism and his extraordinary fame lent this great weight. But even apart from this, there were three main philosophical reasons for favouring reductionism.

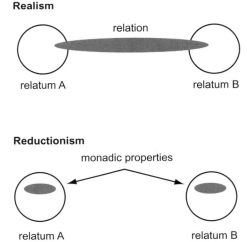

Figure 9.1 *Two views of the ontology of relations. According to realism, the relation stretches between the two relata. According to reductionism, the relation is merely an ordinary one-place property inside each of the two relata.*

First, as mentioned above, our experience with ordinary objects encourages the view that they are primary. Bodies seem to move without being caught in a web of changing real relations. Talk of anything over and above particulars seems preposterous to common-sense philosophers. (They overlook, however, that we always encounter objects involved in relations: in contact, in the world, in space, etc.)

The second barrier to realism was a phenomenon known nowadays as a "Cambridge change". Suppose the top of the taller tree is lopped off, and only 8 metres remain. If a relation were some kind of bridge from one tree to the other, then trimming one tree would change the other. During the transformation of the untouched tree from shorter to taller tree it would be violently disconnected from any bridge-like relation that might connect the two trees. This seems odd. How could a change in one tree instantaneously affect a distant tree? In fact, all trees everywhere would suddenly alter their relations to the trimmed tree. This sort of spooky, invisible change has made the very idea of real relations seem ridiculous.

The third barrier to realism has been the problem of the one and the many discussed above. It is very difficult to say how a bridge-like relation connects or unites the things it relates. Are they one or many? If they are strongly united and become one new individual, then there is no relation, just a particular thing with properties. If they remain many, then there is no relation – just isolated things. Somehow relations are both one and many, but these are contradictories.

During the early 1900s there was a great shift among Anglo-American philosophers who reversed 2,000 years of prejudice and overcame these obstacles to recognizing the reality of relations. This was Russell's great achievement.

Two great, countering pressures outweighed the scepticism about real relations. First, in the 1600s, European mathematicians began to adopt Hindu numerals and Arabic algebra, and thus began to write mathematics in a new language: they used "equations". Earlier mathematics had been written as a series of ratios or proportions or in ordinary language. But writing formulas with an equals sign made them look like representations of relations. When physicist-philosophers such as Descartes adopted this new language and used it to describe the world, it became hard to avoid accepting relations as real. What else were the equations of physics describing?

Russell's victory, however, was especially helped by the invention of the new symbolic logics around 1900. These aped the language of mathematics, and gave philosophers new tools for analysing and studying the various types of relations. Relations were promoted from nonentities to the subject of a new science. Thus this symbolic technology for logic brought with it a profound shift in the basic ontological views of Anglo-American philosophers.

The above objections to realism are now problems about relations and not reasons for rejecting real relations altogether.

> The acceptance of real relations leaves the problem of the one and the many as a deep problem about the structure of relations, which heightens the significance of Zeno's attacks on plurality. If his paradoxes were devices for exposing one–many tensions, then they are relevant to the new realism about relations. They are especially important to any deep theory of spatial or temporal relations.

Zeno and the mathematicians

From Zeno to our own day, the finest intellects of each generation in turn attacked the problems, but achieved, broadly speaking, nothing. In our own time, however, three mathematicians – Weierstrass, Dedekind, and Cantor – have not merely made advances on Zeno's problems, but have completely solved them. The solutions are so clear as to leave no longer the slightest doubt or difficulty. This achievement is probably the greatest of which our age has to boast; and I know of no age (except perhaps the golden age of Greece) which has a more convincing proof to offer of the transcendent genius of its great men.

(Russell, 1901)

Russell used his enormous reputation among philosophers to propagandize for mathematical solutions of Zeno's paradoxes. Russell's views still have a residual influence among today's philosophers, many of whom believe that "mathematics have solved all that". But Russell was wrong, and his views have been overtaken by history.

In essence, there was tremendous optimism during the late 1800s and early 1900s that set theory and the new mathematics of infinity would sweep away the ancient paradoxes and furnish a crystal-clear foundation for all of mathematics. But this revolution quickly discovered that it too was beset by paradoxes, and soon became bogged down in attempts to repair its own premises in ways that would evade a complete collapse. These movements still have some prestige, and set theory is still taught to students, but they really have failed to satisfy the hopes of the pioneers. Now a variety of approaches compete for attention, and there is no consensus that Zeno's problems have been solved; instead, they have simply been transformed into more technical paradoxes. Zeno lives.

CHAPTER 10

Philosophers at war: Newton vs. Leibniz

The Englishman Sir Isaac Newton, one of the greatest physicists of all time, has been reinvented. During the past 30 or so years, historians like Betty Jo Dobbs began to uncover the human behind the scientist and made discoveries that have surprised the world of science.

Newton has often been idolized, but at such a distance that he seemed a cold, remote and austere figure, like the marble statues that depict him. He was famous for basing his science strictly on what he could observe and measure. He mocked other philosophers whose premises and hypotheses were spun out of their own brains, and proudly hissed "I feign no hypotheses". As a professor and later head of the Royal Mint in London, he seemed a ready-made, secular saint for science.

In the 1930s, boxes of Newton's unpublished papers were discovered in an attic and sold at auction. Their surprising contents led to some talk of a cover-up by his family and followers. As historians began to investigate these and other scattered papers, a new Newton emerged. They showed that he spent much of his time working, not on physics, but on alchemy: the magical search for a way to produce gold. Newton was in fact something of a transitional figure. He was half-wizard stoking his furnace and half-scientist covering pages of parchment with his sprawling mathematical calculations. Other papers showed that Newton suffered bouts of insanity. Researchers found that his alchemical notebooks recorded not only the colour, weight and other properties of the chemicals he was mixing, but also their *taste*. Tests on surviving locks of his hair reportedly showed mercury poisoning.

Other investigations showed that Newton, fearing imprisonment or worse, concealed his more radical activities. He befriended the philosopher John Locke before Locke had to flee to Holland. Newton was a Christian heretic, but hid his rejection of the Trinity. Like many scholars at the time he remained unmarried, but his biographer, Richard Westfall, believed the evidence shows that he was homosexual. Newton was a stock-market investor, and lost a fortune when a speculative bubble burst. The new Newton is spectacular: not a secular saint but a richer, fascinating, multi-dimensional human being. None of this detracts from the man or the science. It does represent a real discovery by the historians: the eccentric genius beneath the marble myth.

In the philosophy of space and time, Newton made two monumental contributions:

- *Revival of the atomists' void*
  Newton put the concept of the void at the centre of his new physical theory. Its success eventually reversed the Aristotelian consensus that the concept of the void was incoherent.
- *Invention of a mathematics of change*
  The Greek problem of change and Zeno's paradoxes had shown how difficult it was to form a workable concept of change. In his struggles to predict the motions of the planets, Newton invented a new way to handle change that has had enormous repercussions for philosophical debates about change.

Our goal in this chapter is to penetrate to the core of Newton's arguments for his innovations. Everyone believed that Einstein had finally overthrown Newton's views on space and time but, as we shall see, Newton is making a comeback.

The geometrization of space

When Newton was a student he studied the works of René Descartes (1596–1650), who was something like the Einstein of the 1600s. Descartes was the chief founder of modern post-Aristotelian philosophy, a mathematician and a scientist, who left France for the relative intellectual freedom of Holland. There is a lovely story about Descartes's first stay there when he was just out of the army and still in his twenties. He met another ambitious fellow in the street and they started talking.

Their friendship was cemented when they discovered each shared an interest in combining physics and mathematics. Astronomers had always used mathematics but, until the Scientific Revolution in the seventeenth century, physics was largely qualitative and conceptual. It was a branch of philosophy that emphasized explanations and not precise predictions. Descartes's new friend wrote in his diary: "Physico-mathematicians are very rare, and Descartes says he has never met any one other than myself who pursues his studies in the way I do, combining Physics and Mathematics in an exact way. And for my part, I have never spoken with anyone apart from him who studies in this way". In a nutshell, then, the two new friends excitedly discussed the novel idea that "physics should use mathematics". Descartes went on to discover one of the first mathematical laws of physics and, with figures like Kepler and Galileo, is honoured as a pioneer of mathematical physics.

Descartes could not, however, extend his law into a complete system of physics. His book *The Principles of Philosophy* (1644) was an advance over Aristotle's still-dominant metaphysics but it remained conceptual and qualitative. In fact, Descartes had cooked up a strange mixture of previous systems. He circumspectly advocated the fashionable atomism of the newer philosophers, but also insisted that atoms comprised a plenum like that of Aristotle.

Thus before Newton it was not clear that using mathematics in physics was going to be a successful direction for research. The programme was gathering strength, but its prophets remained a minority. Newton had bragged to his friends in the new coffeehouses that he could calculate the paths of the planets. Working feverishly night after night, however, he began to realize he had more than he thought. His book grew. He added chapters, pestered astronomers for more data and began new calculations. Westfall's biography captures the mood of Newton's almost hysterical energies as he began to suspect that he had *everything*. He had a system of the world. He had God's blueprint for the cosmos. He could predict the orbits of the planets around the Sun, the eerie streaks of the comets, the waxing and waning of the tides, the rise and fall of cannonballs, the dropping of an apple: he could calculate and predict all known motions.

In 1687, Newton's *Mathematical Principles of Natural Philosophy* appeared. The title was a put-down aimed at Descartes's followers, and set the agenda for the future of physics. Unlike Descartes's *Principles of Philosophy*, Newton's method was rigorous and mathematical and carefully limited to the study of material nature. It avoided all discussion of souls and psychology.

This book not only changed our conception of space and time, but it changed for ever humanity's vision of the universe. It showed that the same laws that governed the motions of the planets through outer space governed motions here on Earth and even in our own bodies. It showed that these laws were mathematical, and thus lent themselves to precise measurement and prediction. It showed that the human mind could reach out and comprehend nature, that the mystery and magic of the living world concealed a rational system. In sum, Newton redeemed the faith of the Greek philosophers that reason was at home in the world: that the world was ultimately intelligible. In the long history of the human race, Newton's may prove to be the most important book ever written.

Newton boiled down his entire system into the three compact laws below, from which all the rest followed. They are worth memorizing. The first law was discovered earlier by Galileo, Descartes and others. This was an enormous breakthrough. Most of the motions here on Earth peter out and come to an end: a marble will eventually stop rolling. It took real insight to see that the marble would have naturally continued *for ever* if the force of friction did not slow it. The second law is about "forces", which are just pushes and pulls. It says that a stronger push will create a faster change in movement, and also that a heavier body will react more slowly to a push. The third law is here labelled the "conservation of energy", but the modern concepts of energy and momentum had not yet been invented in Newton's time. He expressed the idea by saying that when one body pushes a second body and gives it motion, the first body loses the same amount of motion in the same direction: "equal and opposite reactions".

Newton's laws of motion
I.   *Inertia*: a moving body will follow straight lines at the same speed unless changed by forces.
II. *Force*: equals mass times acceleration.
III. *Conservation of energy*: for every action there is an equal and opposite reaction.

These are the core of Newton's system, and are some of the most precious words ever written.

As Newton developed his theories of motion, he discovered that the world could not be a mere plenum as conceived by Aristotle and Descartes. It is not hard to see that these laws demanded the existence of some "space" over and above the bodies moving in it. The law of inertia says that bodies will follow straight lines unless deflected by some force. If the theory is correct, these straight lines must exist. There must be, in addition to moving material bodies, a geometric space that houses them. According to Newton, the lines in space tell bodies which way to move. Since the theory best explained all known motions, Newton concluded that the lines and space must be real.

Philosophers call this kind of argument an *inference to best explanation*. If a theory gives the best explanation of something that occurs, then we are entitled to infer that the theory is a correct description. This kind of argument is often used in science and in everyday life, but it is not very secure. Mystery writers construct their surprise endings by arranging for the best explanation of a crime to be overthrown by some last-minute piece of evidence. A claim that rests on inference to best explanation alone is never completely secure.

Newton himself was not satisfied with this kind of argument, and began his book with a long note or "Scholium" on space and time. These famous pages were the most important development in the philosophy of space and time since Plato and Aristotle 2,000 years earlier. In essence, Newton revived the atomists' conception of space and radically transformed it to serve his own theories.

Atomist doctrines were in the air, and creating quite a scandal. In 1633, Galileo had been prosecuted and placed under house arrest in part for his flirtations with atomism; Descartes had to deny that he would even dabble in views so associated with atheism. A generation earlier, in 1600, the philosopher Giordano Bruno had been burned at the stake in Rome for refusing to recant his heresies. In the century after the Protestant churches had broken away from Roman Catholicism, authorities everywhere were in a panic about subversive and divisive philosophies. Atomism was resolutely materialist and seemed to challenge all religions. Newton's embrace of the atomists' void was in keeping with his other radical views.

Newton's *Principia* ignored the paradoxes about change, motion and space, and therefore smuggled them into the foundations of all contemporary physics.

Absolute space and absolute time

I don't know what I may seem to the world, but, as to myself, I seem to have been only like a boy playing on the sea shore, and diverting myself in now and then finding a smoother pebble or a prettier shell than ordinary, whilst the great ocean of truth lay all undiscovered before me.

(Newton, shortly before his death in 1726)

For philosophers of space and time, Newton's Scholium is the Old Testament. Even after Einstein revealed the New Testament of relativity theory, the deep framework of Newton's vision remains basic to all of physics. It was Newton who made the key terms "relative" and "absolute" central to classical theories of space and time. The word "absolute" means "independent" in the sense that a thing is absolute when it does not depend on other things, is free from interference and makes itself what it is ("to absolve" means "to set free"). A king has absolute power when he exercises it himself, independently of a constitution, legislature or foreign allies.

Invariance is, here, a property of appearances. If all measurements of a spacetime interval yield the same result, then the observed interval is invariant. For Newton, "absolute" is a metaphysical term, and describes the reality behind appearances. A thing is absolute when it exists in its own right, when no other thing can alter it.

Newton began the Scholium with a definition of absolute time:

Absolute, true, and mathematical time, of itself, and from its own nature, flows equably without relation to anything external, and by another name is called duration; relative, apparent, and common time, is some sensible and external measure of duration . . .

Newton's metaphor here is very important. He says that time "flows", perhaps as a river does. He further asserts that the passage of time has a constant "speed", that is, that it flows "equably" and uniformly. This seems reassuring, but is also very puzzling. A river flows past its banks. What does time flow past? The speed of a water flow can be measured in units of, say, kilometres per hour. At what speed does time flow? One hour per hour? Newton does not answer these questions.

For Newton, a "relative space" depends on something else. The hold of a ship is an enclosed volume that moves with the ship and depends on it, and is thus merely a relative space. By contrast, Newton thought that empty outer space did not depend on anything, and was therefore an "absolute" space. Relative spaces can move; absolute spaces are immobile:

> Absolute space . . . remains always the same and immovable. Relative space is some movable dimension or measure of the absolute spaces, which our senses determine by its position to other bodies . . . Absolute and relative spaces are the same in shape and size; but they do not remain always one and the same. For if the earth, for instance, moves, a space of our air . . . will at one time be one part of the absolute space, and at another time it will be another part of the same. And so, absolutely understood, it will be continually changed.

Thus a relative space is part of absolute space. But if the boundaries of the relative space move, then the relative space moves with them. An absolute space is not dependent on anything.

Bodies move in space from one place to another, that is, from one part of space to another. But because there are two kinds of spaces, there are two kinds of motions. In a key paragraph, Newton says:

> Absolute motion is the translation of a body from one absolute place into another; and relative motion, the translation from one relative place into another. Thus in a ship under sail, the relative place of a body is that part of the ship or the hold which the body fills, and which therefore moves with the ship. But real, absolute rest is the continuance of the body in the same part of immovable, absolute space.

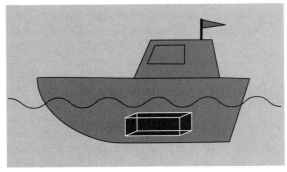

Figure 10.1 *Relative versus absolute space. The space within the ship's hold moves with the ship and is therefore a relative space. The shaded exterior space does not move with the ship and is absolute.*

This can be a bit tricky. All motion is in or through or towards or away from something else. All motion is relative to something. *Thus absolute motion is actually a kind of relative motion. Absolute motion is motion relative to absolute space.*

Newton loudly takes a stand in the Scholium that was at odds with his old reputation. He was often hailed as the father of strict empiricism. This philosophy insists on limiting research to what can be observed and measured. Thus empiricists refuse to investigate God or angels, what makes a poem beautiful or what happened before the beginning of the universe. These are not open to observation and measurement and therefore, they say, should not be part of science.

Modern empiricism has been so enormously fruitful that its advocates sometimes pushed the idea to an extreme. They rejected discussion of anything that could not be *directly* observed, and attacked those philosophers who championed conceptual or linguistic investigations. In these controversies, Newton was used as an emblem of strict empiricism, as a scientist whose great discoveries stemmed from his adoption of empiricism. This image is, of course, completely outdated now. What is peculiar is that even Newton's published papers proclaimed that he was a moderate empiricist. He made a great contribution by emphasizing observation and measurement, and even constructed his own telescopes and other instruments. But Newton thought of himself as a philosopher and also balanced his empiricism with a sense of its limitations.

The Scholium contains a passage in which Newton suggests that science must go beyond what can be directly observed, must go beyond strict empiricism:

> But because the parts of absolute space cannot be seen, or distinguished from one another by our senses, we use sensible measures of them. And so, instead of absolute places and motions, we use relative ones; and that without any inconvenience in common affairs; but in philosophical disquisitions, we ought to abstract from our senses, and consider things in themselves, distinct from what are only sensible measures of them. For it may be that there is no body really at rest, to which the places and motions of others may be referred.
>
> Those who confound real quantities with their relations and sensible measures defile the purity of mathematical and philosophical truths.

Relative spaces are directly observable because their boundaries are (the ship); absolute spaces are not. Relative spaces appear to us;

absolute spaces are the reality behind the appearances. Newton emphasizes that his science cannot be limited to what is directly observable because that would exclude absolute space. Readers of Kant will recognize his distinction between phenomena and noumena: between appearances and things-in-themselves. Early in his career, Kant was a vigorous Newtonian and defender of absolute space, as we shall see.

Remember the slogans: "absolute motion is motion relative to absolute space" and "relative motion is motion relative to bodies or their surroundings".

The bucket argument

Newton was not satisfied with mere definitions of absolute space. He concluded the Scholium with a virtuoso performance, and suggested experiments and arguments *proving* the existence of absolute space. These have had an extraordinary afterlife. They were a direct inspiration to Einstein as he struggled with his theory of gravitation. In different guises, they remain today at the centre of debates over space and time among philosophers. But students sometimes giggle when they read Newton's proposals: they seem silly, almost crude and rustic. These first impressions are wrong. A satellite built by NASA and Stanford University (see Appendix D for their websites) is a high-tech version of Newton's proposals, as will be explained below.

Newton's famous *bucket argument* is now considered a philosophical classic. As their studies progress, philosophers sometimes fall in love with arguments the way others might with a favourite novel, a breathtaking mountain or a moving symphony. As connoisseurs, philosophers hope for arguments with beauty, depth, simplicity – and a bit of mystery. When they find these together, they return again and again to the argument, hoping each time to learn a little more, to push it a bit farther. For all its simplicity, Newton's bucket illuminates the deepest issues in relativity theory and few can resist its allure.

The strategy of Newton's proof is to show that there are certain observable effects that *could only* be caused by absolute space. Newton begins disarmingly. Even though absolute space is not directly observable, he proposes to prove its existence with a bucket. Suppose, he says, that our wooden bucket is nearly full of water and is

Figure 10.2   Newton's famous bucket.

suspended by a good, flexible rope from the tree branch overhead. Suppose we rotate the bucket and twist the rope up as far as it will go without tangling. If we now gently release the bucket, the calm, flat waters will at first remain still within the rotating bucket. As the rope unwinds and the bucket begins to whirl more quickly, the water will gradually be affected by the movement of the bucket and start to spin. As it does, the surface of the water will become *concave*: it will be lower in the middle as the water crowds outwards towards the sides of the bucket.

All this is straightforward, but Newton's genius now notices a subtlety. As the rope smoothly unwinds, the spinning concave water in the bucket will finally catch up with the rotating bucket. Soon they will *rotate at the same speed*. Newton saw here an argument for the existence of absolute space. (Do you?) The argument turns on two key facts: the surface of the rotating water is concave, and the bucket and water eventually rotate at the same speed. In this state, *there is no relative motion between the water and the bucket* – just as a child on a spinning merry-go-round is moving around along with the horses, and thus not moving relative to the horses. Newton's argument can be interpreted as follows:

Newton's bucket argument

A. The motion causes the concavity.   (P)
B. Motion is either relative or absolute.   (P)
C. Thus, either relative or absolute motion causes the
    concavity.   (from A,B)
D. But relative motion does not cause the concavity.   (P)

E. So absolute motion causes the concavity.   (C,D)
F. If something is a cause, then it exists.   (P)
G. So absolute motion exists.   (E,F)
H. If absolute motion exists, then absolute space exists.   (P)
I. So absolute space exists.   (G,H)

Several of the assumptions here are straightforward. For example, motion causes the concavity, A, because the surface of the water is flat before the bucket is released and begins to turn. Newton actually leaps from E to I, but later debates have shown that it is important to fill in these steps.

Laying out the argument carefully like this, however, exposes the biggest assumption. Why does Newton think it is obvious that relative motion does not cause the concavity (premise D)? The Scholium defends this in one key sentence. The concavity persists when "the water rested relatively in the bucket", he says, "and therefore this does not depend upon any movement of the water relative to the ambient bodies". How does Newton make the connection between the water resting in the bucket and the independence from surrounding bodies? Much rests on the answer to this question. If Newton's assumption is sound, absolute space exists and Einstein was wrong.

Newton's idea is this. We know that the bucket itself did not cause the concavity because the water was in the bucket long before it became concave. We also know that the motion of the water *relative to the bucket* did not cause the concavity; this motion disappears when the rotating water catches up with and rests in the rotating bucket. What about the water's motion relative to other bodies? Newton thinks it would be preposterous to assert that the water's motion relative to the tree overhead, the grassy meadow or the distant twinkling stars caused the concavity. First, we could have hung the bucket on a different tree or in a different meadow and still found exactly the same concavity. The concavity does not depend on *which* distant bodies the water is moving relative to. Secondly, there are no means, no causal pathways, for other bodies to affect the water. How could the nearby stream cause the surface of the water in the bucket to curve? Thirdly, the water in the bucket is moving relatively to many, perhaps infinitely many, other bodies. It is moving around the Sun and through the galaxy; it is moving relative to passing birds and ships sinking off the coast of Madagascar. It is absurd to think that this crazy patchwork of relative motions might cause the concavity. These considerations are so obvious to Newton that he feels his assumption D is safe.

We will see in Chapter 15 that Einstein and his sometime mentor Ernst Mach strongly disagreed with Newton, and this led to extraordinary experiments testing Newton's assumption. Could the surrounding bodies have caused the concavity?

> Critics say absolute space is not observable, but Newton argued that its effects are observable. All things are observed only through their effects.

Leibniz's attack

If Newton was the greatest mind in Britain in the late-seventeenth century, W. G. Leibniz (1646–1716) was the greatest mind on the Continent. He is remembered as a philosopher, one of the last defenders of Aristotle's metaphysics, and as a scientist who played a key role in discovering the conservation of energy. He was co-inventor of the calculus and is given credit for inventing the binary number systems used in all our computers today. He was also a visionary logician, pushing forwards towards more rigorous approaches. But Newton and Leibniz hated each other. At a time when men in the upper classes still wore swords on formal occasions and fought duels to avenge any offence to their honour, Newton and Leibniz came as close as one could to coming to blows in a scholarly dispute.

Leibniz was a brilliant opportunist. He had a knack for turning to fashionable subjects and transforming them in unexpected and original ways. During his time at university, he rejected the Aristotelianism of his teachers and briefly became an atomist. But he finally found the atomists' idea of space too absurd and once again took up the idea of Aristotelian substances. He visited Paris in the mid 1670s and was introduced to avant-garde circles of thinkers and writers. At their high-society dinners for wealthy socialites and witty intellectuals, Leibniz quickly learned that the bright young lights in philosophy were studying mathematics. Descartes had died in 1650, but one of his students urged Leibniz to learn a little mathematics. Leibniz read a few essays, including some mathematical work of Newton's, returned home to scribble out some ideas of his own, and two years later invented the calculus.

Leibniz's stunning breakthrough infuriated Newton, who had fully developed calculus years before but was notoriously slow to disclose his ideas and had left them unpublished. He felt, however, that the short essay Leibniz had read contained enough hints, and that Leibniz had therefore plagiarized his ideas. This led to a great long-running controversy on both sides of the English Channel. The English rallied around Newton after a committee report from the new Royal Society in 1711 upheld his claims to priority, but Leibniz's defenders on the Continent were unpersuaded. (It turned out that Newton had secretly written the Royal Society report.)

This celebrated dispute made the second great clash between these titans even nastier. Many years after the publication of his system of calculus, Leibniz publicly attacked Newtonian ideas. He insinuated that Newton was a heretic whose doctrines were destroying religion. Leibniz then turned to the ideas about space and time expressed in the scholium, and levelled a blistering barrage of arguments against the absurdity of an infinite and invisible absolute space. In later years, these attacks made Leibniz a hero to many. He was correct that Newton and the rise of modern science would contribute to the decline of religion in Europe. Moreover, after Einstein overthrew Newton's absolute space in the early 1900s, Leibniz's reputation soared. It seemed he had anticipated Einstein's criticisms, and was simply 200 years ahead of his time.

Leibniz launched his attack because of his friendship with a princess. Leibniz was often at the Court of Berlin where Queen Sophia was his friend and student. There he met the young Princess Caroline, one of the most educated women in Europe, who played a role in leading controversies of the day. Caroline also became a student of Leibniz's and used her power and influence to spread his religious views. She married well. Her husband, a powerful German aristocrat who was the elector of Hanover, later became King George II of Great Britain and Ireland in 1727. From the time she first arrived in England, she again became a chief propagandist for Leibniz's views, as these edited extracts from her letters to Leibniz show:

> We are thinking very seriously of getting your book on theology translated into English. Dr Clarke is the most suitable but is too opposed to your opinions – he is too much of Sir Isaac Newton's opinion and I am myself engaged in a dispute with him. I implore your help. I can only ever believe what would conform to the perfection of God. I have found this much more perfect in your system than in that of Mr Newton, where in effect, God has to be always present to readjust his machine [the universe] because he was not able to do it at the beginning.

I am in despair that persons of such great learning as you and Newton are not reconciled. The public would profit immensely if this could be brought about, but great men are like women, who never give up their lovers except with the utmost chagrin and mortal anger. And that, gentlemen, is where your opinions have got you.

Caroline went on to invite Leibniz to set out his differences with Newton in an open letter. In those days, magazines and academic journals were quite new and scholars often circulated their ideas as letters addressed to a prominent colleague. When Leibniz penned his courtly condemnation of Newton for Caroline, he knew all of Europe would soon be reading it.

Always shy of public controversy, Newton himself refused to reply to Leibniz. Instead, Newton's friend, disciple and sometime spokesman, the Anglican Bishop Samuel Clarke, accepted the Queen's request to defend Newton's ideas in the court of public opinion. Clarke and Leibniz each sent five alternating letters to Caroline. When they were collected and published as a book in 1717 it was a bestseller throughout Europe. Despite the undercurrent of acrimony, this Leibniz–Clarke correspondence is the most valuable discussion of the concept of space between the scholium and the time of Einstein.

Leibniz's vision of philosophy differed fundamentally from Newton's. For Leibniz, our metaphysics should be grounded in deep, clear and simple truths. The philosopher's task was to penetrate down to these fundamental principles and show that all other truths about the world flowed from them. Above all, Leibniz relied on reason, both to find his ideas and principles and to judge arguments based on them. As such, Leibniz is sometimes known as a defender of *rationalism*.

Newton's physical theories, however, were based first and foremost on experience and general patterns found in experience. Newton did not claim to understand the basic causes of these patterns and, indeed, emphasized the modesty of his achievement. He had found formulas that described and predicted experience but did not explain it. Newton desired to know the principles beneath these patterns but was satisfied with the limited (and glorious) progress his creations represented.

Einstein once quipped that most scientists accepted a theory when it was confirmed by experimental data, but that he never accepted the data until it was confirmed by theory. This was the spirit that Leibniz brought to his physics: distrust appearances until reason is satisfied. Leibniz's many arguments were thus designed to expose Newton's theories as philosophical nonsense, and therefore to demonstrate that they could not be fundamental, could not be a final theory. One theme of his attacks was that Newton's theories were incompatible with a now famous principle that Leibniz made the bedrock of his own philosophy. The idea is that "everything has an explanation, nothing is really left to chance":

> *Principle of sufficient reason:* For anything that is, there is a reason why it is so and not otherwise.

The key word here is "reason". Classical philosophers thought of reasons in broad terms. They included sentences, facts, conditions, causes and beliefs. Thus the reason for some flood was that the rains caused the dam to break, and the reason for a prejudice was that they believed in the stereotype. In this sense, reasons are aspects of our inner or outer worlds that lead on to other aspects.

A key distinction in philosophy is that between "necessary" and "sufficient". For example, a cause is necessary to its effect if the cause must be present for the effect to occur (although other factors may also contribute to the effect). A cause is sufficient for its effect if it is powerful enough to bring its effect about (although other causes may independently produce the same effect). The presence of oxygen is a necessary cause of an ordinary fire. Given the presence of oxygen, striking a match is merely a sufficient cause for a fire, because the fire could also have been started by a spark.

Leibniz claimed that there is some sufficient reason for everything that happens, and he built his own metaphysical theories on this principle. This is an assertion about the world. It says that the web of cause and effect is seamless. There are no uncaused events; there is no true chance or randomness. This principle is also an assertion of the world's intelligibility. Since we understand and explain events by discovering their reasons, Leibniz asserts that understanding is always possible: there is always a reason to discover.

It is surprising that such a basic and general principle could be used with deadly effect against Newton's absolute space. Leibniz noticed that the very existence of absolute space contradicted his principle. He agreed with Newton that, if it existed, such a space would be utterly smooth, uniform and homogeneous: the same in every place and in every direction. Newton had both conceptual and physical reasons for this commitment. Conceptually, Newton believed that space was nothing or at least not a body, and could have no properties. These belonged to substances, that is, to the contents of space. Physically, if inertia drove bodies smoothly forwards along straight lines for ever, there could be no bumps or rough patches in space to disturb them. Leibniz, however, saw that the uniformity of space created a problem.

Suppose that God grasped all the matter in the universe, that is, all the contents of infinite space, and shifted it around so that what lay in the east was now west and vice versa. If space was everywhere exactly the same, then this shift would produce no difference at all. Leibniz saw his opening there:

Symmetry argument against absolute space

A. If absolute space is uniform, then there is no reason
   for the universe's orientation.   (P)
B. Absolute space is uniform.   (P)
C. Thus, there is no reason for the universe's
   orientation.   (from A,B)
D. But, there is a reason for everything.   (P)
E. Thus, there is a contradiction.   (between C,D)

Note that the argument itself does not depend on the existence of God. The last premise, D, is a restatement of the principle of sufficient reason.

For Leibniz, the source of the problem and its solution were clear. He believed that the concept of an absolute space was absurd. The argument just exposed a problem with absolute space, and was a reason to reject Newton's doctrine altogether. Thus Leibniz insisted that the existence of a uniform absolute space, premise B, must be denied.

Clarke and Newton were desperate. To save absolute space they had to call in God. They were impressed with the success of Newton's theories, and were determined to defend their uniform absolute space. Thus they insisted on the truth of the second premise. But they were also inclined to agree with the principle of sufficient reason. Like Leibniz, they were committed to the rational intelligibility of the world. Thus they accepted the last premise, and this meant that the first had to go. It was the only way to rebut Leibniz.

Clarke and Newton suggested that even in an entirely uniform space there would be a reason for the universe's orientation; namely, God's will. That is, they suggested that God could, in his wisdom, simply have decided to put some galaxies in the east of the universe and others in the west. This divine preference itself, they asserted, was the sufficient reason. It was the first premise in the argument, A, that should be thrown out to remove the contradiction. Leibniz was horrified at this manoeuvre. He countered that without a ground for choosing an orientation, God's decision was mere whim. Would God have been playing dice during the creation of the universe?

Today, physicists regard Leibniz as the winner of this argument. The technique that he used in the above argument has become one of the most common and powerful strategies of reasoning in advanced physics. Leibniz is honoured as a pioneer for recognizing the importance of this strategy (although the idea of shifting the entire universe was common in medieval debates over space).

Leibniz claimed, in modern terms, that Newton's theory "had a symmetry". Its predictions about the behaviour of bodies remained the same even if their position in absolute space were different. If all bodies were shifted in tandem to a different place ten metres to the left, their behaviour would be the same. The idea of position in absolute space was useless, Leibniz concluded, and should be abandoned.

As we have seen, Einstein practically based his career on arguments about symmetry. He showed physicists that they were important tools for constructing new theories. They could be used to test which elements of a theory were doing work and which were merely excess baggage. Suppose that a theory includes names for several variable quantities (names like "length", "mass", etc.), and that when a theory is used numbers are substituted for these variables (the mass is 3 kg, etc.). In some cases, we may discover that the predictions of a theory remain the same when different numbers are substituted for some particular variable. Einstein said that such a symmetry meant that the variable was useless, was "superfluous structure", and should be cut from the theory. Thus, hunting for symmetries became a useful tool for identifying the useless bits in a theory (such as absolute position or absolute velocity).

More interestingly, symmetries could be used to find new theories. Suppose physicists knew that a variable in an incomplete theory had no effect on its predictions. As they extended the theory to cover more cases, the meaningless variable should remain meaningless. Thus symmetries restrict the ways theories can be extended, they narrow the choices available. As such, they throw a powerful searchlight into the infinite realm of possible theories, and have even led physicists to stumble towards the correct theory. The standard model, the deepest theory of matter at present, was discovered by Glashow, Salam and Weinberg using just these kinds of symmetry arguments, and won them the Nobel prize in 1979.

> Leibniz's principle of sufficient reason says, as Parmenides did, that the world is ultimately intelligible: "reasons" are understandable causes.

Leibniz's alternative vision: the monadology

Leibniz is a hero to those physicists and philosophers who celebrate his rejection of absolute space. But what positive, alternative theory did Leibniz offer? What was his conception of space and how did it evade the criticisms he levelled against Newton? Surprisingly, Leibniz saw so deeply into the perplexing nature of space and time that he violently rejected their existence altogether. For him, space and time were sorts of illusions staged by God: mere phantasms within our souls. His own metaphysics, therefore, ranks among the most bizarre ever defended by a major philosopher.

The key evolution in Leibniz's thought began during his 1672–76 trip to Paris. There he discussed the ontology of relations with other leading philosophers and read Plato's dialogue *The Phaedo*. His surviving notebooks reveal his struggles with the relational paradoxes. Soon after returning to Germany, he laid the foundations for his mature metaphysics, the famous *Monadology*. The key feature of this system was his denial of relations between and outside substances. What does this mean?

For Newton any two places in space were linked by an intervening stretch of space, and the distance between the places was just the length of the space between them. Metaphorically speaking, this stretch of space forms a "bridge" between the places: it is real, outside the places and links them together. As above, call this kind of relation, which has a real existence outside its relata but partially overlaps them, a "real relation". As Leibniz grew to feel the urgency of the problem of the one and the many, he found the idea of bridge-like, real relations absurd and was driven back to a pure substance ontology without any relations at all. Like Aristotle, Leibniz concluded that only substances and their properties existed. In a well-known passage in his fifth letter to Clarke and Newton, he poked fun at the very idea of relations spanning the gaps between substances:

> It cannot be said that both of them, the two relata together, are the subject of a single relation; for if so, we should have a relation in two substances, with one leg in one, and the other in the other; which is contrary to the notion of all properties inhering in substances. Therefore we must say that this relation is indeed out of the substances; but being neither a substance, nor a property, it must be unreal, a merely mental thing, the consideration of which is nevertheless useful.

Thus Leibniz's deeper objection to absolute space is that it is incompatible with a substance ontology. As a network of bridge-like real relations, space is neither a body nor a property of a body.

Leibniz penetrated more deeply than Aristotle into the implications of a substance ontology. Aristotle rejected the space of the atomists, and argued for the existence of a plenum. Leibniz saw clearly that the plenum too was problematic. Aristotle relied on common sense. It was obvious that things touched each other, rested next to each other, and bumped into each other. Likewise, it was obvious to Aristotle that there could be no gaps between things, no stretches of existent nothingness. Thus there was a plenum: a close-knit world of substances nestled in next to each other. Crucially, Leibniz saw that touching and adjacency were *relations*. Suppose that Jack and Jill exist, and in addition they touch. What makes this additional fact true? What is its truth-maker? It could not be Jack and Jill, because they also exist without touching. So touching must be something additional, some sort of relation over and above its relata. But it is neither a substance nor a property. Thus Leibniz concluded, there is no touching.

Leibniz's saw clearly the implications of excluding all real relations from his metaphysics. His substances were lonely and utterly isolated. Each probably contained a soul but was, for Leibniz, completely simple and contained no inner relations and, in fact, no inner differences or distinctions at all. Moreover, each was in effect a tiny universe. There was nothing outside each substance: no empty space, no plenum, no "nothing". Leibniz's substances were not "together" in any sense. They did not reside in the same space, they were not near or far from each other, and they could not influence each other at all. There were no real relations at all.

To reconcile this stark vision with appearances was difficult. We feel that we move through the world, and feel that other things touch us. Leibniz recognized this, of course, and explained that each ensouled substance had a series of images unfolding within it – as if, perhaps, it had a film playing in its mind. These inner "phenomena" contained impressions of touching, movement and causation, but these were, for Leibniz, simply illusions of some sort. Their only reality was as perceptions within the substance. Just as Aristotle thought that substances could seamlessly unify their actual and potential properties, Leibniz asserted that these shifting phenomena within his substances did not compromise their unity. His substances were changing in some sense but nonetheless utterly simple and the same. For both Aristotle and Leibniz, this ability to be both one and many was perhaps the most important characteristic of a substance.

Strangely, Leibniz did accept that there was some coordination between substances. When one of us talks, another would hear. This was not, however, causation. Rather he believed that God has so arranged the "film" playing within each substance that there was a correlation between causes and effects. Continuing the metaphor, this is as if, in a multiplex cinema, a gun was fired in one film and in the theatre next door a gangster fell groaning to the ground. God created "films" that were synchronized. This is Leibniz's famous doctrine of *pre-established harmony*. It is an attempt to reconcile the appearance of cause and effect with the absence of real causal relations. Leibniz thought this was a virtue of his system. In effect, he had argued that, since there were no real relations, there must be a God to pre-arrange all causes and effects. He had proved the existence of God in a new way. Other philosophers have thought this doctrine a desperate and absurd attempt to save his system.

We can learn from Leibniz's metaphysics a philosophical lesson that is extremely important today. The central mystery for us is how a great mind could have found all this plausible? How could a mathematician and scientist deny the reality of the physical world we perceive around us?

Leibniz found his metaphysics plausible because he was horrified by the problem of the one and the many. Any real relation must somehow unite its many relata, and therefore harbours a tension between unity and diversity. Leibniz saw no way to escape contradiction, and banished real relations altogether. Thus spatial, temporal and causal relations all disappear from his metaphysics, and God must be summoned to rig together appearances.

Leibniz was a deeper, and more clear-sighted philosopher than Newton. Leibniz saw difficulties that Newton was happy to brush aside as he constructed his theories. The success of Newton's theories bludgeoned later philosophers into accepting his views on space and time, and overlooking the ontological difficulties that so bothered critics like Leibniz. As we shall see below, these difficulties have been resurrected.

The monadology was the last great gasp of substance ontologies in the philosophy of space and time. Aristotle's core concept of substance continued to be influential for some time after Leibniz, and even survived until the 1800s, but was gradually expelled from mainstream science. For many philosophers, the concept of substance has become a symbol of the medieval scholastic philosophy that preceded modern science: a symbol of obscurity and intellectual stagnation. Leibniz's insight that the concept of substance was needed to suppress the paradoxes of change and the problem of the one and the many was largely lost.

> As Leibniz famously put it, the monads had "no windows": there was no outside for them to look out upon, there was not even nothing to relate them.

The mathematics of change

> In retrospect, whereas the idea of change and variability had been banned from Greek mathematics because it led to Zeno's paradoxes, it was precisely this concept which, revived in the later Middle Ages and represented geometrically, led in the seventeenth century to the calculus ... The objections raised in the eighteenth century to the calculus were in large measure unanswered in terms of the conceptions of the time. Their arguments were in the last analysis equivalent to those which Zeno had raised well over two thousand years previously and were based on questions of infinity and continuity.
>
> (C. Boyer, historian of mathematics)

Mathematics and geometry were long thought to deal with static, unchanging and eternal structures – the forms that are ultimate reality. In Plato's dialogues, geometry is held up as an ideal of eternal and divine knowledge. Although some geometers did study the curves traced out by moving objects (spirals, etc.), generally speaking mathematics could not handle continuous change until Newton's invention of the calculus in 1666. His groundbreaking essay was called "To Resolve Problems by Motion These Following Propositions are Sufficient". The success of Newton's physics has persuaded many that his calculus had somehow resolved Zeno's paradoxes, or at least shown that they were unimportant. This section briefly discusses why that is an error.

The Greeks did not have practical problems with the way they *talked* about motion. They could say that a journey by chariot took three hours and covered ten kilometres; they could agree to meet in the marketplace at noon. Their problems were with *understanding* change, with creating a contradiction-free theory of change. Remember that Zeno argued that we could not walk to a wall because we could not traverse the infinity of intervening points. It is not an adequate solution to insist "But we do reach the wall!" Zeno might agree with this; the problem is to explain or understand how we reach the wall.

In a sense, Newton invented a thoroughly practical way to describe continuous change in a mathematical language. He enabled mathematics to make successful predictions of astronomical and terrestrial motions. Crudely put, however, Newton accomplished this just by making the assumption "But we do reach the wall!"

At the core of Newton's calculus is the notion of a *limit*. This is the idea that, if we add together a half, and a quarter, an eighth and so on to infinity, we will exactly *reach* the sum of one. Zeno would say that the addition will never total to one because an infinity of numbers would have to be added, and no infinity can ever be completed. But Newton's calculus simply assumes that the series does add to one exactly. It assumes that we do reach the wall. The Greek philosophers did not have practical problems with talking about change, and Newton effectively taught mathematics to talk in a practical way about change and continuity. He does not solve Zeno's theoretical problems with change. Newton just assumes the truth of what Zeno questioned.

A *pragmatist* is a philosopher who believes that only practice matters, and might therefore argue that Newton had solved Zeno's paradoxes by showing that they had no practical consequences. But this argument has two premises in need of defence: pragmatism itself, and the claim that the paradoxes will not rear their head in practical ways in a physics deeper than Newton's.

The calculus did not solve, but rather suppressed, Zeno's paradoxes.

CHAPTER 11

The philosophy of left and right

Some boys and girls find it very difficult to learn which is their right and which their left hand. Likewise, when they begin writing, some confuse their p's and q's, or their b's and d's. Kant had the brilliant insight that children are right to be confused. Something deeply puzzling is involved. In a famous argument published in a four-page essay in 1768, Kant diagnosed the children's problem and found in it a beautiful justification for Newton's absolute space.

Kant's startling argument

If two objects have the same size and shape, they are called "congruent". If an object is removed from a place exactly its size, a congruent object can be put in the same place. But your hands are "incongruent": they have different shapes. A left hand cannot be inserted into an empty right-hand glove. This gave Kant pause. Hands have similar parts and yet are incongruent. He called two incongruent objects that have the same parts arranged in the same way, *incongruent counterparts*. They are a pair of counterparts because they are so similar, and yet they are incongruent.

What makes left and right hands different? They each have the same number of fingers, and each of the fingers is attached to a palm. What accounts for their difference? We want to say that the fingers point "in different directions", but surely a direction outside the hand cannot determine the hand's shape.

Hands are fleshy, complicated creatures living in three-dimensional space. Consider a simpler example. The letter "b" consists of a small circle and a vertical line, and looks like a the palm of a left hand with everything but the thumb amputated. Likewise, the letter "d" looks like the palm of a right hand that has lost everything but its thumb. Suppose that the "serifs" have been removed, so that these two letters are exact incongruent counterparts: small circles with a line on the left and right (b and d). Suppose further that these letters can be slid around on the surface of this page, but not lifted up and reattached to it. That is, suppose the letters live only within the two-dimensional plane surface of the page.

Oddly, no matter how the b is twirled around or shuffled back and forth, it can never fill the exact place of a d as long as it remains flat on the page. Kant was deeply troubled by this. Here b and d have the same parts, and each line is attached to a circle. What makes them incongruent? We want to say the little lines "point in different directions", but can the shape of an object depend on which way it is pointing? We tend to think of each object in the world as "independent" in some sense. For example, we think an object's shape surely belongs to it, and is independent of what surrounds it. Kant considered this carefully, and was forced to conclude that the letters were incongruent because of *something* outside.

What makes things congruent or incongruent? Kant made the general assumption that at most three factors are involved. An object has parts. An object also has relations inside itself, that is, between or among its parts. These "inner" relations may hold the parts together and make the object into a whole. Finally, an object is involved in "outer" relations to whatever is outside or surrounds it. Kant began with the simple idea that the letters are incongruent because of one of these three factors:

Incongruency due to outer relations

A. The letters b and d are incongruent. (P)

B. If they are incongruent, then this is caused by some difference in their parts, inner relations or outer relations. (P)

C. So this is caused by some difference in their parts, inner relations or outer relations. (from A,B)

D. But the parts of b and d are the same. (P)

E. And the inner relations of b and d are the same. (P)

F. So the incongruency is caused by some difference between the outer relations of b and d. (C,D,E)

G. If something is caused (directly) by some difference between things, it is caused (indirectly) by the things. (P)

H. So, the incongruency is caused by the outer relations
of b and d. (F,G)

This conclusion is already surprising. Our simple idea that the letters are incongruent because their little lines point "in different directions" has led to a much more profound fact. We might say: the shape of an object depends on something outside it. This is so peculiar we should check the premises. Surely the parts of b and d are the same (D): they each consist of a circle and a line. Some criticize the next premise (E), and say that the inner relations are different, that is, that the circle and line are attached in different ways. But look carefully; this criticism is mistaken. In each case, the line is attached at one of its ends, and intersects without penetrating the circle (i.e. is tangential to the circle). The inner relations are the same. This is what confuses children. No amount of staring at just the b or the d themselves will reveal any difference: same parts, same angles, same kind of connections. The difference must be outside.

Kant has already discovered something surprising, but he has much greater ambitions. He claims that all this leads to a new proof for the existence of space. Aristotle was wrong about the plenum; the atomists and Newton were right to assert the existence of space. He continues the argument as follows:

From outer relations to space

I. Outer relations are outer relations to other objects or
to space. (P)
J. So the incongruency is caused by the outer relations
of b and d to other objects or to space. (H,I)
K. But the incongruency is not caused by outer relations
to other objects. (P!)
L. So the incongruency is caused by outer relations to
space. (J,K)
M. If something is a cause (or a relatum of a cause), then
it exists. (P)
N. So space exists. (L,M)

This is a stunning conclusion. Kant's insight into a child's confusion has led to a powerful new proof for the existence of space.

Mathematicians call the outer relation of an object to the environment its orientation. They say that b and d are incongruent because they have different orientations.

But should we believe Kant? The premise with the exclamation mark (K) is what philosophers call a "strong assumption". This means that a premise contains a powerful new idea, and helps push the argument much nearer to the conclusion. But strong premises are dangerous. They try to do so much that they are often untrustworthy. Compare this to a rock climber scaling a cliff. Every inch the climber moves upwards creates a new choice between safe and incremental moves from one crevice to a nearby one, or long, more dangerous stretches. The difficult "strong moves" may be more challenging and open up new routes, but by making them the climber risks a dangerous fall. Strong premises are similar. They often represent surprising new inspirations, but just as often are a stretch too far and can send an argument crashing down. Will Kant's assumption bear so much weight?

Kant believes his assumption K is obvious. Some of his remarks indicate why. First, he says that the incongruency is due to the letter's shape itself, and shape does not depend on *which* other objects are around. The b on a page would have the same shape even if there were no d's on the page or anywhere else. Secondly, he emphasizes this point with another short argument. This might be called the "empty universe argument". Kant simply assumes that a letter or hand would still have the same shape even if the rest of the entire universe were empty. From this, he reasons that the outer relations on which the shape depends cannot be relations to other objects – because there are no others in such a universe.

Both of these remarks simply restate the idea that shape does not depend on other objects. They do not make Kant's strong assumption seem obvious. Although the structure of Kant's argument is clear, the argument is finally not persuasive. One assumption (K) seems necessary for the conclusion, but is not obvious. In itself, Kant's argument is suggestive and interesting, but not finally a proof for the existence of absolute space.

According to Kant the shape of your hands depends on the universe.

Kant is rescued

Fortunately, later research provided very interesting support for Kant, and showed that incongruency is very probably caused by outer relations to space. With this help, Kant's argument has been rehabilitated and now stands as one of the most provocative arguments for absolute space. The central point is simple. The letters b and d are incongruent only when confined to the surface of this page. No horizontal sliding will allow one into the place occupied by the other. But if we are allowed to lift the letters off the page and rotate them around, it is easy to show they are congruent because they exactly fit into the same place, and therefore have the same size and shape. Thus two objects that are incongruent in two dimensions are in fact congruent in three dimensions. Whether or not objects are congruent *depends on the dimensions of the space they inhabit.*

The same is true of left and right hands. In a strange space that had four spatial dimensions in addition to time, a left hand could be "rotated" into a right hand. A left hand could thus be fitted into a right-hand glove simply by flipping it around.

Another intriguing example is provided by a long, thin, rectangular plastic strip whose end is twisted halfway around (by 180 degrees) and smoothly glued to its other end. This loop with a twist is called a *Möbius strip* after its inventor, the mathematician A. F. Möbius. Surprisingly, a letter b that slides around this strip and makes a complete journey around the loop will return as a letter d (when viewed from the same direction, as if the strip were transparent and the letter were in the surface). That is, the letters b and d are incongruent in an ordinary, flat two-dimensional space, but not in a two-dimensional space with a twist! The incongruency of the letters depends on the overall shape of the space!

Suppose, likewise, that the entire universe had some sort of peculiar twist in it like the Möbius strip. Astronauts travelling in one direction would then find themselves back at their starting point. In

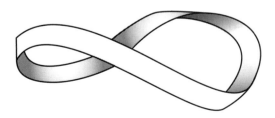

Figure 11.1   *A Möbius strip has one side and one edge. It is two-dimensional like a flat piece of paper, but has a different topology.*

this case, a left-hand glove could be converted into a right-hand glove just by sending it along with the astronauts through the twist. In fact, the astronauts too would return mirror-reversed: their hearts would be on their right sides!

Mathematicians say that a space with a twist in it has a different *topology* from ordinary, flat space. The word "topology" just means the study of place, and is the name of an important branch of mathematics today. The topology of a space is the way its points are connected to each other, and this stays the same if the distances between points are shrunk or expanded. Analogously, a balloon's shape and size change as it is blown up, but its topology doesn't change: the bonds between molecules stretch but do not break.

The fact that incongruence depends on dimensionality and topology very strongly suggests that Kant's strong assumption (K) was correct. The letters b and d are incongruent because of outer relations, but not outer relations to other objects. Since altering the space affects whether or not the letters are incongruent, their shape must depend on the surrounding space, and not on the objects contained in it. Research continues on this subject, but many philosophers think Kant's argument is good evidence for some form of spatial structure over and above the bodies they contain.

After Kant's investigations of the peculiarities of incongruent counterparts, they played an extraordinary role in chemistry and physics. Two molecules that are incongruent counterparts of each other are called "isomers" in chemistry (from the Greek: "iso" is "same" and "mer" is "parts"). Many medicines and industrial chemicals depend on the remarkably different properties of isomeric molecules.

There was tremendous surprise in 1956 when two physicists, Tsung-Dao Lee and Chen Ning Yang, showed that incongruent counterparts play a role in fundamental physics. They studied very fragile subatomic particles, which can be produced by physicists but quickly decay and fall apart. Some of these particles come in pairs of incongruent counterparts; that is, pairs of particles that have the same properties except that their shapes are mirror images of each other (like hands). In a series of dramatic experiments, Madam Wu (Chien-Shiung Wu), a physicist in New York, showed that the lifetime of certain particles depends on whether they were left-handed or right-handed! That is, even the most fundamental physical laws are sensitive to handedness. The excitement about this discovery was so great that Lee and Yang were given the Nobel prize in record time.

Even if we live in a three-dimensional space without twists and thus left and right hands must remain incongruent counterparts, Kant's argument is strengthened by the possibility that more dimensions would render them congruent.

CHAPTER 12

The unreality of time

British philosophy is sometimes celebrated and sometimes satirized as sturdy common sense. It tends to be grounded in facts and logic, and prefers science to mysticism. But for a generation or two during the late 1800s and early 1900s, a loose movement called British Idealism came to dominate philosophy in the universities. The major figures – Bradley, McTaggart, Green and Alexander – often disagreed among themselves, but they typically denied the reality of space and time, claiming that the world of science and appearance was contradictory. They believed instead in some sort of higher, spiritual reality. They were rational mystics.

James McTaggart supported his metaphysical idealism by advancing a famous argument against the existence of time. His attack has survived the rest of his philosophy, and continues to be widely discussed. When the argument was first published in 1908, three years after Einstein's papers on special relativity, debates over the nature of time were quite fashionable. Questions about whether time was another "dimension" and whether the world was really a four-dimensional block universe began to emerge. Independently of Einstein's theories, McTaggart saw clearly that such views might be incompatible with real change. If time is like a spatial dimension, he argued, then there is no such process, no "change", whereby one thing becomes another.

The A-series and the B-series

The truth-maker principle insists that if a sentence is true of the world, then something in the world makes it true. This seems to be common sense and is treated by many philosophers as bedrock, as obviously correct in some sense. But there is a well-known challenge to the principle that was already raised in one form by Aristotle. Suppose that the sentence "Princess Diana died in a car crash" is true. What makes it true? What is the truth-maker for this sentence?

We want to say that the sentence is true because the crash really happened; metal did smash into concrete. But this event occurred in the past. If the past is gone completely, and does not now exist in any way, what makes it true that the crash did occur? Is it our present memories, or the traces of paint still left on the underpass in Paris? This cannot be correct, because Princess Diana would still be dead even if she was forgotten and the underpass scoured clean.

The general problem of statements about the past and the future, and what makes them true or false, is deeply puzzling. There is no consensus among philosophers about their truth-makers; some even doubt whether such statements could be true or false. Perhaps it is not true now that Princess Diana died in the past? For some philosophers, however, this problem leads them to suppose that the past (and the future?) has some form of "existence". The event of Princess Diana's death does "exist" in some sense, and this past event is the missing truth-maker. These philosophers debate the kind of existence that past events might have, but generally suppose it to be a paler, ghostly existence: more "abstract" and less robust than present events.

In his attack on time, McTaggart seemed to take it for granted that past and future events have some sort of existence, and perhaps the truth of statements about the past persuaded him that this was obvious. Thus he speaks as if all events "have positions in time" even when they are far in the past or future. To have a position or any property requires that events exist in some sense. Given this fundamental assumption, he sets to work abolishing time.

Since all events have positions in time, what makes some events earlier or past, and others later or future? McTaggart says there are only two ways of accounting for the order of events in time. Perhaps events are linked by relations into long chains, and these relations make some events earlier and some events later. Thus the marriage of Diana is earlier than her death because there is a relation between the two events that fixes their order. Since the marriage is always earlier than her death, the relation between them is permanent. McTaggart calls the long chain of events linked together by permanent relations a *B-series*. Although he does not use the term, this B-series is very similar to the block universe discussed above (this is easy to remember

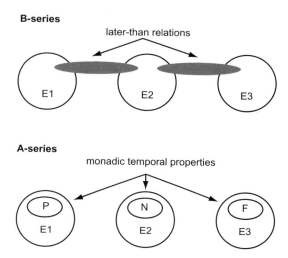

Figure 12.1 *McTaggart's two series. In the B-series, event E2 is made later than E1 by a later-than relation, and event E3 is made later than E2 by a similar relation. In the A-series, the three events E1, E2 and E3 have properties that make them past, now or future.*

since both begin with B). In both, events are static points locked into their positions in space and time, and there is no real change or becoming.

On the other hand, McTaggart says, perhaps there are no such relations, and events simply have the special properties of "being past", "being now" or "being future" (i.e. P, N, and F). Diana's death is earlier than now simply because it *is past*, or it *has past-ness*. The passage of time just is the shifting and changing of these properties. An event that begins with the property of being in the future, fleetingly becomes present, and then has the property of being past. The event of Diana's death never changes – the car always crashes – but its temporal property shifts and changes. McTaggart calls such a collection of events with P, N, and F properties an *A-series*.

In sum, McTaggart starts by saying that time must be one of the following:

- *A-series*: individual events have the property of being past, now or future, and these properties determine their position in time. These properties change.

- *B-series*: individual events are linked into a chain by earlier-than and later-than relations, and this linked chain is the order of time. These relations are permanent.

This terminology is so well-known in the philosophy of space and time that it is worth memorizing. Assuming that all events have positions in time, and therefore have an order in time, McTaggart's distinction seems right. The idea is that any order must be due either to something "between" the events or to something "in" the events. The relations of the B-series are somehow between events and link them together, and each property of the A-series is within an individual event.

> For McTaggart, since all events in the past, present and future exist in some sense, their being is not temporal; their temporality must then be in their properties or relations.

The B-series is contradictory

The above distinction now turns into a dilemma. McTaggart shows that no matter which we choose, we encounter contradictions. His first argument is straightforward:

The B-series implies that time is unreal

A.	Time is a B-series.	(P)
B.	The B-series is events in earlier-than/later-than relations.	(P)
C.	Events in earlier-than/later-than relations are unchanging.	(P)
D.	So time is unchanging.	(from A,B,C)
E.	But time is change.	(P)
F.	So time is contradictory.	(D,E)
G.	There are no contradictions.	(P)
H.	So there is no time.	(F,G)

There are two strong premises here that should be examined closely. The idea that events in earlier-than/later-than relations are unchanging, premise C, is the idea that Diana's marriage is *always* before her death. This order between the events is permanent. The claim that time is change, premise E, shows that McTaggart is aiming to show that there is no becoming, no process in which an individual event loses some properties and gains others. Thus the argument is really aimed at time as a process of becoming. McTaggart is, therefore, correct that in a "block universe" there is no room for true becoming or movement of any kind.

In short, if time is relations, and these relations are unchanging, then there is no true change.

The A-series is contradictory

To save the reality of time, we must therefore place our hopes in the A-series. McTaggart's argument here is deeper and more original, but also more involved. There are two main ideas. The first stems from the idea that the properties P, N and F are contrary properties, and therefore cannot all belong to the same event without giving rise to a contradiction. But, McTaggart emphasizes, they do all belong to the same event: each event has the property of being future, of being now and of being past. Why then is there no contradiction?

When faced with a contradiction, draw a distinction. Clearly, an event has the properties P, N and F *in different respects*. But what are these respects? We want to say that an event has the properties *at different times*. It is future first, and then at a later time exists now, and at an even later time becomes past. But this simple response leads to trouble. The properties P, N and F were meant to endow an event with a position in time, but now to avoid contradiction we must introduce a "meta-time". We can label moments of this new meta-time P', N' and F' (pronounced "P prime", etc.).

McTaggart is clearly correct here. If we think of P, N and F as ordinary properties, then they must belong to events in different respects. But now he pounces. If the meta-times P', N' and F' are also ordinary properties, and also contraries, then we have an infinite regress. That is, a further set of moments of "meta-meta-time" will be needed to prevent P', N' and F' from belonging to an event all at once. Thus P', N' and F' lead to P'', N'' and F'', which lead to P''', N''' and F''', and so on to infinity. Thus McTaggart's first idea is that the properties of the A-series lead to an infinite regress. His second is that this infinity should be rejected.

At each level of the properties, the next level *must* exist to avoid a contradiction. But this means that *all* the levels to infinity must exist to avoid contradiction. That is, the whole infinity of levels must be actual and complete in some sense. Philosophers say that such infinities are *vicious*: to avoid a contradiction in some ordinary property we must assume a towering, actual infinity. This is unacceptable.

The argument is that the A-series leads to an infinite regress, this regress is vicious and thus we must reject the A-series:

The A-series implies that time is unreal

A.	Time is an A-series.	(P)
B.	The A-series is events with contrary properties: P, N and F.	(P)
C.	Thus, time is events with contrary properties.	(from A,B)
D.	If something has contrary properties, it has them in different respects (to avoid contradiction).	(P)
E.	Thus time is events with different respects: P', N' and F'.	(C,D)
F.	But these different respects are also contrary properties.	(P)
G.	Therefore, time is events with an infinite regress of properties.	(E,F, and induction)
H.	Contradiction is avoided only if the infinity is actual (i.e. if *every* set of properties is accompanied by a further set of properties).	(P)
I.	But no infinity is actual.	(P)
J.	Therefore, time is contradictory events.	(G,H,I)
K.	There are no contradictions.	(P)
L.	Therefore, there is no time.	(J,K)

McTaggart's attack on the A-series is a deep argument that sharpens our thinking about time. By combining this with his earlier attack, McTaggart will conclude that, since time must be either an A-series or a B-series but both lead to contradictions, there is no time at all. Time is not real.

> McTaggart is assuming that all the properties of an event except P, N, F and so on, are permanent. Diana will always have died; only the time of the event can change. Thus only P, N, F and so on can be used to fend off contradictions.

CHAPTER 13

General relativity: is space curved?

Errors of thought cost me two years of excessively hard work, until I finally recognised them as such at the end of 1915 and, after having ruefully returned to Riemann's idea of curved space, succeeded in linking the theory with the facts of astronomical experience. Now the happy achievement seems almost a matter of course, and any intelligent student can grasp it without too much trouble. But the years of anxious searching in the dark, with their intense longing, their alterations of confidence and exhaustion and the final emergence into the light – only those who have experienced it can understand that. (Einstein, 1934)

The 1905 special theory of relativity was limited to measurements made by equipment moving without acceleration. The general theory of relativity eliminates this special restriction. To achieve this, however, Einstein had to even more deeply revolutionize our concepts of space and time. Building on the insights of the earlier theory, he now argued that space can be bent by matter.

Thus we have reached a third stage in the philosophy of space and time. The atomists first proclaimed that space or "nothing" existed in order to solve the problem of change. Newton revived this doctrine when, despite the criticisms of Aristotle and Descartes, he needed absolute space for his broader theory. Einstein now completes his revolution with the momentous claim that *space changes*. That is, space has evolved from a static structure proposed to make sense of motion to a structure that itself changes.

Red rubber sheets

In Newton's classical physics, space tells bodies how to move. A body given an initial shove will follow a straight line in space unless deflected by some other force. Einstein thought that this "one-way" influence was peculiar. If space acted on bodies, should not bodies act on space? The germ of Einstein's later theories of space and time, his general theory of relativity, is that this circle is completed.

> *Central idea of the theory of general relativity:* Spacetime tells bodies how to move, and bodies tell spacetime how to curve.

But what is a curved space or curved spacetime? If space is emptiness, or even a kind of nothingness, how could that curve? What would space bend into?

Physicists begin to answer these questions by insisting that only observable entities may play a role in physics. Since space is invisible and we see no lines of latitude and longitude etched across the night sky, the straight lines through space can only be discovered by following bodies around and observing their paths. Thus physicists define a *straight line* through space as the *path traversed by a body moving without interference of any kind*, that is, *moving inertially*.

Suppose, however, that two bodies are shoved along two adjacent, parallel paths in the same direction, but later bump into each other. Newton would say that some force must have pushed them together. If they were moving inertially without disturbance they would have followed two parallel paths, and since parallel lines never intersect, the bodies would never collide. Einstein disagreed, and suggested another possibility. Suppose that the bodies bump into each other because space itself is curved. Suppose that space is crisscrossed in all directions by lines that inertial bodies follow, but that the fabric of space can be bent, twisted and curved. Then bodies coasting along "parallel" paths may indeed bump into each other if the paths converge.

It does sound strange to say that "straight lines curve" or that "parallel lines intersect", but this is just a superficial oddity of physicist's language. They adhere to the definition above even when parallel, straight lines intersect, and prefer simply to say that they have enlarged our notion of what "straight" and "parallel" mean.

Einstein's concept of curved space is often illustrated by the *rubber sheet analogy*. Strictly speaking, it is spacetime that is curved, but this analogy helps us picture a curved space. Imagine a large sheet of supple rubber stretched out and secured along its edges, perhaps like the surface of a large drum in an orchestra. A heavy lead weight placed in the centre of the sheet will sink down into a smooth, circular well. This gives us a picture of what it means to say that "mass causes space to curve". More interestingly, suppose that children begin shooting marbles back and forth along the rubber sheet. Suppose a marble is shot straight but not directly at the lead weight. Instead of following a "straight line" its path will bend towards the lead weight. Either it continues on away from the weight after this deflection, or it will spiral down into the well. There is no significant attraction between the lead weight and the marble. The lead weight affects the marble by distorting the spatial surface that it travels along.

This nicely shows how Newton's gravitational forces are replaced in Einstein's theories by curved spaces. For Newton, bodies move towards each other when they exert attractive forces. For Einstein, they influence each other indirectly by affecting the space between them. Each body curves the space in its environment; when other bodies coast along straight lines they veer toward the centre of curvature. Some say that, in general relativity, *gravitational forces are geometrized away*.

Suppose further that the lead weight on the rubber sheet was moved rapidly up and down. If the sheet were large enough and flexible enough, ripples of upward and downward motion would spread out across the sheet. Perhaps they would look like the circular waves in the surface of a pond caused by a falling stone. Similarly, Einstein's theory predicts that moving masses will cause travelling distortions in the fabric of space: *gravity waves*.

Thus the rubber sheet analogy illustrates the way mass curves space, the curvature of "straight" inertial paths and gravity waves.

Figure 13.1   The rubber sheet analogy. The heavy lead weight pulls the sheet down and creates a circular well.

The rubber sheet analogy is cheating. It assumes that the weight and marbles are held down by ordinary gravity here on Earth. In a real curved space, inertia alone would keep them following along the curved lines of the space.

Eddington's eclipse expedition

The world was convinced of the truth of Einstein's outlandish conception of curved space in 1919. In the aftermath of Germany's defeat at the end of the First World War, the English astronomer Arthur Eddington organized an expedition to observe a total eclipse in South Africa. British confirmation of the theories of Einstein, a Swiss national working in Berlin, would at once advance physics and the cause of world peace.

How might observations made when the Sun was eclipsed by the Moon confirm the curvature of space? Light follows straight lines but, according to Einstein, these lines should bend around and towards heavy masses. Thus starlight travelling closely by and almost grazing the Sun should be slightly deflected towards it (like the marbles above). Ordinarily, the Sun's brilliance would drown out the starlight and make it impossible to observe this deflection. But during a total eclipse, the Moon would just block out the Sun's own light. The images of stars around the edge of the darkened Moon should be slightly out of place because their light was bent on its way to earth-bound telescopes.

During the summer and early autumn of 1919, Eddington measured his blurry photographs and calculated his results. Word began to leak out that his team had confirmed Einstein's predictions about the degree of deflection within experimental error. Back in his office, according to a well-known story, when Einstein was first handed the historic telegram with a preliminary announcement of the results, he glanced at it, set it aside and continued talking to a doctoral student. When she asked about its contents, Einstein's calm report caused great jubilation. Einstein, however, remained calm. Somewhat amused, he said simply "But I knew all the time that the theory was correct". When pressed to admit that the experiment might have given negative evidence, he went on "In that case I'd have to feel sorry for God, because the theory is correct".

142

Eddington announced his results publicly in London at a meeting of the Royal Society, whose president some 200 years earlier had been Isaac Newton. The next day, 7 November 1919, the London *Times* carried the now famous headlines on its front page: "Revolution in Science – New Theory of the Universe – Newton's Ideas Overthrown". From that day, Einstein was a celebrity and space was curved.

Although historians have since cast some doubt on Eddington's first crude results, the bending of starlight is now routinely observed by astronomers. The Hubble Telescope orbiting Earth has produced beautiful images of what is now called *gravitational lensing* (see Appendix D for websites). This occurs, for example, when one distant galaxy sits far behind another nearer galaxy. As light streams around the nearer galaxy, the rays may be bent towards us from several different angles. The telescope will see multiple copies of the distant galaxy arrayed around the nearer one.

Physicists now accept that a substantial number of experiments confirm Einstein's ideas of a curved spacetime. Gravity waves, however, have been a significant exception. Even movements of very large bodies produce extremely weak waves, and they have so far proved impossible to detect here on Earth. In 1974, however, Taylor, Hulse and their colleagues produced the first, serious evidence for the existence of waves rippling through the fabric of space. They studied the motion of pairs of stars orbiting rapidly around each other, and showed that they lose energy at just the rate that would be expected if gravity waves were emanating outwards. In 1993, they won the Nobel prize for this discovery. Several large, ground-based projects are now underway to detect gravity waves originating in outer space.

> After Eddington published a famous mathematical treatise on general relativity, someone asked whether it was true that the theory was so difficult that only three people in the world understood it. Eddington looked startled and asked "Who's the third?"

The path to discovery

The idea that space is curved seems bizarre. Einstein emphasized that the train of thought that led to this conception depended heavily on certain *thought experiments*. In these imaginary situations, Einstein used his reason and intuition to investigate physics without mathematics or experiment, and at times this method made Einstein appear more like a modern philosopher than a hard-nosed physicist. Two of these now famous thought experiments illustrate one route Einstein took to the discovery of general relativity, and also are good examples of the breathtaking beauty of Einstein's arguments.

Suppose that some surveyors live on the surface of a large *spinning wheel* and make a series of length measurements. Since *acceleration* means a change in speed or a change in direction away from straight line motion, every part of the wheel except its very centre is accelerating as it rotates. Such surveyors might, for example, measure the radius of the wheel from its centre to its rim, and also its circumference. For an ordinary stationary wheel, the circumference is about three times longer than the diameter. That is, the length of the circumference divided by the length of the diameter is the number π (pi), which is about $3\frac{1}{7}$. But, Einstein claimed, this would not be true for the spinning wheel.

Remember, he said, the lesson of special relativity: faster speeds mean shorter lengths. That is, there is *length contraction in the direction of travel*. Special relativity applies only to measurements made with rulers and clocks moving at steady speeds in the same direction but, Einstein argued, it also *applies approximately to accelerating bodies*. During very short moments of time, even an accelerating body moves at about the same speed. A sports car may accelerate to high speeds within 20 seconds, but during each of those seconds its speed is more or less the same. Thus during short moments we can apply special relativity to measurements made by accelerating rulers and clocks, and predict that they too will find length contraction and time dilation.

Consider how this affects the surveyors on the spinning wheel, which is, by assumption, a well-formed circle. They measure the radius by laying their rulers along one of the spokes. Since these rulers will lie at right angles to the direction of motion, they are not contracted at all. However, rulers laid along the circumference will experience length contraction as the wheel spins. More copies of the ruler would fit into the circumference. This means that the measured length of the circumference divided by the measured length of the radius will give an answer different to that for the stationary wheel. Instead of a number about three, the result will be much larger. The rulers along the circumference shrink while those along the radius stay the same, and so the ratio increases. Nonetheless, the wheel is a circle: it is the same distance from its hub to its circumference in every direction. This is remarkable. According to Einstein, laws of geometry known since ancient times "do not apply" to rapidly accelerating bodies. In sum, Einstein's thought experiment with the spinning wheel taught him that *acceleration distorts geometry*.

Building on this insight, a second thought experiment led Einstein deeper, toward the core ideas of general relativity. Imagine that an experimenter is in a small room like the inside of a *lift*, and that the room is located in outer space far from any planet or any other source of gravity. Suppose further that a hook and long rope is attached to the outside of the room at its top, and that God or some other being steadily pulls the room upwards. This will cause the room to move up faster and faster with constant acceleration. Anything floating or unsupported in the room will settle to the floor and remain there as long as the acceleration continues.

Einstein realized that, for the experimenter enclosed in the room, the upward acceleration would feel the same as a gravitational force pulling down. In fact, *no experiment performed inside the room could distinguish between an upward acceleration and downward gravitational pull*. Perhaps objects fell to the floor because God was pulling the room up, or perhaps some unknown planet had swum into the neighbourhood and its gravity was pulling everything downwards. No experiment could decide. In sum, Einstein's thought experiment taught him that *acceleration is equivalent to gravitation*. If no experiment can detect a difference, he concluded, they are the same as far as physics is concerned.

The reason for this equivalence is that gravity affects all bodies in the same way: it is a universal force. A gravitational force will pull *all* the bodies in the room down at the same rate, and thus is indistinguishable from an upward acceleration, which tries to pull all the bodies upwards. In contrast, electric forces affect only bodies that carry electric charges. Thus an electric attraction pulling down on the room would affect only some of the objects in the room. The experimenter inside would quickly see that only charged bodies were affected and conclude that an electric force was present. It is the universality of gravity that makes it equivalent to an upward acceleration.

Einstein's line of reasoning reached a stunning climax when he combined the lessons of these two thought experiments. Put somewhat crudely, he triumphantly argued:

Core argument for general relativity

A. Acceleration distorts geometry.   (P: from spinning wheel)
B. Acceleration is equivalent to
gravitation.   (P: from lift)
C. Therefore, gravitation distorts geometry.   (from A,B)

This is the line of reasoning that Einstein used to argue that "matter tells spacetime how to bend": matter is the source of gravitation and gravitation bends spacetime. Thus spacetime is curved and behaves like a flexible rubber sheet.

This is a bewildering, fantastic series of ideas. No one would take them seriously if Einstein had not used them to make some very surprising predictions that experiments later confirmed. We have met one example above. If we assume that light follows straight lines, then the paths taken by light should be distorted by any nearby matter that distorts the geometry in its neighbourhood. This is the effect confirmed by the eclipse expedition and by gravitational lensing. Light does follow straight lines, but the lines are bent by large masses!

Many other predictions followed. Returning to the spinning wheel, Einstein argued that a clock on the rim would run more slowly than a similar clock left at the centre of the wheel. This is just another application of the idea that faster speeds mean longer hours. Since the rim is accelerating, Einstein argued that acceleration also causes time dilation. But since "acceleration is equivalent to gravitation", he concluded that *gravitation causes time dilation*. Clocks that feel stronger gravity pulling them down run more slowly.

In 1960, Pound and Rebka confirmed this claim directly by placing two similar clocks at the top and bottom of a tower on the campus of Harvard University. Since the clock at the bottom was nearer to the earth and therefore felt its gravitational pull more strongly, Einstein's theory predicted that this lower clock would run more slowly. Although the difference was very, very slight because the clocks were so near each other, delicate measurements found just the effect Einstein predicted!

In fact, Einstein took his ideas one step further. Rather than saying that mass causes gravity, which distorts the geometry of space, he asserted more simply that mass is directly associated with distorted geometry. In other words, rather than picturing gravity as something contained within and distorting space, he said they were one and the same thing: he identified gravity with the curvature of space. The rubber sheet analogy helps make this clear. The marbles rolling past the lead weight are deflected by the curvature of the rubber sheet:

there is no need to assume some gravitational force or field that exists over and above the sheet and pulls on the passing marbles. Thus, for Einstein, gravity just is the curvature of space. As before, the forces have been geometrized away.

> Einstein's thought experiments are not a priori reasoning. They mix reasoning and experience.

Equivalence and the bucket

This insight that gravitation was equivalent to an acceleration was key in Einstein's struggle to generalize his earlier theory of special relativity. Remember that this was limited to special cases; namely, to measurements made with unaccelerated or inertial rulers and clocks. In the early theory, Einstein simply did not know how to handle acceleration. Newton thought that acceleration was so strange that it provided the best evidence for absolute space. Einstein rejected absolute space, but simply ignored the problem of acceleration in the early theory. Now his thought experiment suggested a new way to think about acceleration. Instead of pointing to the existence of absolute space, acceleration was the equivalent of a gravitational field. Thus instead of accepting Newton's talk of a mysterious, invisible space containing all bodies, Einstein could say that all effects of acceleration in the room were due to gravitation.

Thus Einstein's thought experiment with the small room was also his answer to Newton's bucket argument. Einstein agreed that the surface of the water was concave, but denied that this was due to accelerated motion relative to absolute space. The concavity was evidence for the presence of some gravitational field pulling the water out to the sides of the bucket. This claim is very much alive and at the centre of contemporary debate, as discussed in Chapter 15.

The shape of the universe

The universe is very, very large. Although light is fast, it takes it about three years to travel from the nearest star to Earth. A typical galaxy like our Milky Way galaxy contains about 100,000,000,000 stars; light crosses from one end to the other in about 50,000 years. In human terms, galaxies are incredibly huge. But they are only tiny specks compared to the whole universe. There may be 50,000,000 galaxies in the universe. Some cosmologists speculate that a beam of starlight would take a hundred billion years to travel through the entire universe. If that is true, then even the Hubble Telescope orbiting around Earth can see only a small portion of the whole universe.

In ancient times, the Roman poet Lucretius argued vividly that the universe must be infinite. Suppose, he said, that there was an end to space. Then we could stand at the brink and hurl our spear across the edge. If the spear rebounded, we would know that there was something beyond the end. If the spear did not rebound, then it carried on into more space. In either case, there must be something beyond the brink, something beyond the supposed end of space. Thus, he concluded, it is not really an end, and space must continue on infinitely. Newton too thought that his absolute space was infinite. But, once Einstein had persuaded us that space can curve and bend, questions about the shape and size of the universe were opened to experimental tests. Interestingly, Einstein raised the possibility that the universe might have a limited finite size but not have any boundary. That is, the universe may be "finite and unbounded". This does not make sense at first, but can be explained by a simple analogy.

Consider the surface of a child's balloon. The surface itself is a two-dimensional curved space. Although the surface has a limited size, say about 50 square centimetres, the surface has no boundary. An ant crawling over the balloon could move forwards endlessly without meeting a boundary. Thus a curved space that turns back on to itself can be finite even though it has no boundaries.

We live in a four-dimensional spacetime, and Einstein considered the possibility that our universe is curved in such a way that it is finite and unbounded like the balloon. This would have a surprising consequence. Just as an ant on the balloon crawling in a straight line would return to its starting point, astronauts travelling in a straight line for a very long time would find themselves back on Earth! This seems crazy, but there are experiments that might provide evidence that this is the case. Some astronomers are pointing their powerful telescopes in diametrically opposite directions, and hope that they might see the same, distant galaxy in both directions. Most think there is little chance of success, but we might be surprised.

There is now a wide variety of experiments being performed to explore the shape of the universe, and more are planned. We may have hard evidence soon.

CHAPTER 14

The fall of geometry: is mathematics certain?

We reverence ancient Greece as the cradle of western science. Here for the first time the world witnessed the miracle of a logical system which proceeded from step to step with such precision that every single one of its propositions was absolutely indubitable – I refer to Euclid's geometry. This admirable triumph of reasoning gave the human intellect the necessary confidence in itself for its subsequent achievements. (Einstein, 1933)

Some seek truth and some doubt it. Some are dedicated to seeking progress in our knowledge of reality, and some find it all too absurd. In the European tradition, the battles between these two warring tribes took place in the shadow of a great fortress. Defenders of truth could raise their fingers over the heads of the sceptics and point upwards to mathematics: a shining crystal palace of certainty surrounded by thick walls of deductions and demonstrations. But the revolution in theories of space and time during the twentieth century finally levelled this fortress. Sceptics have overrun even mathematics. Much of the fashionable relativism that has flourished during the past 30 years took heart from this downfall of mathematics, and with good reason.

Euclid and his *Elements*

Geometry was the glory of ancient Greece. Building on its beginnings in Egypt and Babylon, the ancient Greeks pursued geometry with extraordinary passion and precision for a thousand years, and first built up the fortress of mathematics on firm foundations. For them, geometry was the study of the real properties of real things: it was a branch of metaphysics. Like their other theories, it was object-oriented. They did not, in the first place, think of triangles and spheres as inhabiting a "geometric space". Instead, they typically drew concrete figures in the sand or on their slates, and investigated their properties and inner relations.

The Greeks did more than reveal the beauty of geometry in a thousand different theorems. They organized this knowledge, and invented a new method that grounded it securely in the simplest truths. This "axiomatic method" is one of our most precious inheritances. Even in ancient times, it was applied broadly to physical science (optics) and philosophy (by Proclus). This method is essentially the same as that used in the step-by-step arguments here. It begins by identifying the basic premises, and then carefully illuminates the reasoning that leads from them to some new truth in the conclusion.

One historian has asserted that all the prominent mathematicians in later antiquity were students or scholars in Plato's academy, or students of these and so on. The most prominent of these lineal descendants was Euclid, who lived in Alexandria, Egypt around 300BCE: about 50 years after Plato's death. Euclid's famous book on geometry, the *Elements*, is one of the great books of European culture. Its beauty is twofold. By brilliantly creating and arranging his proofs, he was able to show that the mathematical discoveries of the preceding centuries could be traced back to *five* premises. Just five ideas formed the foundations of the entire crystal palace.

Secondly, Euclid concluded his treatise with the touch of a real virtuoso. Plato had written of the beauty and symmetry of "regular solids", which became known later as the "Platonic solids". These are three-dimensional geometric figures like the cube, whose sides and angles are all the same. Oddly, even though there are an infinity of differently shaped sides that might be fitted together in infinitely different ways, there are only five different regular solids. There are only five ways of building perfectly symmetrical solids with flat sides. At the end of his treatise, Euclid leapt from two-dimensional plane figures into the realm of solids. In the great climax of Greek geometric thought, he proved that no future mathematician would ever discover another perfect solid: that the five Platonic solids were perfect and complete.

Historians do find it difficult to judge how much of the *Elements* is original and how much Euclid merely collected and systematized the efforts of earlier geometers: after Euclid, scribes neglected copying the scrolls of earlier geometers and in time their works were lost altogether.

Euclid's basic premises contained a time bomb, which later was to topple the edifice he so carefully erected. His five premises were supposed to be the most basic and simple truths, grounded in the deepest simplicities of Being. But consider each in its turn:

Euclid's five postulates
I.   There is a straight line between any two points.
II. A line can be continued in the same direction.
III. A circle can be constructed around any point with any radius.
IV. All right angles are equal to each other.
V.   Lines which are not parallel will, if continued to infinity, intersect somewhere.

The first four are plausible basic truths, but the fifth suddenly extends common sense into the great unknown. How would we prove what happens at infinity? What experience or intuition could help us here?

According to legend, Plato had inscribed above the door of his Academy, "Let no one ignorant of geometry enter here".

The rise of non-Euclidean geometries

Already, in ancient times, there was discomfort with Euclid's fifth postulate. Beginning with the Renaissance in the fifteenth century and continuing in the Scientific Revolution in the seventeenth century, the prestige of mathematics rose again and new suspicions were levelled at his mysterious fifth postulate. Many ambitious mathematicians sought to outdo Euclid by cleaning up his axioms by finding fewer or simpler ones that would serve as a more secure foundation for the queen of sciences. Some 300 years of searching produced only mounting frustrations. Mathematicians could neither do without Euclid's fifth postulate or its equivalents, nor show that it was wrong or faulty. It was there, ugly and stubborn, like a wart on the face of mathematics.

In desperation, several innovators finally adopted an indirect strategy. Instead of seeking for a deeper truth behind or underneath the fifth postulate, they proposed to prove it using a *reductio ad absurdum.* They would *assume* that Euclid's postulate was false and, using this reversed axiom together with the other four, would derive contradictions. That is, they would perversely assume that all parallel lines intersect! Surely, they thought, such an abomination would lead to contradictions. By leading this false assumption into a contradiction, that is, by reducing it to an absurdity, they would reveal its falsity. Surely, this would prove that Euclid's postulate could not be false, and was a necessary foundation stone for a true and consistent mathematics.

This result was astonishing, and led to some very deep thinking on the part of Europe's leading mathematicians. They had combined the false premise with Euclid's four other, simple premises and begun proving things, hoping to squeeze out a contradiction. But one theorem led to another and soon they had a large number of new theorems but no contradiction. They continued on, hoping the bad apple they had started with would spoil the whole barrel of new theorems, but could find no contradictions at all. To their surprise, they had soon built up an entire alternate mathematics, as if God had created a psychotic alternative universe and they had stumbled on its strange system of geometry: a world where parallel lines met each other!

Mathematicians soon realized that they could build pictures or models of these strange worlds. The simplest was the two-dimensional surface of a sphere. Consider a globe plastered over with a map of Earth. The lines of longitude cut the equator at right angles and all intersect at the north and south poles. But one definition of parallel lines is that they cut another line at the same angle. Thus at the equator, the lines of longitude are *parallel*, but they nonetheless *intersect* at the poles. In fact, all the largest circles that can be drawn on the globe are parallel – according to this definition – and yet intersect. Unwittingly, the mathematicians had created a new axiom system to describe the geometry of circles drawn on the surface of a globe. The strange universe they had created was not Euclid's, but it was free of contradictions. *It was the geometry of a curved space.*

In the early-nineteenth century, Karl Friedrich Gauss (1777– 1855), one of the greatest mathematicians of modern times, pondered these unexpected developments. He had a daring, tickling insight. A very small patch of the globe appears flat. This is why we used to think the earth was flat. In each small bit of the surface, parallel lines do not meet and Euclid's old geometry holds true. But suppose, Gauss said, that *our universe,* the physical world we live in, is just like that!

Suppose that we experience only a small bit of the universe, and thus believe that parallel lines do not intersect. Suppose that parallel lines extended across the universe far enough do intersect, like lines of longitude at the poles. Suppose we live in a universe that is not described by Euclid's geometry. Suppose the universe is curved. These thoughts must have made Gauss dance.

Although Gauss's thoughts seemed a mere fantasy about lines extending across the cosmos, he brilliantly saw that his ideas could be tested here on Earth. The key was that triangles on a curved space differ from those on a flat space. Both are constructed of three line segments meeting at three angles. In the flat space described by Euclid, the sum of those angles was always two right angles (180 degrees). But this is not true in curved space: *the sum of the three angles in a triangle in curved space can be more than two right angles.* To see this, consider the large triangle on the globe constructed from two lines of longitude that intersect at right angles at the North Pole. If the part of the equator that lies between them is taken as the third side, then a triangle is formed between the North Pole and the equator. Every one of its angles is a right angle; thus, the sum of its three angles is three right angles. The curved space permits lines meeting at large angles to fit together to form a triangle.

Gauss was so seized by this fact that he soon persuaded his friends to test his ideas. They knew that small triangles would appear to be flat, and have angles that added up to two right angles. But triangles that were large enough might begin to reflect any curvature in space, and have angles that added up to more than that. Gauss and his friends hauled telescopes and other apparatus to the tops of three

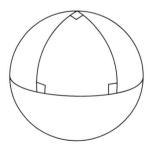

Figure 14.1 The geometry of a curved space. The two lines drawn from the North Pole to the equator, with the equator itself, form a triangle with three right angles.

mountains in Germany. With lights flashing on two of them, and the telescope on the third, they were able to measure the angles between the mountaintops. Repeating this, they found all three angles. Alas, after careful calibrations and calculations, they discovered that, within experimental error, the sum of the three angles was two right angles. Euclid was right! His geometry described the true structure of the world. Defeated, Gauss trudged back down the muddy slopes, not realizing that he had simply been two centuries too early. Although his challenge to Euclid was stillborn, the new geometries blossomed into an exciting sub-speciality of mathematics. Soon new paradises of exotic geometries were being invented and explored in the minds of mathematicians all over Europe. Euclid still reigned, but subversive energies lurked in the shadows.

As we have seen, Einstein worked to extend his special theory into the more general theory, which included gravity, for eight long years, from 1907 to 1915. This was a titanic struggle of late nights, frustrating mistakes and time-wasting failed ideas. At one point, Einstein began grappling with the idea that gravity might distort geometry. This was a breathtaking intuition, but Einstein was a poor mathematician and knew too little of advanced mathematics to express his ideas. Desperate, he finally appealed for help to a friend from his days at university. Now a professional mathematician, the friend surprised Einstein by saying that an entire sub-branch of mathematics had been developed to describe the geometry of curved spaces. The mathematical language Einstein had been groping for in the dark had already been worked out in detail, but Einstein had not known.

This new high-powered language for describing curved spaces had been worked out by mathematicians merely for its sheer beauty. A few of them (like Clifford and Riemann) speculated that Gauss was perhaps correct, and that further experiments should be done to investigate the geometry of the physical universe. But in the main, curved spaces were studied as pure abstractions. Once in Einstein's hands, however, the new language helped him make the final breakthroughs to his general theory. The experiments celebrated as confirmations of Einstein's theory also confirmed that Gauss was indeed correct. The geometry of curved spaces, with triangles whose angles did not add to two right angles, was the geometry of our world.

The lesson is a profound one. The axiomatic method was born out of a desire to isolate the essence of ideas and their relations. Euclid's masterpiece applied the method and surprisingly revealed that assumptions about parallels were a cornerstone of geometry. Two thousand years later, this paid off in a wholly unexpected way: it inspired the development of non-Euclidean geometries and brought Einstein's general relativity to fruition. The step-by-step analysis of arguments is a precious inheritance.

> Mathematicians used to think that they were studying the structure of space or the properties of figures; alternative geometries taught them they were merely studying possible models.

What does curved space curve into?

Anyone first encountering the idea of curved space often asks what it is curved into. Generally, things bend by moving into some unoccupied space. But if the whole universe consists of curved space, *what could it bend into*? Physicists usually reject this question, and this section explores one of the motivations for this neglect.

We usually think of ourselves as three-dimensional creatures living in a three-dimensional world. But suppose there was a two-dimensional universe called "Flatland" populated by dismally thin two-dimensional creatures, the "Flatlanders". They might slide around their world very contentedly and never feel that they had been deprived of a dimension, just as we feel cosy in our three dimensions. Flatlanders might develop a sophisticated geometry, and, indeed, might decide that their space was curved (as if they were, unbeknown to themselves, living on the surface of a balloon). They might notice, for example, that the angles in large triangles did not add up to two right angles. Their measurements would, of course, all take place *within* their world and thus would have to describe the curvature of their space in a language that referred only to their two-dimensional world. It would have to be an *intrinsic description*.

Gauss invented a way of describing a curved space that depended on features and measurements confined within that space. This language is complete, and does not require any reference to what may be outside the space. The Flatlanders, after all, may be correct that their universe is only two-dimensional, that there is not-even-nothing outside their horizontal world. Geometers say that Gauss's intrinsic descriptions need not refer to any outer, *embedding space*.

Physicists have adopted Gauss's viewpoint. Curved spaces are entirely autonomous. Since a curved space can be described internally, curvature does not presuppose any outside space for it to "curve into". In part, this is motivated by their empiricism. If physical theory does not need to mention a structure, if measurements and predictions do not depend on it, then the structure has no place in physics. Embedding spaces are superfluous.

Physicists say our universe can be curved even though there is nothing outside it.

The loss of certainty

So far we have two intersecting stories. Einstein's monumental struggles to extend special relativity led him to believe that space was somehow curved. He did not know that investigations of Euclid's fifth postulate had led mathematicians to the development of an elaborate new language for curved spaces. When Einstein adopted this language in his new general theory, he was able to make precise and surprising predictions. Their confirmation persuaded us that the world was correctly described by these exotic geometries – that Euclid was overthrown. These facts tumbled philosophy into a new world, and must affect the way every philosopher thinks. They mark a new age in the history of reason.

Amid the busy hurly-burly of our ordinary lives, the philosopher's search for permanent truth, for deeper, lasting understanding, seems not only impractical but also hopelessly naive. From Plato onwards, however, philosophers could always point at mathematics as an ideal of certainty and knowledge. They could say that truth was attainable, that they had proud, noble, valuable examples here ready at hand. Under the flag of Euclid's geometry, philosophers could rally the troops and fend off the sceptics. For some 2,000 years, Euclid's axioms were thought true. They were precise insights into the nature of Being, into the structure of our world. The edifice of inferences and theorems he built on his axioms was a model for deriving truth from truth, an ideal for reason everywhere to struggle towards.

General relativity led to a profound re-evaluation of Euclid. Before Einstein, the exotic geometries of curved spaces were often thought to be mere fantasies, games that mathematicians might play during their idle hours. But Einstein showed that experiment favoured these non-Euclidean geometries. It was the world that was fantastic. Thus Euclid's axioms were not insights into Being. There were reinterpreted as mere historical accidents. They were arbitrary starting points chosen by a mathematician with a limited imagination. Just as people who do not travel much might think that the earth is flat, mathematicians studying only circles and lines on their little slates might think that Euclid's axioms were obvious. If they had first studied larger systems like triangles formed by mountains or stars, they might have observed that three angles in a triangle do not always add to two right angles. They might have chosen different axioms.

To add insult to injury, even Euclid's reasoning was found to be flawed. With the rise of more powerful logics in the twentieth century, the *Elements* was carefully scrutinized and found to contain a catalogue of minor errors and omissions. Although all of Euclid's theorems did follow from his axioms, his proofs were sometimes sloppy or incomplete by modern standards. Euclid was cut down to human size.

Mourning the loss of their hero, philosophers retreated. They had thought of axioms as truths, as the deepest, most secure foundations for their systems. Now axioms became mere assumptions, mere premises. They were provisional starting points, which another philosopher might or might not accept. Instead of pillars driven into bedrock, axioms were merely floating ideas selected for convenience on given occasions and disposed of tomorrow.

Non-Euclidean geometries, of course, did not replace Euclid with a new crystal certainty. Once Einstein has shown that experiment would decide which geometry described the physical world, he made all geometry uncertain. Future experiments and deeper theories may show that even these curved spaces are superficial, special cases. Deep down, our world may be neither Euclidean nor non-Euclidean. There is no longer any certainty.

Mathematicians pioneered this new view of axioms, as they were the first to be acutely aware that Euclid had competitors. Among philosophers, Russell loudly propagandized for the new viewpoint in his *Principia Mathematica*, where he emphasized that his assumptions were doubtful and provisional. He claimed only that they were sufficient to derive the conclusions he needed, and not that they were necessarily true in any deeper sense. After Einstein and early work by the philosopher Hans Reichenbach, Euclid's downfall was widely accepted: *axioms became assumptions.*

For many philosophers, these developments represent real progress, a welcome sign that philosophy has thrown off its dreams of achieving truths that escape from human fallibility. Complete certainty was always beyond our grasp, they say, and the myth that mathematicians had found it simply confused philosophers. We are not diminished by Euclid's downfall; we are liberated. Living with a sense that all knowledge is as fragile or as strong as we make it is a mark of maturity.

Einstein transformed not only our image of the physical world, but also our belief in reason and philosophy itself.

CHAPTER 15

The resurrection of absolutes

Philosophy does make progress. The achievement of philosophers of space and time over the past 30 years has been extraordinarily important and far-reaching. The dramatic claims made by Einstein and many other physicists about the death of Newton's absolute space have been rebutted. The nature of spacetime has been substantially clarified in ways that would have astonished the pioneers.

This success is all the more significant because it has taken place in the face of hostility from many physicists. Even today, many or most physicists cling to some of the naive early claims made about relativity theory, which survive as a kind of folklore in the physics community. There are exceptional physicists who contributed to recent developments. But philosophers deserve recognition for penetrating through the fog that surrounded the foundations of spacetime theories and for moving the debate ahead.

Ancient and medieval philosophers debated the existence of universals. Was there, they asked, a single, universal "form of red" present in each red thing and somehow making it red? Realists argued that such universals were needed to *explain* the similarities between colours and all the properties we see around us. Tough-minded nominalists insisted that universals were merely common names, and resisted entities that were not solid, respectable individuals. The controversies below provide a modern parallel to these debates. One side accepts invisible spatial structures to make sense of what we see; the other derides this as extravagant metaphysics and adheres closely to concrete observables. Unlike the ancient debates, which linger still, there is a strong if not unanimous sense that decisive progress has been made here.

159

The debate below is of sweeping importance not only for physics and philosophy but for intellectual culture as a whole. The existence of space as an entity in its own right seems to be an issue for meta-physicians. But the interpretation of relativity theory is at once the interpretation of our deepest scientific theory and of science itself. It cuts quickly to the questions of where we and the universe came from, and whether reason can discern what lies behind appearances. The future is fighting its way out of this debate.

Modern relationalism

Recall, from above, that Leibniz attacked absolute space. He asserted that, since all motion was relative, absolute place or absolute velocity could never be observed. Leibniz had, however, no answer to the bucket argument. In a flash of genius, Newton noticed that the sloshing water in the rotating bucket was independent of surrounding bodies. He argued that this acceleration was strong evidence for absolute space. Many philosophers and physicists found Newton's vast, invisible, unobservable absolute space irritating, and wished to banish it from physics. But the bucket argument proved a thorn in their side. They tended simply to ignore or overlook Newton's insight. They certainly never had a plausible answer to it.

Three hundred years after Newton, this changed with Ernst Mach, an Austrian physicist now remembered whenever we say that a jet plane has flown at "Mach Two". Unusually, Mach was also a path-breaking historian of physics and fully realized the importance of Newton's bucket. Like Leibniz, he detested absolute space; unlike Leibniz, he took up the challenge of the bucket argument. His reply inspired the young Einstein, and opened the way for Einstein's heretical rejection of absolute space. Thus Mach is now recognized as the originator of attempts in the twentieth century to rid physics of Newton's absolutes. We will see below how far they succeeded.

Mach's famous reply to Newton's bucket argument is driven by a strict *epistemological* assumption. Mach was a prominent advocate of *positivism*, an important philosophy in the late-nineteenth century and early-twentieth century, which insisted that all knowledge was based on experience. It was an extreme form of empiricism. Positivists denigrated any knowledge not based on experience as mere "meta-physics", and this term became a label for old-fashioned philosophy. For positivists, these were merely old superstitions and, like belief in witches, had to be left behind by the march of progress. Physics, in particular, had to expel everything not founded firmly on observation and measurement. The following summary of Mach's argument connects this viewpoint to the attack on absolute space:

Mach's reply to the bucket argument

A. The physical cause of the concavity in the bucket is motion. (P)

B. Motion is either relative or absolute (and nothing else). (P)

C. Therefore, the physical cause of the concavity is either relative or absolute motion. (from A,B)

D. But absolute motion is not observable. (P)

E. Physical causes are observable. (P)

F. Therefore, absolute motion is not a physical cause. (D,E)

G. Therefore, the physical cause of the concavity is relative motion. (C,F)

As we have seen, Newton had argued that the concavity *could not* be caused by relative motion. The spinning water was at rest relative to the bucket and surely the concavity couldn't be caused by rotation relative to the distant surroundings, that is, to the tree, stars and so on. With his missionary zeal for positivism, Mach is certain that causes must be observable. This leads him to conclude that the concavity *must* be caused by relative motion, since only relative motions are observable. Thus it must be the tree or stars that cause the concavity. For him, there is no alternative, no option of invoking unobservable absolute space. For Mach, the spinning water slides up against the sides of the bucket because the water is rotating relatively to the distant stars. Somehow their distant masses grab the water in the bucket.

Mach's general philosophy of positivism had led him to a specific view of space and time that philosophers call *Relationalism*. In this ontology, *the only things that exist are bodies and the relations between them.* Here, "bodies" may mean things with matter or energy, and includes fields of energy like those of electricity or magnetism. The key point is that there is no "container space" independent of bodies, no spatial or temporal structures *over and above* bodies and their relations. Thus there are no places that have an existence distinct from bodies. Things are not in places. The motivation for this relationalism is the rejection of unobservables: bodies and relations are observable, while spatial containers are not.

The opposite of this view is *substantivalism*, which asserts that there is some container, some spatial and temporal structure over and above, and containing ordinary bodies. Newton was a substantivalist.

The terminology can be confusing. In ancient philosophy, space and substance were rival solutions to the problem of change. The atomists solved the problem by supposing that a vast, invisible space existed; Aristotle's common sense insisted that only ordinary bodies existed, and that these substances touched each other without gaps in a plenum. However, over time, the word "substance" began to mean anything solid and "substantial": anything existing on its own and independently of other things. Philosophers began to call Newton's space a "substance" when they wanted to emphasize that it existed independently of the bodies it contained.

John Earman usefully notes that relationalism insists that relations between bodies are *direct*, while substantivalism argues for *indirect* relations. According to the latter, the Sun is 150 million kilometres from Earth because the Sun is in one place, Earth in another, and the places are connected by a stretch of space. Thus the relation between bodies goes through non-bodies, that is, spatial structures. Such relations are indirect. A relationalist denies that the distance between the Sun and Earth is constituted by a spatial structure. For example, fields of gravity and electricity stretch between them and a relationalist may say that these somehow just are, or constitute, the separation between the Sun and Earth.

Thus relationalism and substantivalism disagree about whether space and time exist over and above ordinary bodies and their relations. More briefly, they disagree about whether space exists. For a generation now, this question has been at the core of contemporary philosophy of space and time.

Relationalists are tough-minded empiricists who say only the concrete is real. Substantivalists are far-seeing metaphysicians who tolerate unobservables to "make sense" of things.

Mach motivates Einstein

Newton's prestige was so great that Mach's radical relationalism was very liberating for the young Einstein. It gave him the courage to consider whether absolute space and time were really needed in physics, and probably directly contributed to his great breakthroughs. As we have seen, the special theory of relativity of 1905 launched a direct attack on invariant distances and durations, and therefore seemed to dispose of both absolute space and absolute time. But Einstein knew that his revolution was incomplete. The theory was special because it was limited to the special case of rulers and clocks moving at steady speeds in straight lines. The theory applied only to measurements made by devices moving inertially, and not those undergoing acceleration.

The distinction between inertial movement and accelerated movement seems to depend on the existence of space. If there is a physical difference between them, there must be some standard that determines which is accelerated and which is not. But this standard must be space. It was for this reason that Mach was determined to show that acceleration was merely an ordinary kind of relative motion: not relative to absolute space, but relative to other ordinary bodies. Thus, for Mach, the coffee in an accelerating cup sloshes because the cup is accelerating relative to the distant stars.

Einstein was determined to vindicate this insight of Mach's. His work on the general theory of relativity was guided by this belief that he had to eliminate any fundamental distinction between inertial and accelerated motions. Both should be kinds of motion relative to other bodies, and should not be evidence for unseen spatial structures. In 1916, Einstein completed his general theory, and announced:

> In Newton's mechanics, and no less in the special theory of relativity, there is an inherent epistemological defect which was, perhaps for the first time, pointed out by Ernst Mach.
>
> In an epistemologically satisfactory law of causality, the reason given for any effect must be an observable fact of experience – ultimately only observable facts may appear as causes and effects. Newtonian mechanics does not give a satisfactory answer to this question [of why the spinning water in the bucket is concave], since it makes the unobservable cause of absolute space responsible for the observable effects.
>
> The general theory of relativity takes away from space and time the last remnant of physical objectivity. In this theory, both a body moving with uniform motion in a straight line and an accelerating body may with equal right be looked upon as "stationary".

In sum, Einstein thought he had vindicated Mach and vanquished Newton in two steps:

- Special relativity eliminated absolute distances and durations and velocities, but retained absolute acceleration (which was Newton's evidence for absolute space and time).
- General relativity eliminated absolute acceleration, and thus what was supposed to be the last physical evidence for absolute space and time.

The triumphant claim by Einstein that he had stripped space of its "last remnant of physical objectivity" has been extremely influential. Especially in the middle of the last century, and still to a large degree today, Einstein's pronouncement was regarded as gospel.

Mach's positivism led him to deny the existence of atoms since they were too small to be observed. As he lay dying, legend has it that his students showed him a small "scintillation screen" where individual atoms threw off sparks, and he recanted.

Neo-Newtonian spacetime

Philosophers have fought back against Mach and Einstein and largely vindicated substantivalism and forms of absolute space. Although the battle still rages, and many points remain contentious, there is clearly a growing consensus against Einstein and his fellow relationalists. The next three sections briefly introduce this historic rehabilitation of absolute space. Here we discuss the question of whether absolutes can be justified within classical Newtonian physics, and then we return to relativity theory.

Newton's absolute space scandalized good empiricists and positivists. His ghostly, invisible space and unmeasurable absolute velocities were outrageous lapses for those crusading to rid physics of old-fashioned "metaphysics". The core of the relationalist attack on absolute space was the inference:

Even before Einstein's relativity, we knew that absolute velocity is unmeasurable and absolute place is undetectable. This implies that there is no scientific justification for substantivalism: there is no spatial container over and above bodies and their relations.

This assertion that absolute space was merely "superfluous structure" without empirical justification was often used to browbeat backsliding defenders of Newton.

A milestone in philosophy of space and time was passed when a strong consensus emerged that the above inference was a mistake, thus robbing relationalists of a central weapon. One major reason is that philosophers now agree that substantivalism can be slimmed down and stripped of its superfluous structure. This lean and mean substantivalism can withstand empiricist arguments from the nature of motion. Thus *within classical physics* the arguments do not justify abandoning all structures over and above bodies and their relations.

This puts pressure on relationalism. If absolutes are to be abandoned altogether, it must be because of something new about relativity theory. Empiricism alone is not sufficient to banish absolutes.

The strategy for salvaging substantivalism involves three elements. First, concede to Mach that absolute velocities and absolute places are unobservable, and should be expunged from physics. Secondly, shift from considering three-dimensional spaces to four-dimensional spacetimes. Thirdly, strip down the structure of the four-dimensional spacetime so that it has just the properties and relations justified by observation and no more. The result is a theory or model of space and time known as *neo-Newtonian spacetime*. It is substantivalist and therefore "Newtonian" but, unlike Newton's space, it is four-dimensional and therefore a "spacetime".

Relative velocities and absolute accelerations are observable. Before neo-Newtonian spacetime was invented, no one knew how there could be absolute accelerations (as in the bucket) without absolute velocities and absolute space. Acceleration is, after all, just a change in velocity. The key feature of this theory is that it predicts just the needed combination: absolute accelerations but merely relative velocities.

The quickest way to understand the structure of this new spacetime theory is to compare it to a four-dimensional representation of Newton's original absolute space. Newton believed that the universe was only three-dimensional but a *four-dimensional model* of Newton's theory can be built as follows. Imagine there is a four-dimensional block universe that is neatly sliced, and that each slice is a three-dimensional world at an instant. Newton believed that "the same place existed at different times". In a four-dimensional model, this would mean that places on different slices are "the same" in some sense. They are not *one and the same* because they are on different slices, but have *some relation* that indicates that they share something in common. This relation can be symbolized by R(x,y). That is, any two places, say a and b, which are "the same place at different times" have the relation R(a,b). If these relations exist in our four-dimensional model, then it makes sense to say that places persist through time, and this is what Newton meant by absolute space. These cross-linking relations stretching from slice to slice thus provide a four-dimensional model of Newton's picture of space.

Using these relations to keep track of which places are which as time passes, we can define absolute velocities and absolute accelerations. Thus this four-dimensional model has the features that Newton wanted. But does it have too much? Can we modify the model in a way that abandons absolute place persisting through time, but keeps absolute acceleration? In other words, can we drop absolute place from our model but still pick out which movements are along straight lines at uniform speeds, that is, which movements are inertial and unaccelerated?

Suppose now that the relations R(x,y) do not exist in our four-dimensional block universe, and thus places on different slices are just different and unrelated: there is no sameness of place across time, and therefore no eternal absolute space. Instead, suppose there are three-place relations I(x,y,z) that stretch across the different slices. Three places, say a, b and c, have the relation I(a,b,c) just when a body moving inertially would pass through a on one slice, b on a later slice and c on an even later slice. If a body follows a path through spacetime such that any three places along its path are related by the new relations, then the body is moving inertially along the entire path. Any body deviating from an inertial path is accelerating absolutely.

This is the trick. Instead of defining persistent places, we directly define which movements are inertial. That is, instead of keeping track of places through different slices and using this structure to decide which bodies are moving inertially, we simply keep track of which trajectories are inertial.

If the real spacetime of our physical universe had the structure of this neo-Newtonian spacetime, then we expect to see absolute accelerations (which make the water in the bucket and coffee cups slosh) but only relative velocities. Since this is what we do see, we have an argument that this model correctly describes the real structure of our universe (at least in domains where only low velocities and thus no relativistic effects are involved). If this is so, however, then classical substantivalism is rescued. We have a theory that posits a container over and above bodies and their relations but has no undetectable superfluous structure. We have put Newton's absolutes on a diet, and saved them from Mach's empiricist scoldings.

Neo-Newtonian spacetime does not represent a complete victory for substantivalism. Other attacks can be made. For example, some of Leibniz's symmetry arguments apply equally to Newton's absolute space and neo-Newtonian spacetime. It is also true that the plausibility of this model rests on resolving questions about the status of the future and past in a four-dimensional block universe. Nonetheless, a prominent and seemingly persuasive attack has been rebutted. By shifting from Newton's three-dimensional absolutes to a four-dimensional spacetime, those who argue that space does exist in its own right have won an important battle.

> Model builders ask what properties and relations are needed to account for observations; they do not ask what accounts for those properties and relations.

Absolutes in general relativity

As we have seen, Newton believed that the effects of acceleration, like the sloshing of liquids, provided evidence for absolute space. Special relativity retained a peculiar role for acceleration by limiting its predictions to non-accelerating, inertially moving rulers and clocks, and this seemed to endorse Newton's insight. After ten years of labour, Einstein was understandably proud when he claimed to eliminate the "last remnant of objectivity" from spatial structure in his general theory. Many in the physics community still believe that Einstein was correct.

A number of physicists and most philosophers of science now believe that Einstein was wrong. Although his theory has made many correct predictions, and remains the foundational theory for astronomy and cosmology, Einstein *misinterpreted* what his new mathematics implied. It is not true that general relativity eliminates absolutes. This reinterpretation of general relativity represents an important achievement of post-war philosophy of space and time.

There are two main lines of objections to Einstein's claims about general relativity, which can only be sketched here. The first concerns *boundary conditions* and the second *non-standard models*. Recall

167

that, according to the rubber sheet analogy, we may imagine that spacetime is stretched and distorted by the presence of mass and energy. Large masses create curvature; regions that are mostly vacuum are typically flatter. At first it was thought that this made spacetime a kind of property of the distribution of mass and energy, that is, that mass and energy and their relations fully determined all aspects of spacetime.

To see that this is not the case, consider an ordinary drum. The sound made when a drum is struck depends on three things: the location and intensity of percussive whack, the elasticity and tautness of the material stretched across the drum *and* the size and shape of the drum. A small, child's drum and a large drum like those used in orchestras might be covered by the same taut material and struck in the same way, but they will produce very different tones. Thus the sound that emerges is an important combination of local and global factors. The reason is that the vibrations that produce the sound waves are extended across the whole drum, and will therefore depend on the "global" shape of the whole drum. The bang produced by the drumstick is a local occurrence, but the response is global.

In general relativity, mass produces curvature the way that the drumstick depresses the drumhead. The resulting curvature of spacetime, however, depends on the *shape of the whole universe*, just as the drum's tones depend on the shape of the whole drum. Physicists say that the curvature of spacetime depends on the "boundary conditions", just as the vibrations on the drumhead depend on the shape of the drumhead and the way it is tacked down at the edges.

This is important because it means that the distribution of mass and energy does not determine all of the properties of space and time. The overall curvature of the universe depends on mass and energy *and* the boundary conditions. Since these are independent factors, some aspects of space and time are independent of mass and energy. Mach's hopes that all of physics would depend only on the relations between observable mass and energy are thus dashed: as Newton proposed, spacetime seems to have some autonomous aspects, and exists over and above the bodies within it.

General relativity is a *local theory*: it tells how each little patch of spacetime is attached to its neighbours. This sort of theory leaves a great deal of *global freedom*. By analogy, in a chain of iron links, we know how each oval link is attached to its neighbours, but the overall shape of the chain is still very free. It may by stretched out in a straight line or be left in a pile on the floor.

This global freedom is important. It means that general relativity can make very precise predictions about what happens in small regions of space, say the size of a star or black hole, but leave great doubt about the shape of the universe as a whole. Unfortunately for relationalists, this freedom has also given scope for the construction of non-standard models. These are models of the universe that agree at each point with general relativity's local predictions but have bizarre global features. Some of these models prove that general relativity retains a role for absolutes. In particular, absolute acceleration seems to have reared its head again, and confirmed Newton's original claim that accelerations are evidence for spatial and temporal structures independent of their contents. These models are complicated but, when examined in detail, show Einstein's claims to have eliminated the "last remnants of objectivity" from spacetime were premature.

Philosophical victories are rarely clear-cut. No referee blows a whistle to stop play and declares a winner. Inventive minds will always push and probe more deeply. Nonetheless, the bulk of the arguments now favour sophisticated substantivalism over relationalism. The philosophers who led this revolt, Adolf Grunbaum, John Earman and Michael Friedman, fought against considerable resistance from physicists, and indeed against all those who too quickly acceded to Einstein's authority.

We admire the genius of Einstein's mathematics, and the success of its many predictions. But we also see that, as a pioneer, Einstein misread the trail of ideas that led him to his discoveries. We now understand the nature of Einstein's relativity revolution better than he did himself.

> Space or spacetime exists. It is not merely a creature of the matter and energy in its midst.

The bucket in orbit

NASA will soon launch a satellite built by a team based at Stanford University to conduct Newton's bucket experiment in outer space. The motivation for this experiment can be understood by returning to the rubber sheet analogy. Imagine that the heavy weight in the central well is grasped firmly, depressed downwards to grip the sheet, and twisted. The turning weight will form a whirlpool of spiral wrinkles radiating across the sheet and out to its edge. This effect can, however, be produced in the opposite way. Imagine that the weight is left alone in the centre of the sheet, and instead the entire outer edge of the sheet is given a sharp twist. Since the heavy weight will not immediately keep up with the rotating sheet, a similar whirlpool of wrinkles, this time converging on the centre, will form; soon the weight will feel the twist and begin rotating itself.

The twisting rubber sheet gives us a picture of Mach and Einstein's view of Newton's bucket. They claim that acceleration relative to absolute space does not produce the concavity on the water's surface. Instead, they say, it is the rotation relative to the surroundings that causes the concavity. In fact, they add, there is no way to distinguish whether the water is rotating or whether its surroundings are. Just as the rubber sheet suggests, if the universe was rotating around the bucket, the same concavity would arise. Thus the effect is due to the relation between the bucket and its surroundings, that is, the relative rotation. It does not depend on whether the bucket has some fictional absolute motion. There is, they say, no fact of the matter about which is rotating: the bucket or the starry heavens.

Very soon after Einstein published his general theory of relativity, it was shown that the theory did predict that a rotating universe would cause the concavity in the bucket. More precisely, it was shown that mass rotating around a central body would grab the body and produce a rotation. This effect is known as *frame dragging*. The lines followed by bodies moving inertially are known as their "reference frame", and these are dragged around and twisted like the rubber sheet above. Relationalists view these calculations as a vindication of their interpretation of the bucket. Newton's argument has always been a thorn in their side and this, they say, is the nail in the coffin of arguments for absolute space.

Regardless of these debates, the experimental confirmation of frame dragging would be an extraordinarily important test of general relativity. Most tests to date rely on astronomical observations, and therefore on distant objects we cannot manipulate directly. Physicists have proposed that a spherical weight sent into orbit would be influenced by the earth's rotation. On the earth's surface, the effect would be swamped by vibrations. Suspended in outer space, delicate measurements could distinguish the direct gravitational forces from the subtler influences produced by frame dragging. Accomplishing this, however, has required some of the most advanced physics and engineering ever poured into an experiment. The special weight in the satellite is said to be the most perfectly spherical object ever manufactured. It will be cooled to temperatures near absolute zero to eliminate the tiny vibrations of heat energy. (See Appendix D for websites to access for a further description.) The bucket has gone high-tech.

Substantivalists can hope for the success of this experiment without conceding that it counts against the existence of space in its own right. As Earman and others have argued, relationalists need to show not that the rotating stars would influence the water in the bucket, but that rotation would account for all of the observed concavity. This has not been done. Even in general relativity, rotation is absolute. Newton's deep insight into the puzzle of rotational acceleration has survived into the space age.

CHAPTER 16

The resilience of space

The concept of space was born in paradox and seemed to have the flimsiest claim to existence. Although nothing but mere empty extendedness, it helped make motion and change understandable. Aristotle's rugged common sense rejected "space" out of hand, and made do with his plenum of concrete objects. We have now seen that this ancient debate was preparation for the grander controversies over Newton and Einstein's concepts of space. Like the ancient atomists, Newton embraced space to make sense of motion. His law of inertia demanded a world of geometric lines, and the sloshing water in his bucket seemed to make absolute space almost visible. Like Aristotle, the tough-minded empiricists made war on this metaphysical extravagance. Mach, Einstein and contemporary relationalists all fought back against a space existing over and above its contents. Against Newton and Lorentz, they dispensed with "superfluous" structure and pushed physics back down towards concrete objects and their concrete relations.

But now the folklore that surrounds Einstein's relativity theory has been dispersed. Amid Einstein's many triumphs, he did transform and deepen the concept of space. He did not, however, reduce space to its contents. This flimsy nothing has proved resilient. In special relativity, we saw that the defence of absolute space in Lorentz's minority interpretation was not ruled out by experiment. Furthermore, it provided attractive explanations where the mainstream provided none. A philosopher would say that the case for eliminating absolute space there rested on a strict empiricist ideology, and was not compulsory. In general relativity, the case for some features of curved space remaining independent of matter was significantly strengthened. Boundary conditions and non-standard models proved that the anti-substantivalists had not clinched their case.

The theme connecting the chapters in Part II has been the centrality of real relations. Over and above the individuals in the universe, there must be some web of relations stretching between and uniting them. The philosophy of space and time turns crucially upon the nature of these relations. The ancient paradoxes exposed the knot of conflicting tensions underlying relations, and led to Aristotle's rejection of real relations. In Leibniz, we have the last great metaphysician who saw the depth and intractability of these problems, and likewise banished relations from his system.

In Part I we saw that the mainstream interpretation of special relativity turned the basic properties of distance and duration into relations. Here in Part II, the succeeding chapters have made a strong case for the robust reality of spatial relations. From Kant's incongruent counterparts, to the three-place relations of neo-Newtonian spacetime, and then to the role of absolutes in general relativity, relations between concrete individuals were constituted by something non-concrete. In short, spatial relations are as real as the things they relate.

The victory of substantivalism – of real spatial relations – is still in doubt. Physicists remain in thrall to Einstein's premature claims to have eliminated the objectivity of space. Among philosophers, the autonomy of space is still contested. But, from a long-term perspective, real spatial relations have been gaining credibility for some 400 years. Once mathematics had been rephrased in the language of equations, and once physics had adopted this new language, the ancient resistance to relations was rendered implausible. Modern critics of spatial relations retreated to the claim that there were somehow only concrete relations. But even this halfway house has failed to make sense of the physics of motion and change. Opinion is moving toward substantivalism.

If spatial relations are accepted as real, however, future generations will have to contend with the paradoxes they conceal.

PART III

Frontiers

CHAPTER 17

Faster than light: was Einstein wrong?

Peaceful coexistence

For a hundred years, physicists trumpeted the celestial speed limit. Einstein has shown, they said, that nothing travels faster than light. But for a generation now, there has been stunning experimental evidence that hints that some mysterious influences are travelling faster than light.

Contemporary physics rests on two great pillars. Einstein's theories describe the large-scale structure of space and time. Quantum theory describes the small-scale behaviour of matter within space and time: the behaviour of molecules, atoms and other particles. Roughly, one describes the container, and the other the contents. Although research continues, the two traditions are so much at variance that no one has been able to combine them into a single, unified theory or "theory of everything". Quantum theory emerged piecemeal over many years and its development was driven by experimental results and mathematical guesses. Like most committee efforts, quantum theory was a patchwork of conflicting motivations and strategies. There is one central obstacle to unification: even today no one really understands quantum theory.

For many years, relativity and quantum theory led a peaceful coexistence. The mysteries of quantum theory were dramatized by a series of paradoxes, but the theory worked very well and never threatened to contradict and overthrow its rival. But now things are changing. Recent experiments are revealing that quantum theory is even more strange than expected. Sometimes it appears as a great, conceptual black hole that sucks down into it every attempt to clarify the foundations of physics. Now Einstein is threatened with Newton's fate. The theories of classical physics worked well at low speeds but failed for objects travelling near the speed of light. Newton's theories got the predictions right in a limited domain, but were not fundamentally correct. In the long run, Einstein's theories may be celebrated for a host of startling, true predictions, but relegated to history for their partial vision.

The EPR experiments

The experiments that directly threaten Einstein's celestial speed limit involve measurements on pairs of particles some distance from each other. In short, the measurement on the first particle on the left mysteriously "influences" the other particle on the right. Wiggling the particle on the left produces a jiggle on the right. But the experiments show that any "influence" would have to travel faster than light. That is, the particles are far enough apart that a beam of light from the left-hand measurement cannot reach the right-hand apparatus until after it has completed its measurement and found the jiggle. What could cause this? Could some influence be travelling faster than light? The interpretation of every experiment in science rests on assumptions, and these claims are so astonishing that it is best to examine what lies behind them extremely carefully.

In general, when an association or correlation between two events or measurements is found, there may be three explanations. First, there may be a mistake. Perhaps the association was merely an

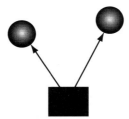

Figure 17.1 *EPR experiments. Two particles leave a common source. A measurement on the left disturbs the particle and influences the particle on the right. If the influence traverses the space between the particles, it travels faster than light.*

accident, a chance or spurious occurrence. If so, further repetitions of the experiments should reveal no further associations. Secondly, there may be a *direct link*. Measurements may reveal an association simply because the first event affects the second. Thirdly, however, there may be an *indirect link* between the events. Perhaps some third event, occurring earlier, sent out influences that created the later association between the pair of measured events. Philosophers say such events have a "common cause".

These three possible explanations provide the framework for the argument that the experiments show some faster-than-light influence:

Faster-than-light quantum influences

A. A correlation between distant measurements is observed.

B. If a correlation is observed, there is a spurious
   association, a direct cause or a common cause.   (P)

C. Therefore there is a spurious association, a direct
   cause or a common cause.   (from (A,B))

D. There is no spurious association.   (P)

E. There is no common cause.   (P: Bell's theorem)

F. Therefore, there is a direct cause.   (C,D,E)

G. If there is a direct cause, it travels faster
   than light.   (P: Aspect's experiment)

H. Therefore, there is a direct cause that travels
   faster than light.   (F,G)

This momentous conclusion threatens to topple our understanding of relativity theory. The argument reveals that it rests on several key premises. The first, B, seems safe. The second, that the association is not spurious, is also simple: the experiments were repeated at a dozen universities and the associations were consistently found. The last two, however, are quite strong and require comment: everything depends on them.

There is now a strong consensus among both physicists and philosophers that there is no common cause (premise E). The basis for this is a famous mathematical proof published by John S. Bell. His result was perhaps the most important development in the foundations of physics between Einstein and the current period of frenetic activity. Indeed, more than anyone else, John Bell triggered the progress now being made. All but a tiny minority of physicists now accept that his proof shows that no possible common cause could produce the observed measurements. It has been studied exhaustively, and several simple expositions have ·been published (see Appendix E).

The next premise, G, gained dramatic support in experiments performed by Aspect and others at the Institute for Optics in Paris. Pairs of distant measurements within the laboratory were made extremely closely in time. Any cause, any force or wave, travelling from one to the other could not complete the trip within the small interval of time between the measurements. Yet the associations between the pairs of measurements were still observed, just as in other experiments. Aspect's and succeeding experiments have provided direct evidence that no signals travelling slower than light could produce the associations.

> In this debate, "influence" is used as (what philosophers call) a "weasel word", that is, a vague word with a slippery meaning used to conceal ignorance. No one really knows what it is that might be travelling faster than light. It is not a cause that can be used to send signals and carries no mass or energy but is apparently not nothing, and so is an "influence" of some sort or another.

Controversy

If the premises based on Bell's theorem and Aspect's experiments are as secure as they seem, there is no choice but to accept the revolutionary conclusion that something is travelling faster than light. Oddly, many mainstream physicists accept both Bell's and Aspect's work but resist this conclusion. How can this be? At first, there was widespread confusion and misunderstanding about Bell's theorem in the physics community. Many physicists had not studied the issue in detail and simply refused to believe that Einstein could be wrong. Even as younger physicists began to realize that quite profound progress of some sort had been made, they tended to give two sorts of reasons for discounting the above argument.

First, everyone agrees that no energy or mass travels between the particles from one measurement to the other. Physicists tend to believe (with good reason) that everything that exists has mass and energy. Thus they argue that if no mass or energy is transferred, nothing at all is transferred. This objection is countered by other physicists who argue that these experiments are very, very strange. They may be telling us that there are indeed things in the universe with no mass or energy (so-called "pilot waves" or "information"). No one has a clear idea about what these might be but clearly, the proponents say, *something* is producing the associated measurements in the experiments.

Secondly, everyone agrees that no messages can be sent from one thing being measured to the other. Usually a cause travelling through space – like a radio wave – is ideally suited to send messages and signals. But in these key experiments, no message can be sent. Many physicists believe that this is evidence against the existence of any faster-than-light causes. But this objection is mistaken. In quantum theory, the results of measurements are fundamentally random. These experiments cannot be used to input and output messages because the result of the first measurement is random. Since we cannot control the input to the system, we cannot control the output. It is a garbage-in garbage-out (GIGO) effect. Thus the failure to transmit messages is due to quantum randomness and not necessarily to the absence of faster-than-light causes.

Many or most mainstream physicists still deny that these experiments threaten relativity theory, but for reasons that seem weak. Philosophers tend to divide into two camps. Some, such as Arthur Fine and Bas van Fraassen, accept the curious associations but, crudely put, say there is simply no explanation for them. They give various arguments but essentially say that explanation has here reached a limit. Nothing travels faster than light and nothing slower than light could produce the associations, and that is the end of the story. This position is made plausible by their general philosophical views, but is obviously frustrating in this special case. Other philosophers hold that something is indeed travelling faster than light. This position was defended for years by the respected but eccentric physicist David Bohm, and was carefully analysed by Jim Cushing. In its various incarnations, this view has won serious reconsideration by philosophers and younger physicists.

An ability to signal would imply a faster-than-light causal process, but the failure of signalling does not imply the absence of causal processes.

Revisiting the majority and minority interpretations

The EPR experiments have momentous implications for the interpretation of relativity theory. In short, they favour Lorentz's minority interpretation.

According to the mainstream interpretation, faster-than-light causation is impossible. There are several reasons for this. One is that the formula for mass increase suggests that anything approaching the speed of light would acquire infinite mass and energy. If the EPR measurements do instigate faster-than-light influences, then there is a lot of explaining to do here. Another reason is that faster-than-light influences would seem to make the paradoxes of time travel a real possibility. If simultaneity is really relative, then such influences could change the past and kill off our grandmothers, and so on.

On the other hand, the minority interpretation can comfortably accommodate such influences. It says that only the present, only the absolute now of the ether, exists. It therefore immediately rules out the time paradoxes: the past cannot be changed if it no longer exists. The minority interpretation insists that the relativity of simultaneity is merely apparent, an artefact of our measuring processes, and faster-than-light influences would favour this view. For a century now, Lorentz has been belittled for clinging to his deeper, explanatory interpretation of relativistic physics. Physicists favoured economy and observability over intuitive understanding. These EPR experiments may mark the rehabilitation of his more philosophical approach.

The EPR debate has, however, produced one significant shift in recent presentations of the mainstream interpretation. It used to be common to assert flat-out that nothing can travel faster than light. Now textbooks are more coy. They say that no "cause" or no "signal" can travel faster than light. This sounds like a minor change, but actually opens up a loophole: the possibility that some things that do not transmit signals travel faster than light.

I conclude this chapter with an odd historical footnote. These historic experiments, which provide the first credible evidence against the mainstream interpretation of relativity theory, were first proposed in 1935 by Einstein himself. As Einstein was developing his theory of special relativity, he also published some papers on the behaviour of atoms and electrons. Some historians, like Thomas Kuhn, now say that these papers were the real start of quantum theory. Before Einstein, Planck had groped towards the basic concept, but it was Einstein who should be regarded as the founder of quantum theory.

Einstein is thus credited by some historians with launching both the quantum and relativity revolutions.

Later in his life, however, Einstein became quite disenchanted with the odd patchwork of ideas that the quantum theory had become. In 1935, he co-authored a now famous paper with two younger physicists, Podolsky and Rosen, which came to be known as the "EPR" paper. The argument of their paper is complicated, but for our purposes can be summarized briefly as follows:

The EPR argument against quantum theory

A. If quantum theory is true, then some causes propagate faster than light. (P)

B. But no causes propagate faster than light (as relativity has shown). (P)

C. Therefore, quantum theory is not true. (from A,B)

Clearly this conclusion is an attack on quantum theory. Essentially they are saying that because quantum theory conflicts with relativity, quantum theory must be nonsense. Most remarkably, however, they detailed specific experiments in which quantum theory seemed to predict faster-than-light causation. These experiments are now known as "EPR experiments".

Partly because of his public attack on quantum theory, which was then both successful and fashionable, Einstein became a sad and isolated figure. For the last 30 years of his life, he was often regarded by other physicists as a has-been, and became the subject of whispered jokes. Even his attack on quantum theory was misunderstood and trivialized. The story circulated widely that Einstein had an old-fashioned mental block against randomness in physics. His line that "God does not play dice" served as a caricature for his views. In hindsight, Einstein knew long before others that the key issue was these "spooky" faster-than-light influences. But even his best friends, like Max Born, could not follow Einstein's reasoning and chided him for being so confused.

In 1964, 30 years after the EPR paper, it was John Bell who revived Einstein ideas and crucially pushed physicists toward conducting the experiments that Einstein had proposed. Even then, however, Bell's paper was lost by the journal and not published for two years. Almost 15 years passed before serious experiments were performed in the early 1980s. These EPR experiments proved that Einstein's premise A was probably correct. Although Einstein has had the last laugh, it may be small comfort. In the long run, quantum theory may undermine relativity theory. We will remember Einstein not for positively creating his own theories but for his penetration into the quantum theory's mysterious, destructive power.

Einstein saw that quantum theory implied faster-than-light signals and therefore was in conflict with relativity, but he concluded there must be some flaw in quantum theory.

CHAPTER 18

The Big Bang: how did the universe begin?

One philosophical question is so exquisitely compact, so breath-takingly deep, that it can only be regarded as a miniature masterpiece. It seems that Leibniz was the first to express it in the haunting words "*Why is there something rather than nothing?*" It is clear that not even "God" could be the answer here, for even if God created all things and even the universe itself, we could still ask why God existed. If the divine existence is pronounced "necessary", we could ask in turn "Why this necessity?"

Some philosophers find Leibniz's question so frustrating and unanswerable that they declare it to be absurd, a grammatical confusion of some sort. Others, however, have felt its sharp bite, its evocation of the "miracle of existence". Modern scientists tend to shun this sort of question altogether. They concentrate instead on "how" questions. They trace how one event caused another, or how one body emerged from more primitive ingredients. *Teleology*, the study of purpose, of ultimate origins and fate, has been expelled from science.

Nonetheless, every human society has struggled to answer questions about the origins of our world, and have believed in what anthropologists call *creation myths*. From the Judaic story of Adam and Eve in the book of Genesis in the Bible, and the Greek myths of Chronus and Zeus, to the Japanese tales collected in the Nihongi, each explains the emergence of our world from a primordial chaos. Modern society prides itself on explaining the world's formation in a scientific way, and the cornerstone of that explanation is the Big Bang.

The first indication that the universe had erupted out of some large explosion was a discovery made in 1929 by the astronomer Edwin

Hubble. Using the largest telescope then available, he made the surprising announcement that distant stars and galaxies are moving rapidly away from us: *the universe is expanding*. In fact, the farther away objects are, the faster they are receding. The most remote objects are moving at large fractions of the speed of light. Through the Second World War and the 1950s, several explanations of these facts were debated, but the controversy was finally settled by surprising new observations.

In 1965, two young radio astronomers from Bell Laboratories in New Jersey were constructing early "satellite dishes", and struggling to eliminate some hissing static in their receiver. They were mystified by its source. It seemed to be coming from all directions in the sky with the same intensity, and this led the engineers to conclude that the source must be within their own equipment, since no transmitter could produce a pattern like that. They checked all their connections, and even cleaned the "white dielectric material" pigeons had left on their antenna, but made no progress at all.

As luck would have it, one of the astronomers heard through friends that physicists from nearby Princeton University (where Einstein had died tens years earlier), had just finished some new, very speculative calculations. The physicists argued that, if Hubble's observations could be explained by a giant, primordial explosion, there should still today be a faint "afterglow" of radio waves filling the entire universe. They were able to calculate the main frequency and intensity of this radiation. The two teams quickly realized that the static in the satellite dish approximately matched the characteristics of the afterglow calculated from theory. Unknowingly, the astronomers had detected the remnants of the Big Bang. The astronomers and the physicists later received the Nobel prize for their historic discovery of this *cosmic microwave background radiation.*

All this jump-started study of the universe's origins. Speculations about the "beginning" had been regarded by mainstream physicists as mere science fiction, but this new hard experimental data moved the subject to the frontlines of scientific research. Since the 1960s, several lines of observational evidence have all converged to make a very strong case for a Big Bang about 15 billion years ago. Most scientists now regard this theory as very well confirmed. For one reason, detailed models of the early fireball can be used to calculate the kinds of debris it spewed out, and precisely predict the proportions of hydrogen and helium that should remain in the stars and galaxies around us. Astronomers have found that the amounts of these elements observed through the universe closely correspond to the predictions. This in turn suggests that we have a good understanding of what happened during the early Big Bang. There is an astounding match between theory and experiment.

If this theory is correct, the original explosion was so hot that only stray particles and the simplest atoms could survive. Any larger atoms formed by random mixing would have been ripped apart in collisions, or bombarded by intense radiation and broken down again into simpler fragments. Thus only the lightest elements such as hydrogen and helium emerged unscathed from the Big Bang. This raises an intimate question. Our bodies are mostly composed of much heavier elements like carbon; likewise Earth contains silicon and other relatively large atoms. Where did these come from?

The generally accepted view is that these were formed much later than the Big Bang. As the universe cooled, scattered atoms were pulled together by gravitational forces, congregated and formed stars. After some billions of years, these stars would age, and some would collapse and explode. Such a *supernova* would be violent enough to ram together simpler atoms into larger clumps, and would fling minute portions of these heavy elements out into empty space before they were broken down again. After generations of stars were born and died, significant amounts of heavy elements would remain floating through space. If these dust clouds again formed new stars, their outer fringes might congeal into planets. Eventually the heavy elements might form complex structures like our bodies. Thus, astronomers believe, Earth and our bodies are ancient ash from stars exploding like fireworks.

Leibniz would insist on asking what came before the Big Bang, but this question makes physicists nervous. They tend to insist in turn that their science merely traces causes: it can only investigate empirical questions. Since the Big Bang was so hot and so turbulent, probably no causal process can be traced back through its origin. Although a few are brave enough to speculate, most would say that whatever came before the Big Bang can be no part of science.

The Big Bang was some 15 billion years ago, Earth was formed some five billion years ago and humans evolved in the past five million years.

CHAPTER 19

Black holes: trapdoors to nowhere

Anyone hauling a boulder to the top of a skyscraper and dropping it on to the street below would expect a catastrophic impact: flying shards of rock and road, streaks of sparks and smoke, the clap and crack of the reverberating bang. Similarly, when a planet, comet or any other material falls into a star, the resulting explosion is often dramatic. It can produce blinding flashes, bursts of high-energy X-rays and gigantic glowing flares of fiery gases.

But, in early 2001, astronomers observing a strange object 6,000 light-years from Earth with the orbiting Hubble Telescope reported that they had seen the opposite. Massive clumps of hot gases many times larger than Earth were being sucked down into a large, invisible object. As they raced downwards, the accelerated jostling heated them, and they glowed and pulsed with incredible energies. Then nothing. The gases just disappeared. There was no explosion, no flashes, no flares – just nothing.

Einstein's theory of general relativity predicts the existence of *black holes*: bodies so dense that their gravity captures everything close by and prevents it from escaping. Not even light, the fastest and most nimble signal known, can climb up and away from a black hole. They are colourless, invisible, wholly black patches in the sky. For this reason, physicists doubted for many years that black holes could ever be seen at all. And if they could not be observed, they doubted they were a serious part of empirical science. For many, they were just science fiction.

Since the 1970s, evidence has slowly accumulated that black holes do exist. Nonetheless, all the observations were necessarily indirect and circumstantial, and sceptics insisted that other interpretations of the data could not yet be excluded. In the past few years, however, the richness and variety of observations have sharply strengthened the case. Many feel there is now overwhelming evidence that black holes exist and are common throughout the universe. The Hubble observations of the disappearing gases were, for one recent example, widely regarded as the tell-tale "signature" of a black hole: nothing else could have so completely swallowed and contained such a violent explosion.

The formation of black holes can be understood in a simple way. The parts of any body attract each other with a very tiny gravitational force. Usually, other forces keep the parts apart and ensure that bodies remain stable. But consider a star shining in the night sky. It is mostly a kind of gas composed of very simple atoms. In its dense centre, these atoms bump into each other and fuse together in mini-nuclear explosions. These generate the heat and light that makes stars so hot. Since heat causes expansion, the energy released pushes the other atoms in the star outwards. Thus the star is stable because of a certain balance: gravity pulls the atoms together, some of them collide and explode, and the resulting energy pushes the atoms away from each other. The inward and outward forces are in equilibrium.

Over billions of years, however, the star will burn up all its atomic fuel and become dim. With fewer explosions inside, gravity will gradually win the war, and compress the star further and further. In very large stars with enormous numbers of atoms pulling each other inwards, no other processes are able to resist the force of gravity, and the star will shrink until it is very tiny. Although the gravitational pull of a single atom by itself is very weak, many atoms concentrated in a small space exert gigantic forces. These would be so strong on our tiny star that nothing could escape its grasp: it has become a black hole.

Even light cannot be reflected off such an object. A portion of any light that struck it might bounce off and begin to race away. But the gravitational pull would be so great that, like a ball arcing upwards and falling down again, the light would gradually turn around and be reabsorbed. This is what makes black holes invisible.

Even though general relativity predicts black holes, Einstein always denied their existence. He repeatedly sought to find physical principles that would block their formation. We can get a glimpse of his reasoning by returning to the rubber sheet analogy for curved space.

A weight on the rubber sheet will bend the rubber downwards and produce a deep well. Crucially, if the same weight is compacted into a smaller space, it creates an even deeper well with steeper sides. This is because there is less rubber directly under the weight and supporting it, and less rubber that needs to be stretched downwards. This can be compared to pushing down on a thin sheet with the flat of your palm and your fingertip: the latter creates a deeper hole with the same force.

According to general relativity, gravity will compress some stars into ever smaller and smaller spaces. This means that the wells in the rubber sheet get ever deeper and narrower. *Eventually, as a star shrinks, the curvature of the well will become infinitely steep*. Thus a black hole is called a *singularity*, which means that the numbers describing it have all gone off the scale and become infinite. When the numbers in their equations blow up and become infinite or develop other pathologies, mathematicians say they have become "singular". What does it mean to say the curvature of the well in the rubber sheet has become *infinite*? The short answer it that no one really knows. We can imagine this as a rip or rupture in the rubber sheet: a place where it is no longer smooth but suddenly has no definite depth, no steepness that we can measure and assign a finite number to.

This is probably what set Einstein so firmly against black holes. His theory made the curvature of spacetime the most basic thing in the world. He pictured the curvature as continuous and smooth, and gave equations that precisely described its flexing. A black hole is not only physically bizarre, but it also represents some kind of breakdown in general relativity. Although the theory predicts that large stars will be endlessly compressed and form black holes, it cannot describe their ultimate, infinite state. Einstein's theory cannot reach into the central core of a black hole.

Zeno's paradoxes entangled Greek philosophy in paradoxes of the infinite. Here we see infinity rearing its head again in our most advanced science. Einstein believed that, if black holes were real, if actual infinities infested his spacetime curvature, his theory would be wrecked. They would show that spacetime curvature was not basic, or that it came to an "end" where it was not defined, or that there was something beyond spacetime. He died believing that predictions of black holes were some kind of miscalculation, some minor misunderstanding that future generations would put right. Thus the confirmation of the existence of black holes has created an important mystery for interpreters of general relativity. If black holes are real and physical, then probably actual infinities are too. In fact, the physicists Stephen Hawking and Robert Penrose proved theorems in the 1970s that roughly say that singularities are inevitable and unavoidable. Since then physicists have begun to grapple with the meaning and mathematics of these infinities more seriously.

John Earman, a leading philosopher of physics, treats this issue in his book *Bangs, Crunches, Whimpers, and Shrieks: Singularities and Acausalities in Relativistic Physics*. He begins with a concession:

> Einstein is surely right that, whatever the technical details of a definition of spacetime singularities, it should follow that physical laws, in so far as they presuppose space and time, are violated or, perhaps more accurately, do not make sense as singularities. This is good reason for holding that singularities are not part of spacetime.

Earman goes on to say, however, that singularities are not a breakdown in general relativity. The theory works well in ordinary, smooth spacetime. Singularities can be regarded as the boundary of spacetime, as its end-points, and perhaps we should not hold it against general relativity that it fails there:

> Contrary to Einstein, I do not think the fact that General Relativity predicts spacetime singularities is necessarily a cause for alarm, and I certainly do not think the prediction of singularities is a signal that the theory self-destructs.

In sum, Earman argues that singularities can be quarantined. They exist and are predicted by general relativity, but will not infect those regions of spacetime free of infinities.

Einstein believed that his theory described the ultimate reality. Thus suggestions that general relativity works only in certain portions of the universe are catastrophic. Earman reflects the views of many contemporary physicists. They expect that general relativity will someday be superseded just as Newton's theories were. Both Einstein and Newton were correct, but only in limited domains. Someday, they believe, a quantum theory of gravity will replace general relativity and, they hope, make sense of singularities.

In the meantime, the hunt for black holes has produced new and breathtaking evidence that they exist, are common and are sometimes unimaginably huge. Astronomers distinguish between black holes that weigh about as much as our Sun and "supermassive black holes". For example, there is a powerful source of X-rays called Cygnus X-1. This system wiggles and gyrates in a way that suggests it is a pair of bodies rotating around each other. One of them, however, is invisible. Observations suggest that it is a black hole weighing about ten times the size of our Sun. This is puny, however, compared to the monsters detected at the centres of galaxies. Galaxies are great, swirling collections of stars that are brighter and more concentrated near their centres. In recent years, compelling evidence has emerged that stars attracted down into the centres of galaxies conglomerate into black holes. These weigh a million or a billion times as much as our Sun. The black hole at the centre of our own Milky Way galaxy is three million times as massive as the Sun.

Black holes exist and give rise to infinities, which suggests that general relativity is not an ultimate theory.

CHAPTER 20

Why haven't aliens come visiting?

Where does life come from? The *theory of evolution* describes how one species slowly develops out of another, how humans evolved from apes, but does not explain the ultimate origin of life. Charles Darwin, who first published his theory of evolution in 1859, was always baffled by this mystery. At one point, even though he was an atheist, he even desperately suggested that God must have "breathed" life into the earliest organisms.

For most scientists, this mystery was solved by the famous experiments of the chemists Stanley Miller and Harold Urey, performed in 1953 at the University of Chicago. In a large, glass beaker in their laboratory, Miller and Urey approximately mimicked the conditions on Earth long before there was any life. They added some simple inorganic chemicals, heated them and shocked them with bursts of artificial lightning. After a week, they opened the beaker to see what products had formed. To their surprise, they found large quantities of amino acids, the simple organic molecules that are the building blocks of our bodies. Although these were not alive, this result proved for many that mere random mixing on the primitive Earth would produce organic molecules and eventually lead to simple life-forms. That is, given enough time and a chemical beaker the size of Earth's surface, *evolution would begin spontaneously.*

Physicists tell us that Earth formed about four-and-a-half billion year ago, and recently fossils of very simple one-cell organisms have been found in Australia that date from less than a billion years later. Since even these organisms were the products of a long period of evolution, the fossils also suggest that evolution started very early, and therefore relatively easily and quickly.

Taken together, the theory of evolution and the experiments of Miller and Urey may solve the mystery of our origins, but they also pointedly raise another question: does intelligent life exist elsewhere in the universe?

If the universe contains a mind-boggling 50 million galaxies each with some 100 billion stars, the sheer force of numbers suggests there is a high chance that we are not alone. The scientist Frank Drake tried to calculate the number of advanced civilizations in the universe using the now well-known *Drake formula* he devised, and found that the universe was so vast that many life-forms must have evolved. But the formula depended on guessing the answers to questions that we were almost entirely ignorant about. How many stars have planets? How many of those are hospitable to life? Even if conditions were right, how frequently would life evolve? What portion of living creatures would develop intelligence, and what portion of them would go on to master technology? Drake made some very conservative estimates, and still discovered that in a universe so vast intelligent life should be common. But his research was widely regarded as speculative, and many decided we were just too ignorant to come to any firm conclusions.

During the 1990s, this debate shifted dramatically. Astronomers invented telescopes and other detectors so sensitive that they were able to search the sky for planets orbiting nearby stars. These are extremely difficult to observe because they are tiny, dark and orbiting around very bright stars. Searching for planets is like looking for moths flying outside a distant lighthouse. Nonetheless, astronomers made an historic, unexpected discovery: *planets are very common*. It is not too much of an exaggeration to say that they found them almost everywhere they looked. Dozens and dozens have been detected around stars not too far away from our Sun. This is surprising and important. Even if planets with conditions favourable for incubating life are a small fraction of all planets, there are still many, many planets where life might evolve across the universe. Thus, this discovery raises the probability of extraterrestrial life, and has led many to change their opinions and entertain the question more seriously.

Critics of the search for extraterrestrial life, however, have some very strong arguments of their own. One has become known as the *Fermi paradox*, named after Enrico Fermi, the physicist who created the first controlled nuclear chain reaction. If, he argued, the universe is so large that advanced civilizations are plentiful, then we should have encountered them by now. At least, we should have obvious evidence of their existence. Even if there are no junk spaceships atop mountains and we are not ruled by intelligent jellyfish, there should be signs of some sort. Although some civilizations might have prohibitions about contacting us, many others would not. This paradox, the tension between statistics that suggest life is plentiful and the deafening absence of clear-cut evidence, has intrigued and bothered many. Where are they?

In the past five years, astronomers have made another historic discovery that may resolve the Fermi paradox in a particularly ominous, unpleasant way. It is a strange story. During the Cold War, the United States launched spy satellites to monitor the entire Earth for secret tests of nuclear bombs. Researchers were surprised by repeated bright flashes of light detected simultaneously by satellites on opposite sides of Earth. After years of secret work, they concluded that the flashes were coming from outer space and disclosed their strange discovery to astronomers in 1973. Since they consisted largely of high-energy light, or gamma rays, these mysterious flashes were called *gamma-ray bursts*.

Astronomers were baffled. The flashes occurred randomly about once a day, and were extremely bright, but no one could locate a source. A similar phenomenon occurs at a birthday party when the room suddenly fills with a camera flash, which fades in an instant. Those looking away from the camera will find it difficult to say exactly where the flash occurred. Since the satellites were not lucky enough to be pointed directly at these flashes, they were unable to pick out a source. At the time, however, astronomers favoured one conclusion: their source must be nearby. House lights seen from afar at night are dimmer the farther away they are. But these flashes were so bright, they must originate within the solar system or somewhere else near our Sun.

After 25 years of inconclusive debate and further observations, collaborators at the Italian Space Agency and the Netherlands Agency for Aerospace Programs sent aloft a satellite specially designed to locate the origins of these strange flashes. It was equipped with cameras with very wide lenses that could continuously monitor very great swaths of the heavens. On 28 February 1997, the satellite caught its first image of a flash. It immediately relayed the precise direction to ground-based telescopes, which swung into action. Within 24 hours, they had pinpointed the source, and made a breathtaking discovery: the source was outside our galaxy. This fact may take some time to sink in. These flashes are extremely bright but come from very, very, very far away. Their sources are extra-galactic. Usually, distant lights are dim. How could this be?

Astronomers could hardly believe their calculations. To fill such great volumes of space with flashes so bright, an explosion would have to compress to within a few seconds all the energy that our Sun emits in ten billion years. It would have to be more powerful than a supernova, an exploding star. It would be the most powerful explosion in the universe.

Astronomers are now debating what mechanism could liberate such incredible energies, and have developed several competing theories. In the meantime, the broader consequences of their discovery are chilling. These gamma-ray bursts are so powerful that they would completely destroy objects near their source, and in fact wipe out life in a sizeable portion of any galaxy in which they occur. That is, any planet roughly in the same neighbourhood of such an explosion would be scoured clean and left a barren, orbiting stone. They thus provide one unhappy answer to the Fermi paradox: although life may arise frequently around the universe, we do not encounter advanced civilizations because they are regularly annihilated by gamma-ray bursts. Without an understanding of their mechanism, we can only guess the chance that a burst may originate closer to home, within our own galaxy. But since life has survived on Earth for billions of years, we have been very lucky so far.

Children growing up today may look to the starry heavens with feelings very different from those of previous generations. Their parents could enjoy the sea of twinkling stars. They were assured that the Sun would shine stably for several more billions of years and that crashing asteroids were unlikely. The discovery of this intergalactic lightning, however, suddenly makes the universe seem a much more hostile place. Moreover, since they travel at the speed of light, these bursts give no warning. If there has been such a massive explosion in our own Milky Way Galaxy, and near our own solar system, the shock wave may now be hurtling toward us with the fury of 10,000 nuclear bombs.

Gamma-ray bursts may be the answer to the Fermi paradox.

CHAPTER 21

The inflationary and accelerating universe

The most exciting and profound new physics, the first glimpses of twenty-first-century physics, are now coming from astronomy. Stunning new, supersensitive instruments and dazzling theoretical models have combined to squeeze revolutionary data from the faintest observations. From satellites in outer space and camps 800 metres from the South Pole, astronomers are mapping the shape of space and reaching back to the birth of time.

Despite its many successes, the Big Bang model led to some new, deeply perplexing puzzles. Suppose our telescopes look at very distant objects in opposite directions. They might be so remote that nothing could travel from one to the other. Even at the speed of light, the journey would take longer than the 15 billion years since the Big Bang. Yet the universe in opposite directions looks pretty much the same; in fact, it is *exceedingly* uniform. The cosmic microwave background, for example, comes to us from the farthest corners of the universe, but is the same whichever way we look, to within one part in 10,000 or more. This is suspicious. What could have coordinated or matched conditions in regions so far from each other? Since this coordination seems to have extended beyond the horizon that light could reach, it was called the *horizon problem*.

There are other big problems. Imagine throwing a stone straight up into the sky. Three things might happen. Ordinarily, the stone will rise upwards, slow down and fall back to Earth. If it were thrown up with enormous speed, however, it would escape Earth's gravitational pull and zip out to infinity. Balanced between these two possibilities, there is a third. If the speed were exactly right, the rock might be slowed down by gravity but never quite enough to make it fall backwards. Its speed would be slower and slower. Far above Earth, where its gravitational field becomes ever weaker, the rock would barely crawl upwards but still manage to continue on toward the stars. Like someone travelling at one kilometre per hour, then a half, then a quarter, and then an eighth of a kilometre per hour, the rock would go slower and slower but never stop altogether. Obviously, this third scenario is extremely unlikely, and depends on the stone's initial speed being exactly on the knife edge between falling back and escaping to infinity.

The Big Bang hurled all the matter and energy of the universe outwards and, likewise, there are three possibilities for what might happen next. First, the matter might expand outwards and then fall back: the *Big Crunch*. Second, it might expand outwards for ever until all the matter and energy were thinly dispersed in a cold and dark infinite space: *Heat Death*. Thirdly, if the critical balance were just right, the universal expansion might slow down to a crawl but never quite fall back. In this case, the universe would become more and more stable. As the mass–energy became more evenly distributed, the curvature of space would become flatter and flatter: the *flat universe*. The problem is that this last scenario is extremely unlikely, but astronomical observations indicate that our universe is indeed flat. How could a huge, violent, turbulent explosion be so finely poised between the Big Crunch and Heat Death? Some called this the *fine-tuning paradox*.

In 1981, Alan Guth, a young physicist, then at Stanford University, proposed a wild theory that would resolve both these and other outstanding problems with the Big Bang in one fell swoop. In a word, he proposed that, early in the first second of the universe's existence, the framework of spacetime expanded extremely quickly. Like a balloon suddenly inflated to a gargantuan size, the universe puffed outward in an instant. This process was dubbed *inflation*. It is not a rival to the Big Bang theory but a modification and addition to it. Guth suggested that the distance between any two points would expand at a rate faster than the speed of light. This does not mean that any *thing*, any mass or energy, travelled faster than light. At each point, light would still travel along at 300,000 kilometres per second, but there might suddenly be much more space between it and its source. The distance between any two points would be stretched extremely quickly. After this brief burst during the initial explosion, the universe would settle down into the steady expansion discovered by Hubble.

Inflation would solve the horizon problem because things that are now very far apart and mysteriously coordinated were once cosy neighbours. This would also solve the flatness problem. Just as any region on a balloon's surface becomes flatter as it inflates, the process of inflation drives the curvature of space to near-perfect flatness. Although it would solve several puzzles about the Big Bang, many cosmologists were sceptical about this extravagant idea. Although Guth had been led to the idea by applying accepted physics to the early universe, the whole seemed rather speculative.

The world keeps surprising us. The great advantage of the inflation hypothesis is that it not only predicts that far-flung regions of the universe will be uniform, but it makes quantitative predictions about the minute residual departures from uniformity. Extremely tiny fluctuations in the microwave background radiation were measured in the early 1990s by the COBE satellite, and were an astonishingly close fit to the predictions. There were still many doubts about inflation among physicists, but in 2000 there were several new and historic reports of observations that further supported the inflation model. Astronomers and physicists triumphantly celebrated the combined achievement of their far-reaching theories and high-precision measurements. Inflation is now probably accepted by most of them, and will be taught as part of the standard Big Bang theory.

Just as it seemed as if contemporary physics was penetrating to the innermost secrets of nature, in 1998 astronomers made a preposterous announcement. The observations were so bizarre and so unexpected that most scoffed at them. It was widely expected that more data or more careful analysis would expose some mistake. When, in 2000 and 2001, more observations were reported, however, they in fact strengthened the case for the first, absurd claim. There is no agreement yet about how to explain these mysterious observations, but if correct they throw the foundations of physics into turmoil. Physicists have been heard to whisper that to make sense of it all we will need a new Einstein.

Imagine that our stone is again thrown overhead, arches high into the sky and then *accelerates out of sight*. That would be absurd. Gravity is pulling the stone downwards. It should be losing energy. How could it speed up? But astronomical teams based at the University of Berkeley and Harvard University have announced just this. The Big Bang threw all the matter in the universe outwards. Both Newton's and Einstein's theories of gravity predict that the expansion must be slowing down to some degree: the mutual gravitational attraction of all the matter in all the galaxies should be pulling them inwards. But measurements of distant supernovae show just the opposite. All the matter in the universe appears to be *accelerating* outwards. Its speed is picking up.

This new acceleration is entirely different from inflation. Inflation is a brief expansion of spacetime that lasted for an instant during the primordial fireball. If the galaxies are even now accelerating away from each other, some new force acting over long distances is at work. This new force would apparently be as permanent and real as the other known forces. But what force could be strong enough to push all the matter in the whole universe outwards? Are there new kinds of forces that our physics knows nothing of? Where would the energy come from? Could there be something "outside" the universe that is attracting our galaxies? Is general relativity just wrong altogether, and a misleading guide to interpreting these observations?

Since ordinary mass produces gravitational attraction, and since mass is energy, physicists say that energy produces attraction. Thus this new, mysterious repulsion, the new push outwards must, they say, be produced by "negative energy". The paradoxical name is really just a label for the mystery. There is no consensus about what new physics will be needed to explain our accelerating universe, and some, perhaps, still hope that the observations are some kind of error.

We return to Einstein again. In 1917, two years after completing general relativity, Einstein applied the theory to the question of the shape of the universe. At that point, however, he believed that the universe was more or less stable; this was a holdover from the traditional belief in the "fixed stars". His theory kept contradicting this belief. As the mass and energy in the universe moved around, the shape and curvature of the universe altered too. Einstein's theory was predicting that the universe would evolve and change over time. Reluctantly, Einstein published a paper showing how his theory, born of so many difficult years of struggle, would have to be modified. In brief, he showed that the theory could be tweaked or fudged to counteract any expansion or contraction of the universe. By adding an entirely new variable, he could stabilize the universe. He called this the *cosmological constant*. When Hubble discovered the expansion of the universe a decade later in 1929, Einstein was red-faced. If he had believed his beloved theory, he could have *predicted* Hubble's historic discovery. He deleted the cosmological constant from his equations and said it had been the "biggest mistake of my life".

What goes around comes around. Now that physicists are struggling to make sense of our new inflating and accelerating universe, the cosmological constant is suddenly back in vogue. By reinserting the constant in the general theory of relativity, and twiddling it up and down, physicists can make their theory match both inflation and the new acceleration. As one physicist said, the constant has become a "panacea": a universal cure for all cosmological puzzles. In fact, to counteract a contracting universe, the cosmological constant would represent just the sort of "negative energy" needed to explain the observed acceleration. Thus it may be possible, by restoring the constant to Einstein's theory, to extend the theory to handle the new observations. Einstein's biggest mistake may be the new physics of the twenty-first century. Time will tell.

CHAPTER 22

Should we believe the physicists?

It must have been around 1950. I was accompanying Einstein on a walk from The Institute for Advanced Study in Princeton to his home, when he suddenly stopped, turned to me, and asked me if I really believed that the moon exists only if I look at it. The nature of our discussion was not particularly metaphysical. Rather, we were discussing the quantum theory . . .   (Abraham Pais, 1982)

There is an old debate in philosophy about whether the world outside our minds exists at all. In the early-seventeenth century, Descartes pioneered the new mechanical and geometrical view of material reality in which every event was determined. But he also believed that we each had a soul and that our will was free. Thus he had to insist that matter and the soul were entirely different: the mind–body split was born. Descartes's critics soon pointed out that a soul confined within the "veil of perception" had no direct evidence that its perceptions were true. Perhaps they were mere illusions or some sort of cinematic film projected by God? Bishop Berkeley went so far as to suggest that there are no bodies outside the mind, and that perceptions were the only reality: "to be is to be perceived". Samuel Johnson thought this was all twaddle. He famously rebutted Berkeley by kicking a stone, as if to say that its reality was painfully obvious.

During the past 30 years, there has been a resurgence of these sorts of questions. Oddly, however, the doubts today grow out of science itself. A number of philosophers, sociologists and historians, and even a few physicists, have proposed that scientific reality is for us a product of social processes or somehow mind-dependent.

Debates over quantum theory have sometimes strongly encouraged these doubts about external reality. A central plank in the theory, the famous *Heisenberg uncertainty principle*, says that the position and speed of a particle cannot be precisely measured at the same time. Initially, this was thought to be a consequence of the smallness of physical particles: any observation of position would *disturb* them and blur their speeds. This interpretation is now known to be false. Instead, there is a consensus now that particles *do not have both a position and a speed at the same time*. That is, when a particle has a precise speed, it has no position in space. Since it is hard to imagine what a particle without a position would be, some draw the conclusion that only observed properties exist. There is no hard little particle moving about independently of our observations. This interpretation was pondered by Einstein in the above quote, and has been advanced by physicists like Bernard d'Espagnat, John Wheeler and others. John Bell's result, discussed earlier, is sometimes interpreted as a proof of these strange views: it suggests to some that properties observed in the "wiggle-jiggle" EPR experiments *could not have existed prior to their being observed*. That is, particles have neither a position nor a speed until observation somehow materializes them.

As the history of science became established as an important academic discipline, it also cast doubt on claims that science had discovered the true nature of reality. In his famous book *The Structure of Scientific Revolutions*, Thomas Kuhn argued that scientists before and after revolutions lived in different "worlds". Their concepts were so radically shifted that they perceived different things, even when making the same observations. The philosopher Larry Lauden went on to make a notorious argument. Since we know, he said, that every scientific theory in the past has been overthrown and proven false, we can infer that even our present ones will be overthrown and are false. Thus there is no reason to believe that scientific theories truly describe reality. Many professional historians of science prefer to study science as a human activity. They regard claims that science has any privileged insight into nature as ahistorical and naive.

Some contemporary sociologists known as *social-constructivists* have been the most loud and hostile critics of science. A loose group led by Bloor, Barnes, Collins and Pickering, known at times as the Edinburgh School, led an attack on science beginning in the 1980s. French sociologists like Bruno Latour continued these onslaughts through the 1990s. They tend to start with the presumption that social reality, our interactions, conversations and writings, are primary. The concepts we use are social products and influence what we see and are able to see. Claims that science is able to escape from the web of social influences and penetrate to some reality beneath seem, to them, suspicious. They analyse such claims as attempts to grab and assert power. In his 1984 book, *Constructing Quarks: A Sociological History of Particle Physics*, Andrew Pickering, a physicist who became a sociologist, suggested that experiments were no longer *tests of theories*. Instead, experiments on subatomic particles had become so complicated that theory was needed to build the equipment and interpret the measurements. Experiments presupposed theory; they were no longer adversaries. In this situation, decisions about which theories to accept could not be decided by experiment alone and, he said, reflected the political rivalries of different communities within physics. "The world" of physics, he concluded, "is socially produced".

Since modern society is so dependent on and dedicated to science and technology, tremendous controversies have erupted over claims that science does not reveal the true nature of reality. Advocates of these views have sometimes been shunned and marginalized. Within philosophy, the debate has stabilized and its protagonists have settled into two warring camps. The *anti-realists* are led by prominent philosophers like Bas van Fraassen and Arthur Fine, while the defenders of science, the *scientific realists*, are led by Ernan McMullin and others.

The very vigorous debate over scientific realism, the belief that science describes reality, has been healthy and productive for both sides. It has generated far-reaching historical and sociological analyses of science. It has discouraged the naive *scientism* or "science-worship" that was common during the Cold War, and which still predominates outside academia. It has forced philosophers to examine their presuppositions, and pushed their theories deeper. In the past, both in philosophy and in science, times of radical questioning and scepticism have often been very fertile. Breathing space was opened up for entirely new viewpoints.

The philosophy of space and time presented in this book generally presupposes that scientific developments have taught us something new and deep. It thus presupposes scientific realism. Scepticism, however, is useful for ambitious philosophers.

Kuhn distinguishes between technology and science, that is, between doing things and knowing things. He agrees that technology has made progress in a sense, but claims that the conceptual justifications for technology have not. After a scientific revolution, new theories are used to rationalize the practices we keep. Thus the practical success of science is not an argument for the correctness of its descriptions: many bad theories have led to successful techniques.

Spacetime diagrams

Introduction

Soon after Einstein developed special relativity, his teacher Herman Minkovski found a simple way to illustrate the strange effects predicted by the theory. If you are comfortable using diagrams and graphs, then learning how to interpret spacetime diagrams will deepen your understanding of relativity.

Relativity theory says that our world is, in some sense, four-dimensional. Time is a dimension and somehow like the three spatial dimensions of height, width and depth. We are used to the idea that three-dimensional objects like cars and houses can be pictured on a flat, two-dimensional piece of paper. But how can we picture a four-dimensional object? Some say that it is impossible, and that our minds are incapable of conceiving four-dimensional objects. Spacetime diagrams use a simple trick: they just omit some of the spatial dimensions. Instead of displaying a three-dimensional object together with its time dimension, they display only one space dimension and one time dimension.

Perhaps you have used graphs where the horizontal axis was labelled "x" and the vertical axis was labelled "y". In a spacetime diagram, we keep the x-axis but label the vertical axis "t" for "time". The diagram thus has one space dimension and one time dimension. Each point on the diagram has two coordinates, (x, t), which can be various numbers like ($x = 4$, $t = 3$). This point thus corresponds to the place marked four (centimetres) and the moment of time when the clock says three (hours). This may seem strange, but remember that

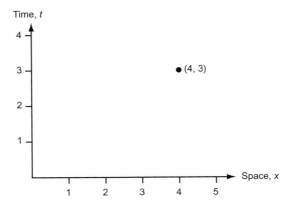

Figure A.1 *A spacetime diagram. The two lines show one spatial and one temporal dimension. The dot marks an event with the coordinates (4, 3).*

we ordinarily think of events as having a time and a place. The opening of a criminal trial is an event. It may begin in the fourth court at three o'clock, and thus might be called "the trial that commences at $(x = 4, t = 3)$". Since every point on the diagram has a place (x) and a time (t), they each represent events: happenings or occurrences at a spot in space and a moment in time.

These simple graphs are useful for diagramming back and forth movements in a single spatial direction. You might imagine cars racing through a narrow, straight tunnel for long periods of time. When they move at very high speeds, their bodies will experience noticeable length contraction and the clocks on their dashboards will slow down. These effects can be clearly illustrated with spacetime diagrams. Anything that moves will visit different places at different times. The series of these events will be represented by a closely packed series of dots on the diagram. This is a path through space and time, and thus through spacetime. Such a path is called the "worldline" of a moving body.

A key idea is that the speed of the motion will determine the angle between the worldline and the axes of the graph. Consider the diagram for a body that does not move at all from one point on the x-axis. Although its x-coordinate is unchanging, the clock keeps ticking and its time coordinate changes as time passes. Thus its worldline is a vertical line: a series of dots with the same x-coordinate and successive t-coordinates. In this case, a speed of zero causes the worldline to form a right angle with the x-axis.

208

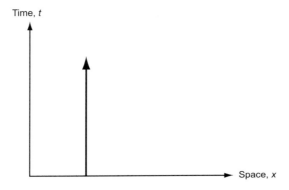

Figure A.2 *The worldline of a stationary body. It remains at the same place (x is constant) while time passes (t increases).*

A car that is racing to the right along the tunnel, that is, in the direction of increasing values for the x-coordinate, will have a world line which tilts to the right. Move your finger along the worldline of A from bottom to top. At each point, your fingertip has an x-coordinate and also a t-coordinate. As you move up the line, the x-coordinate moves through places (say through $x = 2, x = 3, x = 4$, etc.) just as the t-coordinate moves through a series of moments (say through $t = 5$, $t = 6, t = 7$, etc.). Thus the tilted line indicates that at different times A will be at different places: it is moving. Now move your fingertip along the line for body B. Since the line is tilted even more to the

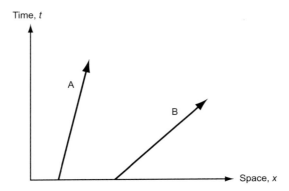

Figure A.3 *The worldlines of moving bodies. Both A and B are travelling to the right but B is moving at higher speed.*

209

right, your fingertip will move a long distance along the spatial axis when it moves only a short way up the time axis. This indicates a high speed: long distances covered in short times. Thus the faster a body moves, the smaller the angle between its worldline and the x-axis. Small angles correspond to high speeds.

Since there is a maximum speed (no body can travel faster than the speed of light), there will be a minimum angle with the spatial axis. The size of this minimum angle will depend on the units chosen on the two axes (seconds or hours, feet or meters, etc.).

Draw the worldlines of bodies moving to the left along the x-axis at various constant speeds. Draw the worldline of a body which changes its speed.

Relativity of simultaneity

With these basic ideas, we can already use spacetime diagrams to give insight into some important features of relativity theory. Einstein showed us that "simultaneity is in the eye of the beholder". We cannot simply assume that time flows at the same rates everywhere in the universe. Instead, we must use clocks and rulers and *experimentally* determine which events are simultaneous.

There is a simple way to show that two momentary events are simultaneous. Suppose that a light flash is set off exactly between the two places where the events occur. If the light waves travelling to those two places reach them just as the events occur, then the events are simultaneous. The reason is that light waves always travel at the same speed. Since the distances travelled by the light going in opposite directions from the mid-point were the same, and the speeds were the same, the times taken were the same. Since the times from the flash to the two events were the same, the events are simultaneous.

Consider the following example. Suppose that we have a long car and place a small light bulb at its exact mid-point. Suppose, further, that we place small clocks at the front and the back of the car and wish to synchronize them exactly. When the light is turned on, we can record the moments when the light first reaches the front and the back of the car. If the clock at the rear shows that the light struck it at noon and the clock at the front shows that it struck a bit later, then the front clock can be reset to remove the discrepancy. This will ensure that the clocks are synchronized, that is, that they will each show one o'clock simultaneously. This simple experiment is illustrated in Figure A.4.

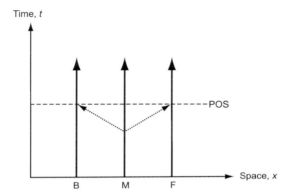

Figure A.4 *Simultaneous events. Lightwaves (indicated by the dotted arrows) travelling from the mid-point, M, of the stationary car strike the back, B, and front, F, of the car. These events are thus simultaneous.*

Here we use a stationary car; in later diagrams it will be set in motion.

In Figure A.4, the back, mid-point and front of the car are all stationary. Thus their worldlines are straight and vertical. The dotted arrow indicates the path taken by the light waves moving to the front and back of the car from the light bulb at the mid-point of the car. The events of the light reaching the clocks at the back and the front of the car are simultaneous. The horizontal dashed line that connects them is called a "plane of simultaneity". (It is a "line" on our diagram because we have omitted some spatial dimensions; the plane would be perpendicular to the surface of the drawing and the t-axis.) All the point events along the plane of simultaneity occur at the same time, as could be shown by other experiments.

On Figure A.4, only one plane of simultaneity is marked by the dashed line. Similar experiments would show that every horizontal line connects simultaneous events. Thus we could cover the diagram with a family of parallel horizontal lines to show all the planes of simultaneity. For example, we could show one line at each second mark.

Einstein's procedure for establishing which events are simultaneous gets much more interesting when the bodies are moving relatively to one another. Suppose the same experiment is done separately on two cars, one remaining stationary as above and one moving rapidly to the right at a constant speed (inertial motion). Both cars can be included in the same diagram (Figure A.5). The key point

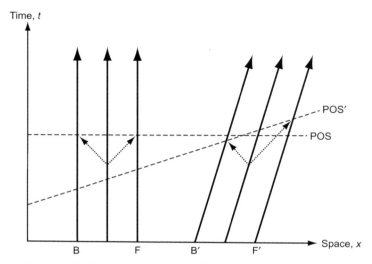

Figure A.5   *Two experiments establish two planes of simultaneity.*

of Figure A.5 is that there are two planes of simultaneity. The experiment done on the moving car indicates that events along the line POS′ are simultaneous, but the experiment done on the stationary car says that events along the line POS are simultaneous. This discrepancy seems odd. It took the genius of an Einstein to claim that the experiments were not at fault. The point is, he said, that there is something peculiar about time itself, namely that simultaneity depends on which sets of moving clocks and rulers are used to measure it. Figure A.5, however, deepens our understanding of this effect. Why does the experiment on the moving car suggest that the plane of simultaneity tilts upwards on the right-hand side?

Consider the light wave moving towards the back of the moving car (which we have at the left of Figure A.5). Since the light wave is travelling to the left, its worldline slopes to the left. And since the rear of the car is moving towards the right, its worldline slopes to the right. The event of the light striking the clock on the rear of the car occurs where the two lines cross each other. Since the light and the rear clock are moving towards each other, it takes very little time for them meet. The light wave moving from the mid-point towards the right of the moving car is chasing the clock on the front of the car. As the light wave advances, the clock races away from it. On Figure A.5, their two worldlines are each sloping towards the right. It takes more time for the light to reach the clock moving in the same direction. Thus, the lines meet and cross each other only after more time has passed.

Crucially, however, a passenger in the moving car may treat the car as stationary. As long as it is moving at a constant speed, its speed is not an objective fact but depends on what standard of rest is assumed. The passengers can assert that the car itself is the standard; that is, they can say that *we* are at rest and it is the *other* car that is moving. Since the two light waves each traversed half the length of this "stationary" car at the same speed, they must have reached the rear and front clocks at the same time. A passenger in the moving car who insists it is stationary, asserts that the two light waves travelled for the same times. The two events where the light waves cross the worldlines, therefore, are simultaneous.

What is the fact of the matter? If the car on the right is really moving, the light reaches the front later because the light wave takes time chasing the front of the car. On the other hand, if the car on the right is really stationary, the light waves reach the front and rear at the same time. According to Einstein, there is no fact of the matter here. Both planes of simultaneity on Figure A.5 are equally legitimate. Since constant speeds are not objective, definitions of simultaneity are not objective. Simultaneity is relative.

Length contraction

We can now use spacetime diagrams to show how the relativity of simultaneity leads to celebrated relativistic effects such as length contraction. Suppose that our car is six metres long when measured by rulers at rest relative to the car. Suppose that it is racing at a very high speed towards a garage that is only three metres long. Will the car fit into the garage? If so, how can the car be six metres long and yet fit into a shorter garage? Can we avoid the apparent contradiction?

In Figure A.6, the vertical lines represent the front and back of the stationary garage and the sloping lines represent the front and back of the car racing into the garage. Move your fingertip along the worldline of the front of the car. When does it enter the garage? When does it smash into the back wall of the garage? A detailed discussion of Figure A.6 will illuminate how the car can have "two lengths at once". First, note that, as above, there are two lines of simultaneity. The horizontal dashed line, POS, is the line of simultaneity for the garage. That is, events along this line were shown to be simultaneous by rulers and clocks that were at rest relative to the garage. The sloping dashed line, POS′, is the plane of simultaneity for the car, and was established by rulers and clocks moving along with the car.

When we measure the length of any object, we find the locations of its front and back *at the same time*. To measure the length of the car, we find where its front is now and where its back is now and then find the distance between these two points. It is no use finding where its front is at noon and where its back is at midnight, because the car may have moved in the afternoon. Thus, lengths are measured along a plane of simultaneity. To find the length of the car on Figure A.6, find the location of its front and then move along a plane of simultaneity to find the location of its back. The distance between these points is the length of the car.

According to Figure A.6, the front of the car enters the garage at the intersection labelled 1, then it hits the back wall of the garage at 2. What is the length of the car when the front touches the back wall of the car? Follow the horizontal plane of simultaneity to 5. This marks the location of the back of the car at the same time that the front is at 2. The distance from 2 to 5 is the length of the car. Note that this distance is smaller than the length of the garage (because 5 is between the front and back of the garage). Thus the car is wholly within the garage.

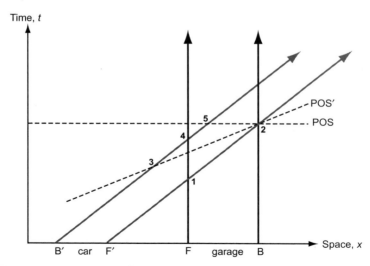

Figure A.6 *Spacetime diagram for a car rushing towards and through a garage.*

Passengers in the car can insist that they are stationary and that it is the garage that is rapidly approaching the car. According to them, the garage is moving rapidly to the left. Likewise they insist on using the sloping plane of simultaneity, POS'.

Since lengths are measured along a plane of simultaneity, they depend on which plane is used. According to the passengers, when the front of the car is striking the back wall of the garage at 2, the back of the car is located at 3. This point is found by starting at 2 and moving along POS' to find out where the back of the car is "at the same time". Thus the length of the car for the passengers is the distance from 2 to 3. Note here that the back of the car is well outside the garage (it does not enter until 4). Thus when the front of the car is touching the back wall of the garage, the back of the car is still outside the garage. The car is much longer than the garage.

We see here that the relativity of simultaneity leads to length contraction. According to one plane of simultaneity, the car is shorter than the garage and wholly inside it when the front strikes the rear wall. According to another, the rear is still projecting outside the door of the garage when the nose of the car hits the wall.

Finally, note that the order in which events occur in time may depend on the plane of simultaneity. If we use horizontal planes of simultaneity (and the vertical t-axis), the car enters the garage at 1, then the rear of the car enters the garage at 4, and only later does the front of the car hit the back of the garage at 2. This is shown on the graph by 2 being above 4, which is above 1. All of this is consistent with the car being shorter than the garage. However, we may alternately use the sloping plane of simultaneity POS' and a family of other lines parallel to it. In this case, the nose of the car enters the garage at 1, and then it hits the wall at 2, and then the rear enters at 4. Note that 4 is later than 2 because it is above the plane of simultaneity through 2: time has passed between the two events. This sequence is consistent with the car being longer than the garage.

Twin paradox

Spacetime diagrams are particularly useful in discussions of the twin paradox (or "clock paradox"). Suppose that one twin stays at home (and thus has a vertical worldline) and the other travels at high speed to a distant star and returns. Since the astronaut twin travels to the right of Figure A.7 on the outbound journey, the planes of simultaneity slope

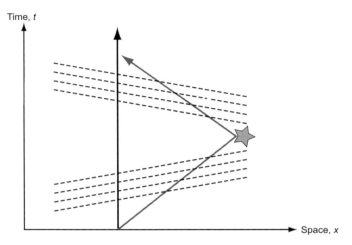

Figure A.7   *Spacetime diagram for the twin paradox.*

upwards to the right; correspondingly, they slope upwards to the left on the return journey. Note that the astronaut twin experiences three periods of acceleration: when leaving Earth, when turning round at the star, and when slowing down at Earth again. These are not shown on Figure A.7, and would correspond to three stretches where the worldline was curved. Between each of the parallel planes of simultaneity, one unit of time passes for the astronaut. Whatever the nature and duration of the periods of acceleration, the astronaut will experience fewer "ticks of the clock" than the stay-at-home twin.

Light cones

Diagrams like Figure A.6 are one major reason why many physicists assert that neither space nor time exists in their own right. Instead, some union of the two exists, which is called "spacetime". Figure A.6 vividly illustrates the fact that length is not an objective property of the car: it depends on which plane of simultaneity is used. The length of a body is a relation to a plane of simultaneity. Spacetime diagrams seem to show us what is real and objective: the patchwork of point events and worldlines in a four-dimensional spacetime.

There is a useful vocabulary for describing the various regions of spacetime displayed on a diagram. Consider the various worldlines that

216

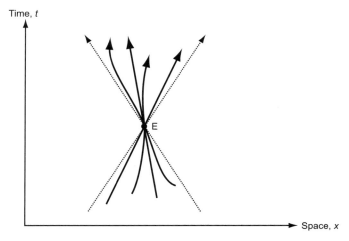

Figure A.8 *A sample of worldlines (bold) and light waves (dotted) passing through a single place and time, event E.*

may pass through a certain place at a certain time (Figure A.8). Here the lines that pass through the event E correspond to bodies moving with different speeds, and so the lines slope at different angles. Since no body may move faster than light, none of the lines can slope more than the dotted lines, which represent the paths of light waves.

The set of all possible worldlines through event E fills out a pair of cones above and below E. Since the sides of these cones are the paths of light waves, the two cones together are called the "light cone" centred on E. The various parts of the light cone have useful names. Since all points on a spacetime diagram represent events at a place and time, the points in the upper light cone represent events that come after E in time and the lower light cone represents events that come before E in time. They are called the "absolute future of E" and the "absolute past of E" because they are after and before E no matter which definition of simultaneity is used. Their order in time is not relative to the choice of the plane of simultaneity.

In the discussion of the car and the garage above we saw that the order of events in time may depend on the choice of the plane of simultaneity. A certain event A may come before or after an event B depending on the plane of simultaneity used for measurements of time. In Figure A.9, all the events outside the light cone of E have this uncertain status. Their time relation to E is not objective. They may be before or after E; they may be in the future of E or in its past. For this

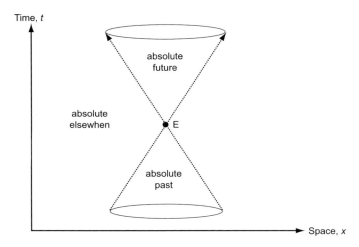

Figure A.9 *The light cone centred on event E, and its parts.*

reason, the region of events outside E's light cone is occasionally called the "absolute elsewhen" to indicate its ambiguous status relative to E.

There are many planes of simultaneity that may pass through event E. Each of them will pass entirely through E's absolute elsewhen, and can never intersect its absolute future or absolute past. The events in the absolute elsewhen are the relative past or relative future of E (depending on the choice of plane of simultaneity).

Of course, there is a light cone around each and every event in spacetime. An event may be in the absolute future of E but in the absolute elsewhen of some other distant event. An event in the absolute elsewhen of E is said to have a "space-like" separation from E. An event in the absolute past or future of E is said to have a "time-like" separation from E.

Time travel

Relativity theory says that every body with mass or energy travels slower than light. If it were possible to exceed that speed, however, we could travel back into the past. To see this, consider three events A, B and C. Assume that B is in the absolute elsewhen of A, C is in the absolute elsewhen of B, and C is in the absolute past of A.

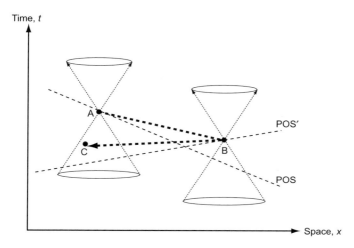

Figure A.10 *Faster-than-light speeds lead to time travel. Astronauts travel into A's future to B and then into B's future to C, which is in the absolute past of A, their starting point.*

To be concrete, suppose that astronauts are in a magical spaceship at the event A. Their ship can travel faster than light but, we assume, moves forwards in time like everything else as it journeys from star to star. Figure A.10 shows the odd fact that two journeys that move forwards in time can combine to produce a trip into the past.

The key here is that two different planes of simultaneity are used. When the astronauts are at A, they use the sloping dashed line labelled POS. According to this definition of simultaneity, B is after A because it is above the line. Thus the astronauts can travel into the future as time passes and arrive safely at the event B. This first leg of their journey is marked by the heavy dotted arrow. Their high speed is indicated by the fact that their worldline escapes from the absolute future of event A and crosses into the absolute elsewhen of A (according to relativity theory, this is impossible.)

Once our imaginary astronauts are safely at B, they are free to adopt another definition of simultaneity (labelled POS'). Since simultaneity is not objective, any definition can be used. Once again they start up their engines and race across to event C (which is in the absolute past of event A). According to their new definition of simultaneity, the event C is in the future of B: it is above the plane of simultaneity on which B is located. Thus faster-than-light speeds permit time travel. They enable the astronauts to escape from their light cone and travel on a roundabout trip into their absolute past. Once there, of course, they could engage in paradoxical mayhem. They could, for example, assassinate their grandparents before they gave birth to their parents. This is why Einstein was heard to say that speeds faster than light would let us telegraph back into the past. Some physicists say that such paradoxes are impossible and, therefore, that these diagrams are another argument for believing that faster-than-light speeds are impossible too.

Block universe

Some physicists argue that relativity theory has shown that the past and future exist in some robust sense. The triangle argument for this conclusion can be illustrated with a diagram similar to the last one, but now all three events, A, B and C, lie on the indicated planes of simultaneity. The three events A, B and C form a rough triangle on Figure A.11. Two sides are portions of planes of simultaneity; since C is in the backwards or past light cone of A, C is in the absolute past of A.

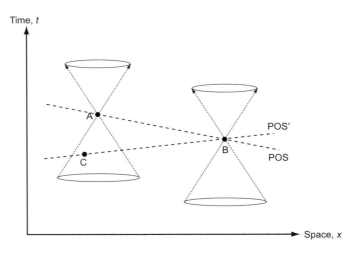

Figure A.11 *The triangle argument. If A and B coexist and B and C coexist, then A and C coexist, but A is in the future of C.*

To avoid solipsism, some events must coexist with A. One candidate is any event simultaneous with A. That is, we provisionally accept that simultaneity implies coexistence. This is suspicious because we are moving from subjective simultaneity (which depends on a choice of measuring instruments or reference frame) to objective coexistence, but the argument is meant to show that any plausible notion of coexistence leads to trouble.

In Figure A.11, since B is simultaneous with A it coexists with A. Using another plane of simultaneity, C is simultaneous with B and therefore coexists with B. If whatever coexists with B also coexists with A (transitivity), then C coexists with A. Thus A coexists with an event in its absolute past. This implies a block universe since the events were chosen arbitrarily.

This argument relies on several strong assumptions and is perhaps best viewed as a challenge to mainstream interpreters of relativity theory. Suppose an event exists. What, then, coexists with it? If nothing coexists with it, then we have solipsism. If only events along some particular plane of simultaneity coexist with it, then this plane is ontologically privileged and is in some sense a return to absolute space. If all events coexist with it, then we have a block universe. None of these responses seems palatable. Is the lesson that "coexistence" should be abandoned? What, then, is the status of spacetime?

Symmetry and Lorentz's minority interpretation

Chapter 3 on the twin paradox claimed that the minority interpretation can explain the symmetry of length contraction. It is useful to work through the details of this explanation, both to appreciate its madcap complexity and its miraculous conclusion. Recall the scenario rehearsed at the end of that chapter: the Jaguar has length d when stationary, but this is contracted to d' when it moves inertially at the speed v. A flash of light begins at the exact mid-point of the car and spreads out in opposite directions to the front and rear ends of the car.

Assume that: (i) the car is really contracted to a length d' (Lorentz–Fitzgerald contraction); (ii) the driver cannot detect this contraction and assumes the length of the car remains d; (iii) light travels at a constant speed *relative to the ether*, that is, the absolute rest frame; (iv) but the light *appears* to travel at the same relative speed in all directions (an empirical fact); and (v) the car is moving to the right, so the rear of the car is to the left. To measure the lengths of objects passing by, the driver notes the locations of their ends at the same time, and erroneously assumes that the flash reaches the two ends of the car in the same length of time (believing that the car is stationary).

Find the real times taken for the flash to reach the rear and front of the car from the mid-point, that is, to traverse half the contracted length of the moving car in either direction. Call these times L and R. In effect, the light races towards the rear at a speed of $c + v$, and towards the front at a speed of $c - v$. The formula "time is distance divided by velocity" gives:

$$L = \frac{d'/2}{c+v} \qquad\qquad R = \frac{d'/2}{c-v} \qquad\qquad \text{[B1]}$$

Find the real distance between the events of the flashes reaching the front and rear ends. When the flash is sparked off, the front and rear ends are a distance d' apart. While the flash travels forwards, the front end travels ahead by vR (distance is rate times time). During the shorter time while the flash travels rearwards, the rear end travels ahead by vL. Thus the distance between the events is the original distance between the two ends increased by Rv and then decreased by Lv:

$$d' + Rv - Lv \qquad\qquad \text{[B2]}$$

Substituting from B1, a few lines of algebra show this distance to be

$$\frac{d'}{1 - \frac{v^2}{c^2}} \qquad\qquad \text{[B3]}$$

But the standard formula for length contraction (Appendix C, equation C2) allows us to replace d' by the uncontracted length d and a square root, which finally leaves

$$\frac{d}{\sqrt{1 - \frac{v^2}{c^2}}} \qquad\qquad \text{[B4]}$$

which is the real distance between the two events of the flash reaching the front and rear of the car in the absolute rest frame (or ether frame).

This can be interpreted as follows. The driver thinks that the car has an unchanged length d, and the onboard rulers confirm this (since they are really contracted too). However, the driver also thinks that the two events are simultaneous, and therefore are also a length d apart (light apparently travels at the same speed in all directions). Thus the actual distance above is greater than the length d measured by the driver. In other words, when the driver's rulers measure a length d, the actual distance is greater by the factor of

$$\frac{1}{\sqrt{1 - \frac{v^2}{c^2}}} \qquad\qquad \text{[B5]}$$

in B4. That is, the car's rulers under-report the actual lengths. Inversely, therefore, stationary bodies appear contracted by a factor of

$$\sqrt{1 - \frac{v^2}{c^2}} \qquad \text{[B6]}$$

This is the same factor as in the standard formula for length contraction (C2).

Thus there is, in reality, an asymmetry. The moving car is really contracted, but stationary bodies passed by the car only appear to be contracted. These effects are, however, exactly equal: the observable effects are symmetric. Thus the minority interpretation can give a convoluted explanation of relativistic symmetries.

Simple formulas for special relativity

Suppose that the duration of an event measured by equipment at rest relative to the event is T. If the same event is measured by equipment moving inertially with a speed v, then the duration according to the new equipment is T'. Let c stand for the speed of light. Einstein predicts that these two numbers are related by

$$T' = \frac{T}{\sqrt{1 - \frac{v^2}{c^2}}} \qquad \text{[C1]}$$

Likewise, if the length of a body is L when measured by equipment at rest relative to it, then it will be L' when measured by relatively moving equipment

$$L' = L\sqrt{1 - \frac{v^2}{c^2}} \qquad \text{[C2]}$$

Likewise, if a body has a mass M, moving equipment will find M'

$$M' = \frac{M}{\sqrt{1 - \frac{v^2}{c^2}}} \qquad \text{[C3]}$$

Equation C3 implies that

$$E = Mc^2 \qquad \text{[C4]}$$

which can be derived as follows. It is approximately true that

$$\frac{1}{\sqrt{1-x^2}} = 1 + \frac{x^2}{2} \qquad [C5]$$

when x is small compared to 1 (check this with a calculator using $x = 0.001$). Substituting into C3

$$M' = \left(1 + \frac{v^2}{2\,c^2}\right)M \qquad [C6]$$

Multiplying M through the parentheses and then subtracting M from both sides gives

$$M' - M = \frac{Mv^2}{2\,c^2} \qquad [C7]$$

The left-hand side is the difference between the mass measured by moving equipment and the rest mass. Call this difference ΔM ("delta em"). Recall that the ordinary expression for the kinetic energy, that is, the energy of motion, is

$$\frac{1}{2}Mv^2 \qquad [C8]$$

Call this E. Then C7 becomes

$$\Delta M = \frac{E}{c^2} \qquad [C9]$$

Or, multiplying both sides by c^2,

$$\Delta Mc^2 = E \qquad [C10]$$

Equation C10 says that the relativistic increase in mass multiplied by c^2 equals the kinetic energy. Einstein argued that, if kinetic energy could produce a difference in mass, then all mass was made up of kinetic energy. This is the first version of the equation derived by Einstein.

Websites

Much of the information available on the web has not been reviewed by scholars, but the following websites are recommended. Addresses were correct at the time of going to press but may change, so the short descriptions provide enough detail to permit finding the material through search engines.

The fun and astonishing pictures produced by orbiting observatories will for ever change our vision of the heavens. Pictures taken by the Hubble Space Telescope are available at the site of the Space Telescope Science Institute: http://oposite.stsci.edu/pubinfo/pictures.html   The Chandra orbiting X-ray observatory is at http://chandra.nasa.gov/chandra.html   The Jet Propulsion Laboratory has pictures on many topics including space exploration: http://www.jpl.nasa.gov

Philosophy resources on the web include two general encyclo-paedias: the Internet Encyclopaedia of Philosophy is at http://www.utm.edu/research/iep and the Stanford Encyclopaedia of Philosophy is at http://plato.stanford.edu/   Two good web directories are the Social Science Information Gateway at http://www.sosig.ac.uk/ and Philosophy in Cyberspace at http://www-personal.monash.edu.au/~dey/phil/   Research articles in the philosophy of science are archived by the University of Pittsburgh at http://philsci-archive.pitt.edu/   Links to online essays in the philosophy of physics can be found at http://web.mit.edu/afs/athena.mit.edu/user/r/e/redingtn/www/netadv/founds.html

The Newton Society is at http://www.newton.org.uk/   There is a good page devoted to Leibniz at http://www.hfac.uh.edu/gbrown/philosophers/leibniz/   Three of the works that introduce his late metaphysics (*The Monadology*, *Discourse on Metaphysics*, *Correspondence with Arnaud*) are online at http://www.4literature.net/

A treasure-trove of many ancient works on philosophy in Greek and English has been made available by the Perseus Project at http://www.perseus.tufts.edu

There are many websites devoted to Einstein listed at http://dir.yahoo.com/Science/Physics/Physicists/ There are pictures and a biography on the American History of Physics history pages: http://www.aip.org/history/einstein/ Einstein's own popular exposition, *Relativity: The Special and General Theories* is online at http://www.bartleby.com/173/

There are both popular and advanced expositions of relativity available online. See Yahoo's lists and particularly Relativity on the Web at http://math.ucr.edu/home/baez/relativity.html

For general information on physics, including recent news and educational resources, see http://physicsweb.org/TIPTOP/

There are several sites with advanced reviews of important topics in physics. See Living Reviews at http://www.livingreviews.org and the review section of the Particle Data Group's site at http://pdg.lbl.gov/ and Net Advance on Physics at http://web.mit.edu/afs/athena.mit.edu/user/r/e/redingtn/www/netadv/welcome.html

The Gravity Probe B experiment on frame-dragging is described at http://einstein.stanford.edu/

Information about recent observations on the accelerating universe can be found at the website of the High-Z Supernovae Search at Harvard at http://oir-www.harvard.edu/cfa/oir/Research/supernova/HighZ.html and at that of the Supernova Cosmology Project, at http://www-supernova.lbl.gov/public/ The journal *Physics Today* has some relevant articles online; see http://www.physicstoday.org/pt/vol-54/iss-6/p17.html and http://www.aip.org/pt/vol-54/iss-7/p16.html

Physicists make many of their advanced research articles freely available on the web, and students might take a peek at this miraculous Republic of Letters in cyberspace. There is a huge archive at http://uk.arXiv.org/ There is a good review of the observational evidence for black holes (written at an intermediate level) in paper 9912186. Stanford maintains a database of publication information about recent articles, which can be searched by the citations of a paper and the references in a paper; see http://www.slac.stanford.edu/spires/

Guide to further reading

Easy reading on relativity

Kip Thorne's *Black Holes and Time Warps* (Norton, 1994) is fun and readable. Einstein's own introduction *Relativity: The Special and General Theory* (Crown, 1961) uses simple algebra (available online). There is an excellent, popular introduction to the Big Bang in Alan H. Guth, *The Inflationary Universe: The Quest for a Theory of Cosmic Origins* (Vintage, 1998).

General books on the philosophy of space and time

For introductions, Barry Dainton's *Time and Space* (Acumen, 2001) is excellent, and is a worthy successor to the long-standard, Lawrence Sklar, *Space, Time, and Spacetime* (University of California Press, 1974). Graham Nerlich's *The Shape of Space* (Cambridge University Press, 1994) is useful and engaging. For collections of readings, see N. Huggett (ed.), *From Zeno to Einstein: Classic Readings* (MIT Press, 1999), R. Le Poidevin and M. MacBeath (eds), *The Philosophy of Time* (Oxford University Press, 1993), and the older J. J. C. Smart (ed.), *Problems of Space and Time* (Macmillan, 1964). For advanced surveys, the best are Michael Friedman's *Foundations of Space-Time Theories* (Princeton University Press, 1983) and John Earman's *World-Enough and Space-Time* (MIT Press, 1989). For books devoted primarily to the metaphysics of time, see Tooley's *Time, Tense, and Causation* (Oxford University Press, 2000) and W. H. Newton-Smith's *The Structure of Time* (Routledge, 1980).

General books on the history of theories of space and time

Ancient

R. Sorabji, *Time, Creation, and the Continuum* (Cornell University Press, 1983). Andrew Pyle, *Atomism and its Critics: From Democritus to Newton* (Thoemmes Press, 1997).

Medieval

Edward Grant, *Much Ado About Nothing: Theories of Space and Vacuum from the Middle Ages to the Scientific Revolution* (Cambridge University Press, 1981). Pierre Duhem, *Mediaeval Cosmology: Theories of Infinity, Place, Time, Void, and the Plurality of Worlds* (University of Chicago Press, 1985).

Modern

Parts I and II of Edmund Husserl's *Crisis of the European Sciences* (Northwestern University Press, 1970) are a provocative reading of Galileo's geometrization of space and its impact on modern epistemology.

Einstein's writings

Einstein's original papers on the special and general theories are surprisingly accessible, and should be read or skimmed by all students. Several key papers are included in the inexpensive *The Principle of Relativity* (Dover, 1952) including Minkovski's 1908 paper and others. Einstein's own introduction, listed above, is quick reading and a useful snapshot of his approach. A readable collection of his non-technical, personal and political writings can be found in C. Seelig (ed.), *Ideas and Opinions* (Bonanza Books, 1954). Einstein's collected works are being published by Princeton University Press.

Biographies of Einstein

There is not yet a definitive, scholarly biography. A. Folsing, *Albert Einstein* (Penguin, 1997) is recent and readable. A. Pais, *Subtle is the Lord: The Science and Life of Albert Einstein* (Oxford University Press, 1982) is a lively, technical work by a prominent physicist who worked with Einstein.

Introductory textbooks on relativity

With some tutorial help, I like to start students with Einstein's 1905 paper on special relativity and his 1916 paper on general relativity (both in the Dover reprint volume). Alongside these, David Bohm's *The Special Theory of Relativity* (Routledge, 1996) is simple and treats the Lorentz interpretation in parallel with the standard introductory topics. Less philosophical, but also short and sweet is R. H. Good, *Basic Concepts of Relativity* (Reinhold, 1968), which uses only simple algebra; E. F. Taylor and J. A. Wheeler, *Spacetime Physics* (W. H. Freeman, 1966) is also simple and conceptually clear. P. C. W. Davies, *Space and Time in the Modern Universe* (Cambridge University Press, 1977) is readable and uses little mathematics. At the next, higher level is Wolfgang Rindler, *Essential Relativity: Special, General, and Cosmological* (Springer-Verlag, 1977).

Intermediate and advanced textbooks on relativity

Ray D'Inverno, *Introducing Einstein's Relativity* (Clarendon Press, 1990) is simple, clear and fairly attentive to foundational questions. B. F. Schutz, *A First Course in General Relativity* (Cambridge University Press, 1990) is simple and clear and uses the newer geometric approach. Physicists prefer texts like R. M. Wald, *General Relativity* (University of Chicago Press, 1984) and S. H. Hawking and G. F. R. Ellis, *The Large Scale Structure of Space-time* (Cambridge University Press, 1973). There is a mammoth but philosophically fascinating text by C. W. Misner, K. S. Thorne and J. A. Wheeler, *Gravitation* (W. H. Freeman, 1973), which should be avoided by beginners but is essential browsing for advanced students. (Several texts are available on the web.)

Lorentz's minority interpretation

Start with Bohm's text listed above. Lorentz is defended in Elie Zahar's *Einstein's Revolution: A Study in Heuristic* (Open Court, 1989). There is important historical material in Arthur I. Miller, *Albert Einstein's Special Theory of Relativity: Emergence and Early Interpretation* (Addison-Wesley, 1981). Lorentz himself gives a very clear explanation of his views on the symmetry of relativistic effects in his *Lectures on Theoretical Physics* (Macmillan, 1931), especially in chapter 2 of volume 3.

Atomic bombs

Max Jammer, *The Concept of Mass in Classical and Modern Physics* (Harper Torchbooks, 1961) is excellent and readable (and contains a chapter on electromagnetic mass). I have followed the conventional treatment of relativistic mass, but this is criticized in Lev. B. Okun, "The Concept of Mass", *Physics Today*, June (1989), 31–6. Richard Rhodes, a novelist with a physics degree, became a historian and wrote a thrilling and disturbing book *The Making of the Atomic Bomb* (Simon and Schuster, 1986); the sequel *Dark Sun: the Making of the Hydrogen Bomb* is also recommended. Both of these give good, detailed, non-technical explanations of how bombs work. Jonathon Schell, *The Fate of the Earth* (Stanford University Press, 2000) pessimistically explores our future with the bomb.

The block universe

Although all textbooks on relativity assert that it is a four-dimensional theory, they curiously avoid discussing what this might mean. Here is a sampling of philosophical articles on the subject: H. Stein, "On Relativity Theory and the Openness of the Future", *Philosophy of Science* 58 (1991), 147–67; H. Putnam, "Time and Physical Geometry", *Journal of Philosophy* 64 (1967), 240–47; D. Dieks, "Discussion: Special Relativity and the Flow of Time", *Philosophy of Science* 55 (1988), 456–60; R. Clifton and M. Hogarth, "The Definability of Objective Becoming in Minkowski Spacetime", *Synthese* 103 (1995), 355–87. The quotation from Einstein on the static four-dimensional continuum (p. 60) is from a late appendix added to his book *Relativity* (p. 150, see above); the Gödel quote (p. 61) is from his article in *Albert Einstein: Philosopher, Scientist* (Library of Living Philosophers, 1949). The useful John Earman, *Primer on Determinism* (D. Reidel, 1986) discusses the difference between fatalism and determinism.

Twin paradox and time travel

David Lewis's article "The Paradoxes of Time Travel" is in the *American Philosophical Quarterly* 13 (1976), 145–52, and is collected in Le Poidevin and MacBeath (eds), *The Philosophy of Time*. The experiment with Boeing jets was reported in the journal *Science* 177 (1972), p. 166. See also the general texts above, and especially Thorne, *Black Holes and Time Warps*.

Ancient philosophy of space and time

The standard collection of the Presocratics for philosophy students is G. S. Kirk, J. E. Raven and M. Schofield, *The Presocratic Philosophers* (Cambridge University Press, 1983). Careful but sometimes one-sided analyses of their positions appear in Jonathan Barnes, *The Presocratic Philosophers* (Routledge, 1979). Aristotle's *Physics* discusses infinity (Book Gamma/III, 4–8), place and void (Book Delta/IV) and Zeno (Book Zeta/VI, 9 but see also Book Theta/VIII, 8 at 263a11); the best English translation is by Richard Hope (University of Nebraska Press, 1961). David Sedley explores an alternate interpretation of the atomist's void in "Two Conceptions of the Vacuum", *Phronesis* 27(2) (1982) 175–93.

Zeno's paradoxes and infinity

In addition to the publications in the previous section, A. W. Moore, *The Infinite* (Routledge, 1990) is a good, introductory survey for philosophers. There is an excellent revisionist history in Shaughan Lavine, *Understanding the Infinite* (Harvard University Press, 1994).

Aristotle

See the recommendations in the previous two sections and J. Barnes (ed.), *The Cambridge Companion to Aristotle* (Cambridge University Press, 1995). Sorabji (see "General books on the history of theories of space and time", above) discusses Aristotle on time, change and motion.

Newton

An excellent general introduction for students is I. B. Cohen and R. S. Westfall (eds), *Newton* (Norton, 1995). The best biography is Richard S. Westfall's *Never at Rest* (Cambridge University Press, 1980); he condensed this for the general reader in his *The Life of Isaac Newton* (Cambridge University Press, 1993). Sklar, Earman and Friedman (see "General books on the philosophy of space and time", above) discuss Newton's views at length. See also B. J. T. Dobbs's *The Foundations of Newton's Alchemy: The Hunting of the Greene Lion* (Cambridge University Press, 1975). I. B. Cohen and Anne Whitman (trans. and eds), *Newton's Principia* (University of California Press,

1999) has been newly translated and edited. For a more scholarly introduction to all aspects of Newton's thoughts, see the excellent *Cambridge Companion to Newton* (Cambridge University Press, 2002), edited by I. B. Cohen and G. E. Smith.

Leibniz

The debate with Newton over space and time is in H. G. Alexander (ed.), *The Leibniz–Clark Correspondence* (Manchester University Press, 1956). The best introduction to his mature metaphysics are the three short treatises: *The Monadology, Discourse on Metaphysics* and *Correspondence with Arnaud*. These are available in, for example, *Philosophical Texts* (Oxford University Press, 1991), and are also available online.

Incongruent counterparts

For an excellent semi-popular introduction to this topic see Martin Gardener's *The New Ambidextrous Universe* (W. H. Freeman, 1991). For an excellent collection of philosophy articles see James Van Cleve and Robert E. Frederick (eds), *The Philosophy of Left and Right* (Kluwer, 1991). See especially the article by Van Cleve, which is a useful survey and lays out arguments in the style of this text. I also recommend Jill Vance Buroker's *Space and Incongruence* (D. Reidel, 1981). Among general texts on space and time, Nerlich and Earman discuss this topic.

McTaggart

The argument can be found together with some responses in the recent Le Poidevin and MacBeath (eds), *The Philosophy of Time*. It appeared originally in *Mind* **17** (1908), 457–74 and later in his *The Nature of Existence* (Cambridge University Press, 1927). Tooley's *Time, Tense, and Causation* has a recent discussion and references to some important articles on McTaggart.

Euclid and non-Euclidean geometry

The old but lovely edition, Thomas L. Heath (ed.), *Euclid's Elements* (Dover, 1956), is very readable and crammed with interesting commentary. A useful introduction to modern approaches to geometry can be found in E. Moise, *Elementary Geometry from an Advanced Viewpoint* (Addison-Wesley, 1990). Many books chronicle the rise of non-Euclidean geometry.

Substantivalism vs. relationalism

Start with Sklar, then see Nerlich, Earman, and Friedman ("General books on the philosophy of space and time", above).

Quantum paradoxes

There is a good collection of fairly accessible articles by philosophers, including Mermin's elementary exposition of Bell's theorem, in Ernan McMullin and Jim Cushing (eds), *Philosophical Consequences of Quantum Theory* (University of Notre Dame Press, 1989). Many of the classic papers on the foundations of quantum theory are collected in J. Wheeler and W. H. Zurek (eds), *Quantum Theory and Measurement* (Princeton University Press, 1983). J. S. Bell's essays, including a simpler derivation of his theorem, are collected in *Speakable and Unspeakable in Quantum Mechanics* (Cambridge University Press, 1987). Einstein's attitude to quantum theory is discussed in Arthur Fine, *The Shaky Game: Einstein, Realism, and the Quantum Theory* (University of Chicago Press, 1986).

Black holes

Start with Thorne, *Black Holes and Time Warps*. M. Begelman and M. Rees, *Gravity's Fatal Attraction: Black Holes in the Universe* (Scientific American Library, 1996) is written at the same semi-popular level with little mathematics.

Big Bang and cosmology

Start with Guth, *The Inflationary Universe*. Michael Berry, *Principles of Cosmology and Gravitation* (Cambridge University Press, 1976) is short and uses only elementary mathematics and physics. L. Bergstrom and A. Goobar, *Cosmology and Particle Astrophysics* (Wiley, 1999) is a good textbook for advanced undergraduates. Original papers on the Big Bang are collected in J. Bernstein and G. Feinberg (eds), *Cosmological Constants: Papers in Modern Cosmology* (Columbia University Press, 1986).

Extraterrestrial life and gamma-ray bursts

There are many books and websites on the possibility of extraterrestrial life. Gamma-ray bursts are discussed in the physics textbook, Lars Bergstrom and Ariel Goobar, *Cosmology and Particle Astrophysics* (Wiley, 1999). The Fermi paradox is discussed in Ian Crawford, "Where Are They?: Maybe We are Alone in the Galaxy After All" in *Scientific American* July (2000), 29–33; there has been a flurry of popular articles on the dangers of gamma-ray bursts, such as Oliver Morton, "The Universe is Savage", *Prospect* January (2000) (available online).

Scientific realism

The claim that quarks are somehow social products is in Andrew Pickering, *Constructing Quarks: A Sociological History of Particle Physics* (Edinburgh University Press, 1984). A good, early snapshot of the debate can be found in J. Leplin (ed.), *Scientific Realism* (University of California Press, 1984).

Feminist philosophy of science

Begin with the Oxford Reader, E. Fox Keller and Helen Longino (eds), *Feminism and Science* (Oxford University Press, 1996). Helen Longino, *Science as Social Knowledge: Values and Objectivity in Scientific Enquiry* (Princeton University Press, 1990) is excellent. There are two useful anthologies: Nancy Tuana (ed.), *Feminism and Science* (Indiana University Press, 1989) and Ruth Bleir (ed.), *Feminist Approaches to Science* (Pergamon Press, 1989). An interesting and readable study of sexism in the history of science is Londa Schiebinger, *The Mind Has No Sex? Women in the Origins of Modern Science* (Harvard University Press, 1989). Evelyn Fox Keller's essay collection, *Reflections on Gender* (Yale University Press, 1996), contains an interesting article on paradoxes in physics and the male personality. Her biography of the biologist and Nobel prize winner, Barbara McClintock, is also recommended: *A Feeling for the Organism* (W. H. Freeman, 1993). Elizabeth Fee's essay "Women's Nature and Scientific Objectivity" appeared in R. Hubbard and M. Lowe (eds), *Women's Nature: Rationalisations of Inequality* (Pergamon Press, 1983). Finally, see Londa Schiebinger, *Has Feminism Changed Science?* (Harvard University Press, 2001).

Cultural studies of space and time

Stephen Kern, *The Culture of Time and Space: 1880–1918* (Harvard University Press, 1983). Michel Foucault's essay "Other Spaces" is collected in *Aesthetics, Method, Epistemology: Essential Works of Foucault: 1954–1984*, volume II (New Press, 1999). The Panopticon is discussed in Michel Foucault, *Discipline and Punish* (Vintage Books, 1995). The social production of space is discussed at length in E. W. Soja, *Postmodern Geographies: The Reassertion of Space in Critical Social Theory* (Verso, 1997). For more recent work see M. Crang and N. J. Thrift (eds), *Thinking Space* (Critical Geographies) (Routledge, 2000).

Inflationary and accelerating universe

Start with Guth, *The Inflationary Universe*. The article by Guth and Paul Steinhardt in Paul Davies (ed.), *The New Physics* (Cambridge University Press, 1989) has an elementary mathematical introduction to inflation. Einstein's article on cosmology is in the Dover reprint volume listed above. There are good articles on the new observations concerning inflation and acceleration by Bertram Schwarzchild: "Cosmic Microwave Observations Yield More Evidence of Primordial Inflation", *Physics Today* July (2001) and "Farthest Supernova Strengthens Case for Accelerating Cosmic Expansion", *Physics Today* June (2000). These are available online.

Perspective and the representation of space in art history

There is a short introduction to perspective in Morris Kline, *Mathematics in Western Culture* (Oxford University Press, 1953), chapter 10. For a readable, provocative survey try Samuel Y. Edgerton, Jr, *The Heritage of Giotto's Geometry: Art and Science on the Eve of the Scientific Revolution* (Cornell University Press, 1991). Erwin Panofsky, *Perspective as Symbolic Form* (Zone Books, 1991) is still an important and influential essay. For a broader history see Martin Kemp, *The Science of Art: Optical Themes in Western Art from Brunelleschi to Seurat* (Yale University Press, 1990).

Index